Making Men in the Age of Sail

CHARLES J BIGGER
LONDONDERRY
SHIPBUILDER & ENGINEER

Making Men in the Age of Sail

Masculinity, Memoir, and the British Merchant Seafarer, 1860–1914

Graeme J. Milne

McGill-Queen's University Press
Montreal & Kingston • London • Chicago

© McGill-Queen's University Press 2024

ISBN 978-0-2280-2129-2 (cloth)
ISBN 978-0-2280-2130-8 (paper)
ISBN 978-0-2280-2183-4 (ePDF)
ISBN 978-0-2280-2184-1 (ePUB)

Legal deposit second quarter 2024
Bibliothèque nationale du Québec

Printed in Canada on acid-free paper that is 100% ancient forest free (100% post-consumer recycled), processed chlorine free

Funded by the Government of Canada | Financé par le gouvernement du Canada | Canada

Canada Council for the Arts | Conseil des arts du Canada

We acknowledge the support of the Canada Council for the Arts.
Nous remercions le Conseil des arts du Canada de son soutien.

McGill-Queen's University Press in Montreal is on land which long served as a site of meeting and exchange amongst Indigenous Peoples, including the Haudenosaunee and Anishinabeg nations. In Kingston it is situated on the territory of the Haudenosaunee and Anishinaabek. We acknowledge and thank the diverse Indigenous Peoples whose footsteps have marked these territories on which peoples of the world now gather.

Library and Archives Canada Cataloguing in Publication

Title: Making men in the age of sail : masculinity, memoir, and the British merchant seafarer, 1860-1914 / Graeme J. Milne.
Names: Milne, Graeme J., author.
Description: Includes bibliographical references and index.
Identifiers: Canadiana (print) 20230586554 | Canadiana (ebook) 20230586597 | ISBM 9780228021308 (paper) | ISBM 9780228021292 (cloth) | ISBM 9780228021841 (EPUB) | ISBM 9780228021834 (ePDF)
Subjects: LCSH: Merchant mariners—Great Britain—History—19th century. | LCSH: Merchant mariners—Great Britain—History—20th century. | LCSH: Seafaring life—Great Britain—History—19th century. | LCSH: Seafaring life—Great Britain—History—20th century. | LCSH: Masculinity—Great Britain—History—19th century. | LCSH: Masculinity—Great Britain—History—20th century. | LCSH: Autobiography. | LCSH: Great Britain—History, Naval.
Classification: LCC HD8039.S42 G74 2024 | DDC 359.0094109/034—dc23

This book was designed and typeset by studio oneonone in Minion 11/12

For Mum and Dad

Contents

Preface

This book uses seafarers' memoirs to explore what it meant to be a man in the later era of the British commercial sailing ship. The fact that a whole book can be written about this theme, using one kind of source, points to the wider lessons we can learn from maritime life and work at the turn of the nineteenth and twentieth centuries. Any of the chapters could be the core of new research, and I hope the material here might inspire scholars to pursue those projects.

A book like this can only be written because dedicated people keep our archives and libraries open, sometimes in the face of considerable odds. They are increasingly custodians of digital resources as well as, and sometimes instead of, paper. Thanks, then, to everyone at Ancestry.com, the British Library, Gale, HathiTrust Digital Library, Internet Archive (archive.org), Liverpool Central Library, Manchester Central Library, Project Gutenberg, ProQuest, University of Liverpool Library, University of Manchester Library, and (for their valued assistance with the photographs) University of Washington Libraries, Special Collections.

I am very grateful to everyone who talked through ideas, sources, and approaches, read draft chapters, or helped in so many ways while I was writing this book. In particular, thanks to Richard Baggaley and his colleagues at McGill-Queen's University Press, and to the press's anonymous readers, whose constructive reports were much appreciated.

The following images are all from University of Washington Libraries, Special Collections, Wilhelm Hester Photograph Collection (PH Coll 318), an unusual set of photographs taken on board arriving vessels in the Pacific Northwest between the early 1890s and mid-1900s. Photographs of working conditions at sea in this period are even less common, but for examples see: Sager, *Seafaring Labour*; Jones, *The Cape Horn Breed*; Barker, *The Log of a Limejuicer*; and Clements, *A Gipsy of the Horn*.

At the wheel of *Dimsdale*, in port.

Judging by other photographs of *Dimsdale* in the same collection, this is either an officer-apprentice or the captain's son. Although proud to take this role, steering a ship was a physical and mental challenge for young sailors. Two Able Seamen (ABs) were often required to control the wheel in heavy seas, one standing on each of the platforms visible in this image.

University of Washington Libraries, Special Collections, PH Coll 318.216, Hester 10329.

The view from the wheel.

Looking forward from *Dimsdale*'s wheel, showing how limited the view was: when the sails were in use, visibility was worse still. This image gives a small sense of the responsibility carried by the man (or boy) at the wheel. Diligent lookouts and careful teamwork were necessary to keep the officers on the afterdeck informed of what lay ahead.

University of Washington Libraries, Special Collections, PH Coll 318.214, Hester 10332.

The apprentices' 'half-deck.'

Accommodation on *Lynton*. These are probably apprentices' quarters, known generically as the 'half-deck,' with four bunks, and sea-chests for seating. The photograph has been carefully composed, with the binoculars and sextant on the table representing the tools of the would-be officer's trade. There is a painting of the ship on the back wall, along with a photograph of a woman; other framed images are just visible in the upper bunks.

University of Washington Libraries, Special Collections, PH Coll 318.458, Hester 10528.

The main cabin.

The captain of *Cleomene* sits in his ship's main cabin. Intended to impress merchants, fellow captains, and guests when the ship was in port, this space could also intimidate recalcitrant seafarers. The cabin was under the afterdeck, hence the skylights, and was the heart of the captain's territory on the ship. Tables like this were sometimes used for laying out the bodies of dead seafarers prior to being sewn into canvas for burial at sea.

University of Washington Libraries, Special Collections, PH Coll 318.178, Hester 10300.

The 'Old Man' and his apprentices.

Captain Jolliff and the officer-apprentices on *Australian*. The apprentices are 'brassbound,' with their buttoned jackets, caps with shipping company crest, and white collars; one carries a telescope. This paraphernalia was central to their self-image as future ships' officers. Their dirty hands and battered boots, however, point to the daily realities of hard work.

University of Washington Libraries, Special Collections, PH Coll 318.62, Hester 10213.

The crew of *Australian.*

The same apprentices on *Australian*, this time in their working clothes. The crew behind them have a common age profile: if the majority look to be in their twenties and thirties, the rest are the men our authors called 'old shellbacks.' While most wear ordinary caps, some favour more individualistic headgear, common in descriptions of sailors.

University of Washington Libraries, Special Collections, PH Coll 318.63, Hester 10211.

A crew prepares for shore leave.

An unusual photograph capturing the crew of *Glenesk* mostly in their formal clothes, presumably prior to going ashore. It is hard to distinguish sailors from officers, defying the common claim that sailing-ship mariners dressed with flamboyant excess in port. The captain, his wife, and their dog could just as easily be from the prosperous middle-classes in any occupation.

University of Washington Libraries, Special Collections, PH Coll 318.350, Hester 10440.

Sailing-ship men.

The unnamed crew of an unnamed ship, but all the 'types' identified by our authors are here to be filled in. The confident young captain sits in the centre with his cigar; on his right, the experienced first mate; on his left, the younger second mate with the ship's cat. Standing rear left, the tall senior apprentice; rear right, the boyish first-voyager. The Black seafarer on the right wears the clothes of a cook or steward. Standing in the centre with his arms crossed is the powerfully-built Able Seaman with his pipe; to his right, the grey-bearded 'old shellback.'

University of Washington Libraries, Special Collections, PH Coll 318.723, Hester 10777.

Making Men in the Age of Sail

Introduction

It might seem odd to write about 'the age of sail' in a book set at the turn of the nineteenth and twentieth centuries. Was that not the age of steam? After all, steamships had been growing in importance since the 1840s, and ocean steam tonnage using British ports had already overtaken sail in the 1870s.[1] But the transition to steam took decades, and some British firms continued to use sailing ships on long-distance trades until the Great War. Many seafarers spent their entire careers in sail, long after the majority of the seagoing workforce was employed in steam. The shipping industry remained conservative, training its officers in sailing ships even when it was clear that they would soon move into steam. In the end, though, sail did vanish from the British merchant fleet, and quite suddenly. That provoked a sense of loss, and the age of sail become a phenomenon to be memorialised. When some of the last sailing-ship mariners wrote their memoirs, they sought to differentiate themselves from men who had known nothing but steamships, and to define their identity as veterans of a lost craft. In that cultural sense, the age of sail only became significant in the early twentieth century, when it was almost gone.

As they charted the final phase of the transition from sail to steam, seafaring memoir-writers revealed broader uncertainties and insecurities of their times. They illuminated the backward-looking, anti-modern tendency of British culture, but also its counterpart: the technological entrepreneurship that drove successive industrial and social transformations. In particular, memoirs offered conflicted visions of what it meant to be a man, and highlighted tensions between the old, rough, seafaring masculinity that authors had grown up with, and their later identities as men of reason, science, and business.

This introductory chapter offers a brief survey of the maritime world encountered by our authors when they first went to sea. It considers how life and work in late-period sailing ships exposed attitudes toward masculinity and manliness, in an era of change and challenge to those ideas. Finally, it introduces the memoir-writers whose books are the foundation of the chapters that follow, and explains how autobiography both moulded and revealed the class, national, and gender identities entangled in seafaring men.

THE LATER AGE OF SAIL

The transition from sail to steam entwined technological change with economics, work, business, society, and culture. Most research conceptualises the transition as the rise of steam, placing steam shipping at the heart of trade and imperial expansion from the middle of the nineteenth century.[2] The steam sector grew through decades of innovation in shipbuilding and engineering; by enabling globalised networks of business, finance, trade, and migration; and, crucially, through the creation of new workforces for the ships themselves and their related firms and industries.[3]

What happens if we shift attention to the other side of the transition, to life and work in the sailing-ship sector as it was gradually eclipsed by steam? Historians have long recognised that sail was not frozen in time by the invention of the steamship.[4] Across the second half of the nineteenth century, builders and owners replaced wooden ships with composite wood and iron, then iron, then steel. Sailing ships built in the 1890s carried much more cargo than those of a generation before, yet with far less capital commitment than steamers, or the costs of fuel. They offered cheap carriage for bulk goods like coal, grain, or wool on the long-distance routes between the Pacific and Europe. Oceanographic and meteorological research enabled faster voyages, while better information improved cargo-handling and business processes.[5] Sailing-ship owners made continuing profits, and Britain still had the world's single largest sail fleet at the start of the twentieth century, even if most British shipowners had long since moved into steam.[6] The Great War finally brought an end to British deep-water sail, but some Nordic operators carried on using sailing ships on the old grain routes in the 1920s and 1930s.[7]

As well as efficiencies of scale and process, the last generation of British sailing-ship owners demanded economies from their workforce. They recruited many sailors from lower-waged countries, reduced crew sizes, and rarely invested in labour-saving technology for handling ropes and sails.[8] The impact of these efficiencies on seafarers was harsh. The routes around the Cape of Good Hope and Cape Horn, and across lonely stretches of the South Atlantic, Indian, and Pacific Oceans, exposed sailing-ship crews to dangerous sea conditions. In the later weeks of long winter passages, seamen endured sleep deprivation, malnourishment, injury, and sickness, far from land or any possibility of assistance. The British state's statistics show that more workers died on ships than in coal mines every year in the 1890s and 1900s, despite the much larger size of the mining labour force, and crew losses in the sail sector were two or three times the already high rate for steamship mariners.[9]

We already know a good deal about later sailing-ship crews, thanks to research by labour and economic historians since the 1980s.[10] Employment on sailing ships was regarded as a young man's occupation, to be followed by marriage and jobs on shore or in steamships, although there were always seafarers who never made those transitions. Sailors were capable and adaptable workers, yet did not fit well with the distinctions between skilled and unskilled labour found in shore industries, and it is telling that general histories of the British working classes rarely mention seafarers. In politics and industrial relations, seafarers appear alternately militant and apathetic, a challenge for trade unions to organise, and resistant to rules and codes of behaviour.[11] Sailors faced huge obstacles to accessing health care, training, and education.[12] The crews of British sailing ships were nationally and ethnically diverse, raising questions for an industry that claimed to be an expression of British identity and tradition, and seafarers offer important insights into mobile, transnational workforces.[13] The public image and reputation of the merchant seaman was also a powerful cultural phenomenon in the late nineteenth century, especially when he became embroiled in moral panics about drink and vice in the waterfront districts of major seaports.[14]

For all that, many aspects of the lives of British sailing-ship mariners at the turn of the nineteenth and twentieth centuries remain unclear. Recent maritime scholarship has concentrated mostly on other time periods, or on other nations' fleets. The seventeenth and eighteenth centuries – eras of piracy, the slave trade, and naval warfare – have held particular attention, and this remained so in the various 'turns' toward global and cultural studies taken by historians in the early twenty-first century.[15] We also have important work on American sailors, some of which has a valuable emphasis on memoir and masculinity, but again its periodisation mostly stretches from the Age of Revolution to the American Civil War; there is a substantial related thread of writing about American whaling crews.[16] Nordic seafaring is perhaps best studied of all, with a consistent output of work in recent decades.[17]

Research on British seafarers has often focused on the Royal Navy, and this raises important issues. The nineteenth century saw a growing gulf between commercial shipping and the fighting navy. Historians of earlier eras write of a world where any sailor might join a merchant ship only to find himself press-ganged into service on a warship, or captured and recruited by pirates in an age of endemic violence and conflict.[18] By the time our authors went to sea later in the nineteenth century, institutional, occupational, and geopolitical seascapes were very different. The Royal Navy had transformed itself into a professional, technocratic force of steel-built and steam-driven warships that no longer had to coerce merchant sailors; indeed, it pioneered the recruitment and training of a modern naval workforce on continuous contracts. Official propaganda and press boosterism represented the naval rating as a steady man, defending family and nation, albeit one who was supposed to know his place in the British class hierarchy.[19] This peacetime navy had little connection with everyday commercial shipping, and certainly not with the last sailing-ship seafarers. Indeed, some of our memoir-writers complained at the time that merchant seamen were undervalued, misunderstood, or simply ignored by nautical commentators, most of whose emphasis was on the Royal Navy.[20]

To be fair, our authors also muddled the chronology of merchant seafaring. Commercial sail's long persistence created an illusion of continuity, and authors often extrapolated romantic myths from earlier periods – usually a jumble of naval and mercantile stories – onto their own careers. They were conscious of that mix of stability and rapid change, but valued being the latest link in a long chain of maritime Britishness. While having this emotional commitment to the past, however, our authors were also determined to show the reading public that their skills, experience, and character still had relevance in the early twentieth century. They wanted to show that their own time at sea was not just an epilogue to the age of sail, nor a prologue to the age of steam. By discussing maritime manhood in the decades before 1914, when both seafaring and masculinity faced dramatic change, this book also seeks to demonstrate a renewed importance for that period. The seafarers who worked in the last merchant sailing ships ought to be studied in their own right, and this book explores how some of them tried to mould a public vision of seafaring through their memoirs, in an era of overlapping and complicated transitions.

MARITIME MASCULINITY

Why study masculinity through the lives and memories of sailing-ship mariners? In part, because that is what many seafaring memoir-writers set out to do. If they rarely used the theoretical language of identity and gender, they were nonetheless preoccupied with the behaviours, beliefs, strengths, and weaknesses of men. Furthermore, they assumed a vital connection between seafaring and manliness. To give just one example from the authors featured in the following chapters, Bill Adams thought the link was inescapable: 'thank God for a hard life, a man's life – pray God for the manhood to endure it.'[21]

Contemporaries saw the sailing ship as a quintessentially male environment. The vast majority of sailors were men, but more than that, their work was perceived as masculine. Hard physical labour in dangerous conditions, venturing far from home, and expertise with traditional crafts and tools were all culturally coded as male activities. Even when women first started working at sea in large numbers, well into the twentieth century, those gendered assumptions restricted them to catering and service roles on passenger steamships.[22] An adventurous, mobile life carried strong manly connotations, although nation-states feared the uncontrolled transience and disruption associated with extreme masculinity, and it is no accident that frontier societies have proved revealing case-studies for gender scholars.[23] Seafaring was also embedded in wider forces with ascribed masculine characteristics, including exploration, trade, imperialism, and national rivalries. Practically all the national myths about British nautical prowess had male protagonists, whether historical (Drake, Raleigh, Cook, Nelson) or literary (Robinson Crusoe, Midshipman Easy, Long John Silver). The Victorian sea was considered a man's world at all levels, and our authors fitted the narratives of their own careers into that heritage.[24]

As even that list of nautical heroes suggests, however, there was never a single definition of what it meant to be a seafaring man, but some characteristics persisted over long periods and moulded the image of the seaman in popular culture. The 'manly sailor' who faced the elements with courage and aplomb, and 'Batchelor Jack' with a wife in every port, were embedded stereotypes, cultivated by writers, shipowners, seafarers, and politicians alike. The character of the seafaring workforce was central to debates about the industry's dangers and inefficiencies, with seafarers being portrayed as stoic, childish, noble, and feckless depending on polemical need.[25] Much of this representation was based on a muddle of ideas about seafaring, manliness, and freedom that had been evolving in British and American politics and literature since the Napoleonic Wars.[26] Throughout the decades covered by our authors' memoirs, the seafarer's craft and skill, encompassed in the nebulous but charged idea of 'seamanship,' was at the heart of the industry's soul-searching about the transition from sail to steam.[27]

An awareness of multiple kinds of seafaring masculinity connects this book with a key finding of the past generation of historical research: there is no single, monolithic masculinity. In any culture and period there are many interpretations of what it is to be masculine, some of which will overshadow, even dominate, others. This is expressed as a 'hegemonic' masculinity against which the rest of humanity – men, women, and children alike – are measured, and measure themselves in a kind of coerced aspiration. Definitions also change over time, because the historical construction of gender is a continuing process rather than an event.[28] Among our questions, therefore, is how these varying meanings of masculinity were realised by individual seafarers, between and among the sailors making up a crew, and between seafarers and their wider society.

Existing research reveals the complexity of what we might call the 'indicators' of masculinity: how was masculinity defined and judged? The favourite affirmatory terms in the Victorian era were 'manliness' and 'manly,' attached to a broad range of idealised behaviours and characteristics. The manly body was important, with a focus on physical strength, muscularity, bearing, grace of movement, health and hygiene, speed and suppleness, in varying combinations over time. The masculine mind mattered too, and in closely-related ways: the discipline and self-control that could be exercised over the body's actions was a common indicator of manliness, tied to issues of rationality, intelligence, and appropriate emotion.[29] As this suggests, masculinity also had a far-reaching imaginary level, through which cultural visions of manhood circulated in novels and newspapers, creating mass perceptions that fed back to the individuals who read them. Boys in particular encountered heroic manly role models at all levels, from their own friends, through characters in adventure fiction, to the nation-moulding mythologies of the school curriculum.[30]

Indicators imply judgements, not least because masculinity never stood in isolation from other cultural forces, and especially from class and social status. Historians have long demonstrated the complexities of the British class system, not least in its strange blend of rigidity and fluidity, and in the way that all classes divided their own members, let alone others, into good and bad segments.[31] Middle-class men might concede that their physical strength was inferior to that of manual labourers, for example, but they compensated with military and associational leadership, codes of gentlemanly behaviour, and mastery of elite sports.[32] At the same time, the boom in athletics and body-building among the middle classes in the late nineteenth century shows that they did not neglect physical prowess as an aspect of their masculinity. They privileged their sculpted bodies, achieved through their own efforts, over what they thought were 'natural' bodies for which workers could claim no credit.[33]

Elites also disparaged the lowest class of men for lacking even the muscularity of the stereotypical labourer, when a new factory-and-slum underclass came to embody physical as well as moral degeneration, and was deemed unfit for military service in the imperial wars of the late nineteenth century.[34] Working men pushed back, creating a complex associational culture that emphasised responsibility and aspiration. Often, their own organisations adopted codes of discipline around alcohol and sexual conduct that were stricter than those of employers.[35] Fundamental to all these indicators were statements about rougher versus more refined forms of manhood, but those distinctions evolved over time, and were often contested. Temperance campaigners and evangelical Christians offered high-profile challenges to rough masculinity, but so did the growing ranks of urban professionals, who had their own standards and expectations.

Defining masculinity therefore requires constant reference to others. The obvious comparison is with women, but arguably most men in the past took for granted their gendered difference from, and assumed superiority to, women. Their more pressing concern was how they compared with other men. Powerful voices denied some men their manhood altogether; more often, victims were accepted as male, but of the wrong sort, whether weak, cowardly, or childish. On the other hand, those whose manliness was accepted by dominant men gained social status. A sorting process often took place in teenage years, when boys were tested against standards of manliness in the workplace.

Evolving ideas of masculinity in the nineteenth and early twentieth centuries were intimately connected with changes in society, economy, and culture. Men's roles were challenged by women's rights movements, by mechanisation and de-skilling in factory employment, and by expectations that boys would spend longer at home or at school before moving into manhood. The domestication of men seemed positive if it led to sobriety and respectability, but provoked stigmas about hen-pecked husbands.[36] At the same time, manliness was reinvented for the purposes of imperial expansion, not least through the new athletic and character-building culture of the public schools, youth organisations like the Boy Scouts, and newspapers and magazines intended to mould the masculinity of boys from all social classes.[37]

Historians of sexuality have also identified this period as one of particular change and challenge to indicators of manly belief and conduct. In the late nineteenth century, western societies adopted increasingly strict definitions of sexual identity, classifying a 'normal' form of sexuality involving attraction between men and women, and stigmatising same-sex relations. All of our authors lived and wrote in this heteronormative culture, whatever their personal beliefs may have been. Over the course of the twentieth century, sexual preferences and behaviours became more public and more debated. Queer theory challenged the simple binary divide between heterosexuality and homosexuality, and urged the acceptance of a wider range of individual choices and identifications over any external classification. Debates over sexuality and gender increasingly took place in a febrile political atmosphere. Historians face ethical dilemmas in assigning labels to individuals whose own views are unclear, and rooted in a very different society and culture. Sexuality is inextricable from all the other aspects through which masculinity is constructed – perhaps especially class, work, ethnicity, and age – but because it has become such a strong cultural-identity marker in the twenty-first century, particular care needs to be taken in reading definitions back into past lives.[38]

All this suggests that we need to be open to many definitions and meanings of masculinity as we approach the sources. Sometimes, our authors discussed manliness in so many words, but we still need to ask what they meant, and try to understand the context of their beliefs. Often, masculinity was assumed and implied, mostly expressed through tales of courage and cowardice, class, rank, and power, race and nationality. Seafaring men were surrounded by long-standing myths, perpetrated in part by their continuing assertion of a historical identity, both as men and as seamen. Seafaring also takes us beyond familiar shore-based models of work and family into a rougher kind of masculinity that had to find its place and role in a changing economic order, and which was appropriated by men of all classes seeking to affirm their own manliness.[39] Maritime memoirs offer us a powerful source for the ways in which our authors sought to represent themselves and their shipmates, moulding a public image of seafaring men.

LIVING AND WRITING THE SEA

The Victorian boom in memoir-writing was a publishing phenomenon that encouraged a great variety of people to recount their lives to the reading public.[40] The trend grew and diversified into the twentieth century, and seafarers were just one of many groups using memoirs to define, and sometimes to defend, their sense of purpose and identity.[41] Many academic disciplines now use autobiography as source material, perhaps most prominently for literary, rhetorical, and historical studies. This has led to a new awareness of the complexity of life-writing's relationships with other ways of looking at the past, and not least with the methods and approaches of historians.[42]

This book uses published memoirs because they are, by definition, public statements of their authors' views and recollections. Memoirs may well carry factual information about seafaring, but they are not neutral documentary texts. Rather, their unique attribute is in painting whatever portrait of life under sail their authors wanted to convey to the reading public. All of our authors intended their words to be read by an audience beyond their own friends and families, and those with major publishers knew that their books might sell widely.

By the same token, this book does not use sailors' diaries or letters, because unpublished materials could not have influenced that broader public image of the mariner. It would be tedious to repeat the point throughout the book, but we should remain conscious that we are dealing with carefully-crafted impressions of seafaring and of seafaring men, created by our authors for that purpose. This book is not so much about life in sail as it is about how a group of former seafarers sought to represent that life and those who lived it.

Initial scoping for this project identified more than three hundred published, book-length memoirs by British merchant seafarers covering the era of the sail-to-steam transition, and this finished book uses evidence from forty-one authors. Memoir-writers are always a select group, because only a tiny minority of people ever publish their life stories, so it is rarely possible to approach this material with any kind of statistical sampling. Accepting that, historians prioritise breadth and richness of testimony, recognising that autobiography, for all its apparent randomness, gives us a seam of personal reflections, attitudes, and beliefs that is otherwise unavailable. The pioneering scholars who uncovered working-class life-writing revealed a plethora of human variation and individuality, and this has since become clear across all social groups, occupations, and classes.[43] The biases and distortions of autobiography become its strength. Drawn from a range of time, space, and experience, maritime memoirs reveal how the image of the seafaring man was created, and how it evolved.

While our authors had varied experiences, they shared a number of characteristics, the implications of which run through the book's analysis and conclusions. Most obviously, all were men. We do have some women's voices from sailing ships in the nineteenth century, but they were mostly passengers, or the wives or daughters of ships' captains, and their testimony tends to be private, in the form of letters or diaries.[44] In addition, all our authors' testimony is what gender theorists call heteronormative; in other words, the overwhelming assumption in their writing – to the point that they did not see any need to explain it – was that relationships between men and women are the natural and normal expression of sexual orientation. Only on very rare occasions do authors even hint at anything else, and we need to interpret such testimony in the context of that dominant, hegemonic cultural definition of male sexuality.

In terms of nationality, our authors were born in many parts of Britain and its then-colonies. Most highlighted their particular origins early in their memoirs, often to claim that the maritime character and culture of the places where they grew up had been an inspiration to them. All our memoir-writers were white; there are no published autobiographies of Black British seafarers in this time to compare with that of Harry Dean, for example, or with the magazine articles of James Williams, both African-American seafarers. Historians need other sources to find the voices of Black seafarers, and even then, few of those who have left any testimony worked in merchant sail in the era being studied here.[45]

Socially, seafaring memoir-writers were relatively privileged, just as the great majority of those who published life-writing tended to be in this period, at least by the time they wrote their memoirs. A few had humble beginnings, however, and only acquired education and economic security later. Maritime memoir in this era was overwhelmingly a middle-class, rather than a working-class or aristocratic, genre of life-writing. The implications of all these characteristics will be considered in more detail throughout the chapters.

Table 0.1 offers a summary of our authors' names and key dates. The years in the 'Apprentice' and 'Boy/OS' columns show when each author first went to sea, either as an indentured officer-apprentice, or as a ship's boy or Ordinary Seaman. Those were the most common ways to begin a seafaring career, and candidates taking the Board of Trade exam to qualify as second mate needed four years of sea experience through any of those routes.[46] Authors who passed their exams for second mate, first or only mate, and master mariner have the relevant years entered in the next three columns. These show when men gained their certificates, and do not necessarily mean that they worked as officers, although the great majority did. The final column has the year of publication for that author's memoir.[47]

Perhaps the most striking pattern to emerge from table 0.1 is the way our authors went through a rapid series of transitions at a young age. As the key dates indicate, it was common to go to sea as a boy of fourteen, and then have to grow into being a man, a seaman, and (for most authors) a junior officer

Table 0.1 Summary of memoir-writers featured in this book

Name	*Born*	*Apprentice*	*Boy/OS*	*Second mate*	*First/Only mate*	*Master*	*Memoir*
Bertram M. 'Bill' Adams	1879, Sevenoaks	1897	-	1901	-	-	1936
John Bain	1839, Nairn	-	1853	1861	1864	1866	1897
James Platt Barker	1874, Cheshire	1889	-	1894	1896	1897	1934
Albert Bestic	1891, Dublin	1908	-	1913	1915	1917	1958
James Gordon Bisset	1883, Liverpool	1898	-	1903	1905	1907	1958
Edgar Theophilus Britten	1874, Bradford	-	1892	1897	1899	1900	1936
Frank Thomas Bullen	1857, London	-	1869	1878	1880	-	1899
Reginald 'Rex' Clements	1885, Norwich	1903	-	1908	1910	1913	1924
William Caius Crutchley	1848, Hertfordshire	1863	-	1867	1869	1876	1912
Hans de Mierre	1890, Manchester	1905	-	1909	1911	1913	1971
Walter Ernest Dexter	1873, Birkenhead	1888	-	-	1896	-	1938
Charles Chubbuck Dixon	1873, Nova Scotia	-	1891	1896	1897	1899	1933
H.F. 'Fred' Farmer	1875, England	-	1894	-	-	-	1925
Clifford Fenton	1885, Cheshire	1901	-	1906	1907	-	1934
Melbourne Garahan #	1887, Australia	1903	-	-	-	-	1922
Bertram Fox Hayes	1864, Birkenhead	1880	-	1885	1887	1889	1925
Henry Hughes	1875, Wales	-	1890	-	-	-	1940
John Joseph Madden Jardine	1867, Liverpool	1881	-	1885	1887	1889	1924
William Herbert Sidney Jones	1887, London	1905	-	1912	1913	1917	1957
John Fryer Keane	1854, Whitby	1868	-	1873	-	-	1883
Charles Herbert Lightoller	1874, Lancashire	1888	-	1892	1895	1899	1935
William Robert Lord	1849, Chepstow	-	1861	1867	1869	1871	1894

John Masefield	1878, Herefordshire	-	1894	-	-	-	1944
Arthur Mason	1876, Ireland	-	1894	-	1899*	?*	1922
John Mason	1864, Orkney	-	1881	1890	1892	1894	1928
Ernest Pryce Mitchell	1862, Cornwall	-	1877	1883	1884	1887	1934
Henry Young Moffat	1844, Edinburgh	-	1861	1868	1874	1876	1910
Leslie Noel Morton	1896, Birkenhead	1911	-	1915	1917	1922	1968
Liam O'Flaherty	1896, Ireland	-	1918	-	-	-	1930
John Edward Patterson	1866, Yorkshire	-	1878	-	-	-	1911
Charles Protheroe	1863, London	1878	-	1883	1887	-	1903
Robert Ramsay	1851, Lanarkshire	-	1865	1871	?*	?*	1930
John Thomas 'Jack' Randell	1879, Newfoundland	-	1895	1904	1905	1907	1930
Arthur Henry Rostron	1869, Lancashire	1885	-	1890	1893	1894	1931
Walter Runciman	1847, Dunbar	1861	-	-	1868	1871	1924
Charles Stevens	1847, London	-	1860	-	-	-	1892
John Georgeson Sutherland	1871, Waterford	1887	-	1892	1894	1897	1922
Francis 'Frank' Symondson	1854, London	1872	-	-	-	-	1876
Alan Villiers	1903, Australia	-	1918	-	-	-	1949
John Wilson	1837, Durham	-	1856	-	-	-	1909
Frank Worsley	1872, New Zealand	1887	-	1892	1896	1900	1938

Notes: Authors' dates of birth, apprentice registration, and officer qualifications come from two key sources compiled by the British state in the nineteenth century, and now searchable via Ancestry.com: UK, *Apprentices Indentured in Merchant Navy, 1824–1910* (original data in Registrar General of Shipping and Seamen, Index of Apprentices (BT 150), The National Archives); and *UK and Ireland, Masters and Mates Certificates, 1850–1927* (original data in Registrar General of Shipping and Seamen, Certificates of Competency and Service (Masters and Mates) (RSS/MC), National Maritime Museum, Greenwich).

pseudonym of Charles Melbourne Jackson

* qualifications gained in the United States

? date unknown

- did not work in this role/gain this qualification

over the course of five or six years. That intimate connection between youth and seafaring created a particular kind of memoir. For those who succeeded, the sheer romantic adventure still struck them as remarkable decades later. Youth could be a time of achievement and responsibility, not just of dreams and aspirations. It is no accident that one of Joseph Conrad's best-known short stories has that one-word title: 'Youth,' written in 1898, conveys his sense of a world open to men in their late teens and early twenties, working as second mates on sailing ships in dangerous, thrilling circumstances. Among our authors, Walter Runciman knew of no other trade where 'a youngster can approach the top of his profession in nine or ten years.'[48] Walter Dexter looked back at his 'eager, restless, inquiring youth – youth which had taken the world as its oyster.'[49]

All this can make maritime memoirs even more youth-focused than life-writing in general. Authors recalled extraordinary experiences in their initial years at sea, and stressed how fundamental those were to the making of seafaring men. Several books are solely about first voyages; most others prioritise early years and skim over subsequent careers. While many authors later took pride in managing the routine business of commercial shipping during their years as captains, only a few wrote about that in the same detail. Youthful experiences were not just a prelude to the achievements of adulthood, and short periods of time mattered. We will see that authors felt strongly about the difference a few weeks or months could make to their seafaring skills, how important it felt to become the ship's senior apprentice, or to be assigned responsible new duties. Although writing later in life, when perceptions of time alter, and years merge into decades, our authors had not forgotten the speed at which they moved, and wanted to assert the value of that adventurous youth.

Four in five of our authors became ships' officers. A few, like James Bisset, Edgar Britten, and Bertram Hayes went on to be well-known captains and commodores of major steamship lines, while others had successful lower-profile careers. However, those who became officers did so by different routes, and this varied with time. Officers were increasingly drawn from the middle classes by the end of the nineteenth century, and the formal apprenticeship became the dominant way to enter the profession.[50] Our authors who went to sea before about 1880 were more likely to start as ships' boys or Ordinary

Seamen than as officer apprentices; after that date, the reverse was true, and more so with each decade.

This preponderance of officers meant that there were inevitable distances between memoir-writers and the sailors they remembered. Commentators at the turn of the century were clear, for example, that most apprentices were a class apart. The novelist Norman Duncan wrote a perceptive article in 1910 about the way they sent letters to seamen's mission pastors, keeping them informed of their adventures – just as young gentlemen would write to their old masters in the public schools, sharing tales full of stiff upper lips, understated perils, and tributes to 'decent chaps' lost overboard.[51]

Other gaps grew over time. Seafarers from humbler backgrounds, who had 'improved' themselves to become officers, often went on to acquire middle-class learning and status, well removed from their former shipmates. Even the few memoirs we have from men who never became officers show substantial education and reading, which distanced them from their peers. At the same time, all seafarers started with hard, dangerous work on deck and aloft, regardless of their intended future paths. When they came to write their memoirs, authors claimed an intimate knowledge of ordinary seafarers' attitudes and worldviews, whatever their own social status.

A few were more explicit, positioning their motives for writing memoirs in their own class and occupational standing, and the knowledge they thought that gave them. Fred Farmer, for example, who worked as an Ordinary Seaman in the 1890s, wanted his memoir to counter what he saw as the weight of writing 'from the cabin end of the ship.' Farmer used the affectionate slang 'shellback' throughout his book to make clear that he was writing of a particular kind of sailing-ship mariner, consigned to history by the time his book appeared in the 1920s. From the beginning, he stressed the mixture of class, masculinity, and morality encompassed in perceptions of the seafarer: 'the shellback did not conform to our ideas of what a gentleman should be; he was an unlovely being, a drunkard and an outcast: but in the battle against wind and wave he was a hero.'[52] Still, the fundamental distinctions of education and eloquence apply; the very fact that Farmer wrote a memoir pushed him into a different world from his shellbacks, and we cannot necessarily accept his assertion of greater authenticity than the captain-writers he claimed to be refuting.

Although the memoirs used in this book are varied, they are almost all affirmative of seafaring as a career, and as an essential part of British national character. They fit into broader autobiographical 'types'; most are coming-of-age and rite-of-passage narratives, while many resonate with the tramp and hobo tales that achieved some popularity early in the twentieth century, in which men gained nobility by defying the convention and conformity of urban life.[53] Few are the outright exposé form of autobiography, although Frank Symondson's criticism of the shipping industry's treatment of apprentices is a useful example. Likewise, only John Wilson's is really a religious conversion narrative, once a very common type of life-writing; others, though, do follow that format in more secular ways, with authors confessing to drift and disillusion, followed by a move onto the right track. As the leading scholar of an earlier period of seafarer memoir-writing put it, maritime autobiography is often hybrid.[54] The next section considers in more detail how seafaring memoir fits in the wider publishing landscape of the period.

PUBLISHING SEAFARING MEMOIR

As noted, this book seeks to explain how some seafarers used memoirs to publicly represent their careers, and those of their shipmates, in the last era of the British commercial sailing ship. Of course, publication is never a guarantee of readership and reception, and it is worth trying to assess the popularity of seafaring memoir as a genre. The memoirs used in this book normally attracted several reviews each, across such journals as the *Spectator*, *Times Literary Supplement*, *Nation*, *New Statesman*, and *Academy*, as well as in local and national newspapers. Most were positive. This points to a substantial, well-known genre taken seriously by people far beyond the shipping industry. The earliest memoir used here appeared in 1876, the last in 1971; the 1920s and 1930s saw the numerical peak. By the late 1930s, one reviewer was referring to 'the seemingly endless output of old sailormen's reminiscences,' and it was far from over then.[55]

In addition, many maritime memoirs were published by major London presses. They were pitched as mainstream non-fiction, advertised in newspapers and journals alongside works of history and biography, and priced at ten to fifteen shillings in the 1920s; all of this suggests a serious middle-class readership. A few received grander treatment, such as James Bisset's three-volume memoir tracing his career from sailing ships through to captaincy of the largest Atlantic liners.[56] Many British seafaring memoirs were picked up by leading American publishers also, implying an active transatlantic market over decades. D. Appleton & Co., New York, published Frank Bullen's memoir in 1899, in the same decade as it handled high-profile authors like Rudyard Kipling, and a broad range of scientific and medical texts. Thirty years later, Appleton published Robert Ramsay's memoir. A few authors worked with local publishers, mostly in seaports; William Lord's memoir was published in Leith, for example, and John Mason's in Kirkwall. Such books were less often reviewed in the national literary journals, although local newspapers noticed them. All in all, the autobiographies of merchant seamen seem to have been an attractive proposition to publishers, reviewers, and the reading public over several decades.

Chronologically, our authors' careers reflect the long transition from sail to steam, and then the lengthy afterlife of memoir publishing that can stretch decades beyond the events being described. As table 0.1 reveals, the earliest writers went to sea between the 1850s and the 1870s, and had already published their memoirs before the Great War. They joined an industry in which sail remained common. When men like Frank Symondson or Frank Bullen wrote about the harshness of sailing-ship work, they were in part calling for the reform of conditions that still affected many thousands of seafarers. Other authors of that generation, senior captains like John Bain and William Lord who published in the 1890s, believed that seafaring had already been much improved by safety legislation.

The rest of our authors, publishing from the 1920s onwards, were already commemorating life in sail, rather than reporting its continuing development. Still, they based their memoirs on varied experiences. When men like Madden Jardine and John Mason went to sea in the 1880s and early 1890s, they joined a sailing-ship sector that was constructing much larger vessels, and they were already nostalgic about the classic clipper ships of the 1860s. If most seafarers their age moved into steam after a few years, some, like James Barker and Charles Dixon, could still have substantial careers as captains in sail before then.

Young seafarers who joined the industry in the late 1890s and 1900s suspected, and often feared, that their large metal sailing ships were the last iteration of sail technology. If they wanted a career in shipping, men like William Jones and Hans de Mierre would probably have to join a steamship company immediately after their apprenticeships. By the time the last of them wrote their memoirs, the age of sail was half a century in the past, yet they still felt strongly that it needed to be explained and memorialised.

This periodisation of maritime memoir matters because of the time-shifting power of life-writing. Authors might assume that their memories remain constant and unchanging, but in reality the meanings that an author ascribes to events are always an amalgam of what happened at the time, and of all the influences that society and culture have pressed onto their thinking since – the memories of a succession of former selves, edited and revised by the process of aging. Authors can change their minds between living an experience and reflecting on it decades later; they will also be aware that the society around them receives and interprets ideas and events differently over time.[57]

This is especially important in seafaring memoir for two reasons. First was the realisation that Britain's deep-water sailing fleet would not be revived with the return of peace in 1918; the few remaining sail owners from before the war had moved to steam or abandoned the industry, and had no successors. This finality created both demand from a curious public, and a supply of memoirs from retired seafarers – what one reviewer called 'the impulse to self-expression of those who see their day and generation passing unrecorded.'[58] However much our early authors predicted the end of sail, it was not yet a reality in the way that it became for our later writers.

The other factor was the war itself. Commentators thought the Great War had crystallised debates around Britishness and the sea, in a flurry of soul-searching about the unappreciated courage of the merchant seaman. Archibald Hurd, in the official history of the conflict, argued that centuries of heritage defined the merchant seafarer as 'no ordinary man' engaged in simple trade and distribution of goods; rather, seafarers were 'a great brotherhood' whose traditions stretched back 'in unbroken and glorious sequence, to the early days of British history.'[59] Although the great majority of seafarers during the war had served on steamships, this desire to commemorate and mythologise fitted naturally with nostalgia for sail.

There was another reason connecting 1920s memoir-writing back to the Great War, and then further back to the sailing ship. On one level, it is absurd to equate peacetime working at sea with fighting in war, but in other ways it is not so strange. Some of our authors believed it. John Masefield wrote of the 'indescribable look of high endurance, which used to mark the sailing-ship seaman,' and claimed to have seen no one else with such faces, except some of the soldiers of the Great War.[60] In addition, because of the war, popular culture suddenly had to wrestle with issues that seafaring communities had known about long before. Men died and were buried far from home; others went missing; most came back changed, physically and mentally. They learned to live and work with diverse comrades in difficult circumstances, and built intense friendships and loyalties. They believed their actions spoke for a better kind of Britishness, and a better manhood, although most tried not to boast of it.

Seafaring memoir-writers mixed autobiography, biography, and history, interweaving their own memories, the stories told by their shipmates, and historical texts. Some had read exploration, travel, and oceanography books along with the popular literature that celebrated famous clipper-ship passages.[61] In so doing, they forged a history of seafaring that spanned decades before, during, and after their own time at sea, and claimed to be saving a heritage that might otherwise be forgotten or misrepresented. Some struggled to convey their own self-image and how to relate to those around them, a common issue in autobiography at the boundaries of social classes.[62] Brought up on a Victorian literature of manly heroism, improvement, modesty, and the triumph of personality and character over adversity, memoir-writers had to confront those assumptions about manhood when living and representing their own lives, and those of the men they sailed with. They had to balance the desire to portray themselves as self-made, independent men against cultural taboos about seeming to be self-obsessed and egotistical.[63]

Autobiography can also be a kind of folklore, a published manifestation of the oral traditions that provided authors with their memories in the first place, as seafarers' stories evolved from being recent anecdotes to becoming legends and then deeply-embedded myths.[64] Memoirs challenged, but also contributed to, the assumption that sailing-ship mariners were an isolated 'folk,' prone to being romanticised by outsiders.[65] Writing about the sea and seafaring is always mythic; ancient voyage narratives like Homer's *Odyssey* remain debated for their melding of folklore, history, and personal testimony, and their remorseless influence on writers ever since.[66]

More broadly, memoirs raise questions about how historical texts are created, how their meaning evolves over time, and how accounts can differ without authors setting out to deceive. Scholars value memoirs for insights into an individual's perceptions and beliefs, and not necessarily as empirical narratives. At the same time, audiences still hold memoir-writers to that factual standard, with regular scandals about 'fake' autobiographies.[67] We are still left with the fallacy of extrapolated authenticity – just because an author is meticulous about facts does not guarantee any deeper understanding or awareness of the people, events, or concepts he is describing, nor any commitment to a wider truth. Writers know that readers can be seduced by detail, falling for the air of authority that we are taught to associate with intricacy, and especially with dates, numbers, and specialist language.

Of all the literary genres our authors had to be conscious of, sea fiction was the most problematic.[68] It should be stressed that while sea fiction was often autobiographical in its inspiration and content, the works used in this book were sold as memoirs rather than novels. Even so, early memoir-writers already suspected that the reading public struggled to tell fact from fiction in sea-writing. They were careful to pay tribute to well-known novelists, in an ironic appropriation of literary conventions to lend credibility to their own experiences. Frank Bullen, for example, praised 'writers like Kipling, Cutcliffe Hyne, Joseph Conrad, and Clark Russell,' while insisting his own work was non-fiction.[69] William Crutchley referred to being 'great cronies' with 'my friend Mr. Clark Russell,' who wrote 'inimitable books'; John Wilson, recalling an Atlantic storm, stated that 'if I had the pen of a Clark Russell I might describe the waves as they ran like great hills.'[70]

Later authors worked, and wrote, in a maritime world that the public increasingly imagined through Joseph Conrad's novels and sea-stories.[71] Arthur Bestic and James Bisset both invoked the same phrase of Conrad's to capture their feelings of awe and excitement in deep water, and Hans de Mierre even described one of his old second mates as a 'conradesque' character.[72] Conrad was imitated and parodied in his day, and even his friends gently lampooned his tales of storms and self-discovery.[73] But that is just testimony to his impact, and it is telling that reviewers often compared maritime memoirs with Conrad's novels, rather than with other memoirs, or with works of marine science.[74]

Indeed, some maritime memoir-writers muddied genre distinctions further. Frank Bullen was a prolific writer on many subjects, for example, while John Patterson and Arthur Mason wrote sea novels, and Bill Adams and Walter Runciman published volumes of sea stories. James Bisset wrote magazine articles and was an active lecturer to Rotary Clubs. In most cases, their memoirs only came later in life. Such men therefore spent years writing and rewriting their time at sea, creating and moulding themselves and their shipmates as characters in their books. Much, perhaps all, of their work can be read as autobiographical, even if only their later books were explicitly sold as autobiography.[75] By then they had, in a sense, done a lot of our thinking for us. For that reason, it is all the more important in this book to include testimony from those who wrote nothing other than their memoirs, and who might give us a less filtered and rehearsed insight, even if they in turn had been influenced by many literary forms along the way.

Some of our authors sought authenticity precisely by denying literary polish. They claimed another affirmatory, manly stereotype, taking on the persona of the bluff, straightforward seafarer who spoke simply and honestly. Henry Moffat wrote in 1910 that he had produced 'a sailor's yarn, told in plain, unvarnished, but let me add, truthful language.'[76] When Arthur Mason began writing in the 1920s, he hoped that 'no one would sneer at the simplicity of an old sailor.'[77] Later that decade, John Mason stressed that he wanted to write 'as plainly as possible, in the plain everyday language of the sea, without any pretence to literary merit.'[78] Reviewers expected this: one critic commended William Crutchley for writing in a 'vigorous and masculine style,' while another thought that 'literary pretensions' had ruined Walter Dexter's book.[79] James Barker even delegated the writing of his memoir to his son, insisting, 'I am a deep water sailor, not an author!'[80] However, Barker's career points to a need to control every detail around him, so we can be sure he dictated the text, even while feeling it necessary to deny writing it.

Finally, memoir-writers were often explicit in contributing to a nationalist mythology around seafaring and Britishness. They represented these 'simple sailors' – the authors themselves, and the men they had worked with – as symbols of a bolder kind of Britishness, but one that contained tensions and paradoxes. Historians have revealed the ubiquity, but also the vagueness, of assumptions about Britain as a maritime nation. Contemporaries complained that most Britons were ignorant about life and work at sea, and scholars have demonstrated the sheer complexity of factors that somehow added up to a recognisable Britishness.[81] Authors looking back from an era of world wars, economic depression, and perceived national decline were tempted to put the lost age of sail on a pedestal of wishful thinking. The old shellback, like King Arthur, might one day return to save the day. When our writers took on that wider mission, creating a cultural narrative for a manly seafaring endeavour steeped in national symbolism, their memoirs offer us valuable ways into understanding the foundations of heritage, memory, and identity.

1

Seafaring Boys

The first step in making seafaring men was making seafaring boys. Most of our authors initially went to sea in their early to middle teens, but many memoirs start before that, with childhood dreams. The idea of a boy running away to sea was entrenched in history and literature, and this chapter explores the would-be seafarer's journey from those inspirations through to the reality of the first voyage. Memoir-writers often gave this phase disproportionate weight. Boys built a maritime fantasy for themselves at home and school, but standing on the deck of a large sailing ship for the first time was always a startling experience. Boy sailors on deep-water ships left family, home, and community behind with no way of changing their minds for many months, and joined crews of strangers about whom they had already conjured a formidable mythology. While putting away childish things is a staple of autobiographical writing in general, our authors thought seafaring created a particularly dramatic example.

Seafaring boyhood was a phase in itself – not yet manhood, but no longer childhood.[1] While boys may have wanted the transition to manhood to happen faster, they recognised that as boys they had freedoms denied to both children and responsible adult men. Most writers came to regard a tough initiation as a tempering, formative experience that turned them into men and seamen, although a few recalled their early days at sea as being full of suffering and exploitation. As steam eclipsed sail, young seafarers at the beginning of the twentieth century were already conscious that the meaning of maritime boyhood was changing. By the time they wrote their memoirs, many thought they had been the last boy sailors in the mould of Raleigh, Nelson, and the other heroes of their childhood reading. This gave them an intense nostalgia for their own careers, rooted in the myths of manly, sea-going Britishness that had started them on the path in the first place. Their accounts offer unusual insight into Victorian and Edwardian ideas of masculine adolescence, and the accepted roles and behaviours of boys.

VOICES FROM THE PAST

Childhood dreams of going to sea were encouraged by a literary culture focused on adventure, exploration, empire, and ideals of heroic masculinity. While Defoe's *Robinson Crusoe* (1719) remained a popular text, the Victorian publishing industry revived shipwreck and piracy stories for young readers. In these, white British boy sailors would take command of survivors and lead them back to civilisation, demonstrating effortless authority over women, foreigners, and even British men from the lower classes. Although they differed in detail and sophistication, books like Ballantyne's *The Coral Island* (1858), Verne's *Dick Sand: A Captain at Fifteen* (1878), and Stevenson's *Treasure Island* (1881–83) featured boy heroes who left their 'stay-at-home' contemporaries far behind. Such writers created a vision of independence and opportunity, in which boys prospered away from petty authority, feminine influences, and the dullness of routine employment.[2] If our authors later felt the need to distance themselves from fictional sea-writing, they recognised that their childhood selves had absorbed the frontier masculinity of such work.

There is, however, a striking anachronism to the maritime consciousness our memoir-writers absorbed from their childhood reading. Many cited Frederick Marryat's novels, which were based on his service in the Napoleonic Wars and published in the 1830s and 1840s. One of our early authors, John Patterson, read Marryat in the 1870s, and this provoked his 'unalterable intention of becoming a sailor.'[3] Two decades later, Rex Clements's inspiration for going to sea was 'romance and much reading of *Robinson Crusoe*.'[4] When Clifford Fenton's mother finally agreed to let him go to sea in 1901, he revelled in the thought of following 'Drake, Blake, Hudson, Nelson.'[5] Alan Villiers, one of the last of our authors to go to sea, grew up in the decade before the Great War reading Marryat's novels, and also biographies of Cook, Flinders, Bligh, and Nelson.[6]

This obsession with fictional and idealised images of an older maritime world worried parents and mentors. Villiers's father told him that seafaring 'only seemed adventurous because I was building up my ideas of it from my own imaginings, fed on books, and the sight of ships in a safe port.' The first mate of a Norwegian ship told him even more plainly: 'Don't let the books fool you, my boy. There's no sailor writing them.'[7] But of course sailors were writing – the early memoirs featured in this book were published before our later authors went to sea, and were clear about the hardships of seafaring life at the end of the nineteenth century. For all the changes to shipping across the century, boys going to work in the later years of sail embraced an archaic and mythologised nautical worldview through their childhood reading.

If literary visions of seafaring seemed rooted in the distant past, some family and personal inspirations were also based on experiences of decades before. Intergenerational oral traditions created a rich combination of knowledge, attitudes, and moral standards that were passed down to children, and seafaring families were no exception.[8] Walter Runciman, for example, reported a key moment with his grandfather and two great-uncles in 1855, when he was seven years old. He remembered them as tall, strong, and genial men, 'magnificent specimens of manhood,' who told matter-of-fact tales of their service in Nelson's navy without boasting or grievance. Runciman decided that being a seafarer was every British boy's duty, and identified with the boy sailors who played important roles in his uncles' stories.[9]

It seems not to have mattered to Runciman that his uncles had been in the Royal Navy, while all his own testimony assumed that he would be a merchant sailor. This is common in memoirs. Tales of the Elizabethan 'sea dogs' Drake and Raleigh, of piracy and its suppression, and the cult of Horatio Nelson permeated English history lessons for most children, and navy expansionists were vocal in the era of great power tensions late in the nineteenth century. Although some of this encouraged boys to join the navy itself, much of it created a generic sense of maritime destiny, and of exemplary seafaring manhood as national character.[10] Indeed, maritime classics had little to say about seafaring of a kind relevant to modern commercial shipping, and their focus on individualism, leadership, and dramatic action bore scant relation to the routine, collaborative hard work our authors would experience at sea. Few complained of being misled. Looking back, most accepted that childhood visions of seafaring were unrealistic, elitist, romanticised, and militaristic, but that the right kind of boy would value inspiration over measured advice.

As a result, some of our authors managed to combine a surprising degree of drift with their aspirations to become seafarers. Bill Adams, growing up in the 1890s, devoted even more memoir space than most to his childhood visions, and recalled building an image of British maritime heroism from meeting a nephew of Admiral Pellew (a popular hero of the Napoleonic Wars), then by seeing Spanish ships in harbour that made him think of the age of Drake, then again through a formal education that stressed empire and triumph, ancient and modern. In addition to a list of classical authors, he cited *Treasure Island* as his schoolboy reading. When the time came to leave school, however, he had no clear path. He unsuccessfully applied for a job in the paymaster's department of the Royal Navy, which he vaguely supposed might lead him into some seagoing role. He then secured an apprenticeship with a commercial shipowner.[11]

Walter Runciman's encounter with his sailor uncles has another lesson for us. The resulting discussions drew a gendered line through his family and its decision-making. His mother rejected any glamorisation of seafaring, recounting how her relatives had been taken by press-gangs and lost at sea, and how she had insisted that her own husband find work on shore. Where Runciman saw freedom and manliness, his mother saw coercion and degradation. Although Runciman denied that his determination to go to sea wavered, he gave a good deal of space to his mother's arguments, crediting her with maintaining the family's moral direction around hard work and education as the route to improvement.[12] It troubled Runciman that exercising what he saw as a boy's right to go to sea, to become a man and an honourable inheritor of Britain's nautical traditions, would put him in conflict with his mother.

Authors across our period stressed their mothers' views and actions. Robert Ramsay recalled how his mother took him to the shipping company office to sign on as a boy sailor in 1865, and he appreciated this support rather than resenting any slight on his ability to manage his own affairs. Soon after, Ramsay thought that having his sisters and their friends kiss him goodbye on the quayside enhanced his manliness, rather than making him look like a child. He was careful not to cry when he hugged his mother, though, because he knew the crew was watching.[13] Pryce Mitchell squared the circle by insisting on both his independent right to go to sea in the 1870s, and his unashamedly sentimental attachment to his mother. He recalled how his mother was 'far braver than I' at their first leave-taking, and the comfort he took from packets of lavender she had secreted in his kit.[14] When James Bisset made an abortive attempt to stow away on a sailing ship in 1897, he was 'appalled at the enormity of the crime I was about to commit against my loving parents, especially my dear mother.' It took another year to persuade them to let him go to sea, and Bisset stresses several times his appreciation for his parents' financial support in paying for his indentures and fitting him out for sea. Nor was he embarrassed to have his mother negotiate his kit with the outfitters, hailing her wisdom and common sense.[15]

Some parents accepted that their sons would go to sea, but took steps to delay the event, trying to build knowledge and maturity, and perhaps hoping that the boy would grow out of a passing phase. Jack Randell felt it was 'the most natural thing in the world' for him to go to sea because 'we Randells have been sailors as far back as our records go.' He claimed that his ancestors had sailed with all the British maritime greats from Drake to Nelson. When it came to his own teenage years, however, his parents slowed him down, negotiating a gradual acquisition of seagoing experience. They let him work on a fishing schooner every summer so long as he spent winters safely at home, bribing him with gifts of a horse and a shotgun. By the time he was sixteen and had completed school, his parents evidently believed they had managed his energies and aspirations well, and Randell was sent to sea with his brother, who was already a ship's captain.[16]

Parents were disciplinary as well as loving influences, and authors felt the tension between obedience and conformity on the one hand, and youthful adventure on the other. Their careers raised the awkward truth that deference at home and in school was not a necessary prerequisite for seafaring success, and perhaps not even a desirable one. Again, this seems consistent over decades. Henry Moffat told of running away from home in the 1850s, fighting back against a schoolmaster, and forging a letter from his mother so that he could run away to sea at the age of twelve. For all that, his memoir is affectionate towards his family, and he saw no tension between such behaviour and his eventual respectability as a ship's captain.[17] Frank Worsley devoted the first two chapters of his memoir to describing an outdoor childhood in 1880s New Zealand, during which he claimed to find 'civilized life very irksome.'[18] By the time he wrote his memoir, Worsley had already published two books about his role in the 1914 Shackleton expedition to the South Pole, so he hardly needed to establish his adventure-seeking credentials. Nonetheless, he seems to have felt a wild childhood was an essential preface to the story of his first voyage as a boy sailor.

Disagreements with fathers are common in memoirs. Melbourne Garahan recalled his father making a speech about his poor conduct, and how this would be addressed by sending him to the training ship *Worcester*. Garahan's father spoke of the behaviour expected of men, rather than just the usual strictures about the obedience of boys: 'you must understand that there is nothing unmanly or humiliating in being subject to discipline.'[19] The irony was that being sent away suited boys like Garahan, not because they necessarily agreed with that disciplinary philosophy, but because the maritime world offered them alternative fathers. Edgar Britten remembered a symbolic sequence of events. As a six-year-old passenger at sea with his mother, he got into a fight with another boy, impressing the ship's captain with his 'pluck.' A dozen years later, his parents refused to let him go to sea, so he ran away, and claimed to have met that same captain on the docks in Liverpool. This new father figure found Britten his first job on a ship.[20]

Ultimately, parents struggled to compete with the idea of seafaring as birthright and vocation. John Bain, one of our earlier authors, got his first job at the age of eleven with a Poor Law tax inspector, and soon confessed to his superior that he wanted to be a sailor. At that point, Bain recalled, 'a strange, wistful, far-off look came into the old man's face as if the memory of an old dream had been suddenly awakened.' Bain discovered that the inspector's hobby was working out navigation problems, concluding that, 'I never could rid myself of the idea that the old gentleman had been born to be a sailor, but by some mischance had missed his destiny.' It would seem absurd had Bain written of his employer's destiny to be a tax inspector, but such language underlines seafaring's unusual hold on the imagination, as well as Bain's sense that he must avoid the old man's fate and go to sea himself. Even then, Bain worried about his mother's wishes, and waited at home until she agreed; he claimed that her approval was a great sacrifice to her, and made him determined to do well as a sailor.[21]

All these authors were conscious of conflicting forces acting on them, their families, and their wider society and culture. Going to sea was a radical disruption, likely to inflict deep hurt on mothers especially, yet it was also a long-standing tradition for boys steeped in a maritime imaginary. Writers often gave careful, respectful accounts of parental arguments, and felt the need to pay due regard to the views of elders. Most were writing as retired ships' captains, so could not really advocate anything else. But if loyalty to parents was a valued trait in young boys, so was a bold character. Seafaring had a cultural pull on boys that few occupations could match, despite – or perhaps because of – that temporal disconnection between the modern industry and the seemingly timeless mythology surrounding boys who ran away to sea.

IN SEARCH OF A MARITIME SELF

Children, and especially boys, had a licence to treat the outdoor world as an adventure playground in the nineteenth century. Along with the often-cited romantic ruralism of fields, woods, and streams, urban children had access to industrial spaces that would later be restricted on safety grounds, and those growing up near the coast had harbours, the sea, and boats at their doorsteps. Looking back at these childhood explorations, authors claimed the risk-taking persona of the would-be seafarer, stressing that they had supplemented their reading of the maritime classics with a more active path to the sea, and in particular one that involved spending time around working sailors.

Walter Runciman and Liam O'Flaherty were very different writers, but they offer similar reflections on growing up near the sea, and being inspired by its impact on the people around them. When he wrote his memoir in the 1920s, Runciman was a major shipowner recalling a childhood on the north-east England coast in the 1860s, when the coal-and-iron industrialisation of the district was still underway.[22] To him, the North Sea, 'in all its divine magnificence and its angry and sullen moods,' was a looming presence, full of danger and menace, yet irresistible.[23] O'Flaherty, who became one of Ireland's best-known novelists, grew up in a fishing village on the Atlantic coast half a century later, but to him also the sea was 'the greatest living thing in my environment.'

For both men, the effect of those forces on their elders, and particularly the seafaring men, formed their own aspirations and ideals. Runciman would listen to fishermen as they pondered the fate of ships struggling to make headway offshore, thrilled to be 'allowed to stand on the outskirts of the group.' Being tolerated by such men raised the prospect of making the transition from a small and delicate child to a seaman. O'Flaherty made a different point, eulogising the sailors and fishermen of his childhood, but drawing a sharp contrast between that kind of maritime life and the one he encountered. A modern sailor was, in his view, 'a slave of the sea,' a man who lived as an outcast from the land, and when O'Flaherty made his way to the London docks in search of work, he felt 'as strange to that mode of life as one who had never seen the sea.'

For Bill Adams, meeting working seafarers while still a child on shore in the 1890s was crucial to his evolving identity. He recalled a series of such encounters, including one of the earliest and most formative, when a sailor shouted 'hey, shipmate' to him. Throughout his memoir, Adams returned to that word as the mantra of the true sailor, fundamental to the well-being of a crew and vessel at sea, but also to him as an individual. His next lesson was a bewildering introduction to sailor philosophy and behaviour. As a thirteen-year-old, Adams tried to stop a man beating a woman in the street, and had to be rescued by passing sailors. One of them lectured him on the proper etiquette of getting involved in other people's affairs, and on how to tell whether a fight was fair or not. Adams was selecting an inexorable string of events that steered him toward a seafaring self. Elsewhere he admitted that most of his visits to the docks were solitary experiences because 'sailors seemed never to have much to say to a young lad.' He made his own influences, latching onto every exotic place-name, and absorbing an intense sensory environment of shapes, smells, and sounds: the tar, brine, and sails, the craft and technology of figureheads and rigging, the sailors speaking their 'unintelligible language.'[24]

The first thirty pages of Adams's memoir are therefore a powerful statement of how a boy became obsessed with going to sea, and of his developing self-image as a shipmate-to-be. But Adams's book is also a reminder that memoir-writers easily create a false sense of inevitability. For every boy who went to sea, there were many who shared their aspirations but who took different decisions. Sometimes we get tantalising glimpses of roads not taken. Henry Williams, for example, grew up in the busy port of St Ives, the son of a man who had been at sea in his youth. Early in his memoir, he wrote a single sentence that presumably hides a great deal of disappointment and trouble: 'at the age of fifteen I began to think of the future, and my first thought was naturally for the sea, but after a few coasting voyages I gave that up and all idea of a seafaring life.'[25] Williams opted instead for an administrative career in railway and dock companies, and refrained in the rest of his memoir from drawing any lessons from that seafaring experience.

Indeed, a few of our authors stand in direct contradiction to those inspired by a nautical vocation. Frank Bullen, who became one of the most prolific maritime writers of the era, remembered his initial reluctance to go to sea in the 1870s. He had no illusions about the nature of seafaring life and work, having seen the suffering of sailors on shore, but his home life was worse still. Following the break-up of his parents' marriage, Bullen lived with an aunt and acquired a good reading education until her death when he was nine. He then struggled for three years before an uncle took him to sea. Bullen went because it offered him food and accommodation; he had no affection for the life or for his uncle, and his account is unusual in downplaying any initial attraction to the sea.[26] Bullen's route into seafaring was probably very common, even normal, for poorer boys who had limited options when growing up in port towns.

Most of our authors, however, grew up in the middle classes, and had a more deliberate and structured path toward their first voyages. Officer apprentices had the luxury of making detailed preparations, helped by family and friends, and many authors recalled how this made them conscious of a key transition. Being fitted out with clothing and equipment for a sea voyage had a crucial practical purpose, given that months would pass before the next opportunity to stock up on essentials, but that was often overshadowed by its symbolism. Authors remembered their visits to a marine outfitter as an initiation into a material world that immediately marked them as sailors. Boys being kitted out for a first voyage already felt very different from their schoolboy selves of a few weeks before. That equipping was also the last occasion when their fantasies of sea life remained intact. When preparing for all their subsequent journeys, hard-learned experience drove their choices and priorities.

Three accounts, decades apart, point to an unchanging ritual as newly-outfitted apprentices prepared for sea. In 1863, William Crutchley signed his indentures and then 'went back home to display to my lay acquaintances and the world of Margate in general, the full glory of blue cloth and brass buttons.' 'Upon mature consideration,' he wrote, wearing the brass-bound uniform was the best moment of his career, eclipsing even his first command.[27] Later, in 1881, Madden Jardine built a seagoing image of himself from the successes of slightly older role models, and the symbolic paraphernalia and behaviours of seafaring. 'Many a heroic school-mate' had overcome opposition at home to go to sea. They would then return in their brass-bound uniforms to lord it over those left behind and impress 'all the girl chums.' To Jardine, an apprentice on shore was unmistakeable – 'his breeze and his swank and his ten degrees roll' – but he was also part of a larger destiny. Looking back, Jardine believed that he had grown up in the 'high water mark' of the great age of seafaring, that his own port of Liverpool hosted the 'flower of England's Merchant Fleets' in its miles of docks, and that ships' apprentices were a personification of something triumphant. It all added up to a view of his future that had no patience for the safer alternatives, not least the 'tall office stool' occupied by respectable boys of his class.[28]

Finally, in the 1900s, William Jones cemented his seafaring self-image in the days between being accepted as an apprentice and joining his first ship. He had been constructing it for years, befriending the sons of watermen and fishermen, and going as a 'volunteer member' of the crew on their fathers' vessels – Jones's wording seems carefully chosen there, keen to stress that he was part of a group of seafarers, and never just a passenger. A former school-mate, just returned from a Cape Horn voyage, provided Jones with a list of equipment, and he rushed up to London to acquire it. The novelty of the oil-skin suit and sou'wester hat was 'a great thrill,' but it was the brass-buttoned jacket and company cap that he wore on a tour of his local friends and relatives. In addition, 'photographs had to be taken' of him in both uniform and oilskins. For Jones, promenading around Southend waiting for orders was 'one of the most exhilarating of my experiences of over fifty years in or connected with ships. It was a period in which imagination could soar, unhindered by reality.'[29] His mother's advice on cleanliness, and her help in packing his sea-chest, became the last link with life on shore, and then Jones went to the docks by himself, to avoid any emotional scenes on the quayside. He drew the line between shore and sea, and between his old life and his new one, well inland at the point where he left his family.

Some transitions took longer than others, especially when parents insisted on their sons attending a nautical training school. There was great ambivalence about this. For all their qualms about the risks of going to sea, families could not afford years of theoretical education that would be unsuited to any other career. It was better to find out if the boy had the practical and physical attributes of a seafarer first, before teaching him navigation.[30] There was class anxiety, too. While the Thames training ship *Worcester* and its Mersey counterpart *Conway* catered to the middle classes, most institutions were created under Industrial Schools legislation, intended to push boys from the lower classes into work as ordinary seafarers.[31]

Some boys thought schooling just slowed down their aspirations. James Barker was dismayed when his father sent him to a navigation school in the 1880s rather than letting him go straight to sea. He had little to say about the curriculum in his memoir, and while he conceded that navigation training had 'proved invaluable,' Barker thought most knowledge of seamanship was 'self-acquired.'[32] We will come back to that revealing individualistic mindset in later chapters.

Others, though, saw nautical school as formative. Melbourne Garahan and John Masefield were cadets in *Worcester* and *Conway*, respectively. The fact that their ships never left port seems irrelevant as they recount their induction to maritime life. *Worcester* showed Garahan the meaning of the maths he had neglected at school; now that he could apply it to learning about navigation, it became fascinating. Garahan claimed that these institutions had transformed the quality of merchant officers, building character at least as well as the great public schools.[33] Masefield's dreams became populated with nautical paraphernalia. Visiting the Liverpool Sailors' Home outfitting department, he was captivated by a display case of cap badges showing shipping company flags before donning his own uniform and cap. This initiation into maritime iconography was profound; as Masefield put it, 'Having thus branded myself … the time had come to proceed to the ship.'[34] Both boys went to sea for real later, but their idea of themselves as seafarers was forged in those days of leaving home and joining the training ships.

By the time they were writing their memoirs, our authors could have been forgiven for skipping over their chronology, and forgetting that a year seems much longer, and carries many more complicated meanings, to a boy of fourteen than it does to a man of sixty. It is striking, then, that most gave a lot of space to those small milestones on the way to becoming a seafarer. Rapid transitions were the hallmark of the early stages of a seafaring career, and many authors wanted to explain that those began on shore, in a set of deliberate actions by which they constructed their would-be seafarer's identity.

FIRST VOYAGES

Most of our authors were between fourteen and seventeen when they went to sea, which was in line with the pattern across the shipping industry. Some earlier writers started younger, but average ages increased from the 1890s, when parents insisted that boys stay in school before starting an apprenticeship. Still, authors and commentators agreed that boys should go to sea in their early to middle teens if they, and the industry, were to gain the most advantage from youthful enthusiasm and adaptability. John Mason, who worked on a wide variety of vessels from the 1880s, thought it best to start at fourteen, and certainly no older than eighteen. He believed that 'young boys, as a rule, have not the sense to get scared, and they become so inured to hardships and dangers aloft and on deck that they take them as they come and think nothing of it all through life.'[35]

Although he went to sea more than two decades after Mason, William Jones had similar views. In his opinion, 'the young and healthy mind, and active body, of a fifteen-year-old boy become adjusted with surprising speed to the intricacies of a new situation,' and even in the first week or two at sea a young sailor with the proper attitude could become useful.[36] As we will see, Jones could be very critical of the working conditions imposed on seafarers, but he did not doubt the basic premise of his career path, its starting point in the sudden immersion of boys into difficult, dangerous work, and the ability of suitable boys to cope with this. Jones looked back at his first apprentice voyage as justification for the practice of sending boys to sea, albeit in a well-managed way – one had to be the right kind of boy, the prototype of a balanced manhood.

First voyages inculcated three key lessons, discussed by our authors as a process of initiation, when boys joined a working environment that was also a way of life. The first was taking and knowing their place, which of course was at the bottom of the ship's hierarchy, even if they had expectations of rapid advancement. Second was loyalty to the ship. Third was a broader loyalty to the craft of seafaring. All these were played out within a community of men and boys that could be supportive and fraternal as well as disciplinary, and with notable variations depending on whether the new sailor was a ship's boy or an officer-apprentice. As has been noted, many authors made their first voyage the largest single part of their memoir, devoting far more space to it than they did to later years and decades at sea. Authors used 'first-voyager' to describe themselves and others in this situation. A few also labelled the older boys as second- or third-voyagers, but most did not – there was a real sense that anyone who went back to sea after the first voyage was well on the way to becoming a seafarer.

Such transitions were common on the route to manhood. Scholars have shown that leaving behind the domesticity of childhood was not only about leaving mothers and feminine influences, but also fathers and kinds of manhood unsuitable for the boy's new career.[37] Some of our authors remembered the powerful symbolism of the moment, albeit with a guilty conscience. Walter Dexter, for example, later thought he had been callous for saying a 'hasty goodbye' to the sick father he would never see again, but 'I was to take my place among men, and to battle alongside them, against whatever might come.'[38]

Taking that place was never straightforward. Authors who had constructed an officer-like image for themselves often recounted having their airs and graces deflated. Most played up, for comic effect, the gap between an apprentice's vision and the rougher reality, but at the time it must have been less humorous. James Barker reported arriving on board, proud of his brass-buttoned jacket and imagining himself an admiral. Announcing that he was 'James P. Barker, the new apprentice,' he got a response 'like a blast of dynamite' from a 'piratical looking fellow with a black beard.' This turned out to be the ship's mate, who called Barker 'Jimmy,' and insisted on being called 'Sir.'[39] Albert Bestic's arrival on board was almost identical: wrongly assuming the mate who questioned him was a shabby, limping caretaker, he was also pulled up and lectured about how to address his superiors.[40] In writing about these events, authors were claiming to have been boys able to join the rough society of seafaring men, and later tell a yarn against themselves.

Those who started as ships' boys and Ordinary Seamen reported mixed experiences at the hands of crews and officers. Some sailors showed a remarkable level of sentiment toward their youngest shipmates. Although boys were expected to grow up quickly on board, childlike behaviours could gain the sympathy of the crew initially. Charles Stevens, for example, joined in the leisure activities on his first ship in 1860 by wearing a blue shirt and a sailor's cap given to him by his mother, and singing a song called 'A Seaman's Life is the Life for Me.' He reproduced the lyrics in his memoir and concluded that these 'expressed the boyish feelings of my heart.'[41] They are a music-hall stereotype of seafaring boldness and freedom, alongside attachment to his mother and the expectation of a watery grave. It seems strange that a thirteen-year-old would deliver such a performance to real sailors, but Stevens did not report any mockery. Sailors sometimes adopted boys almost as pets or mascots, and while boys were keen to grow out of that, it could make for some early security in a new environment.

At the other extreme, some first experiences at sea were exacerbated by bullying and ill-treatment. Although Frank Bullen sailed on his uncle's ship, far from seeing his uncle as a father figure, Bullen fell out with him and sought refuge with the sailors in the forecastle. From that point on, the crew took charge of Bullen's education: 'the one aim, apparently, of every man forrard was to so fit me for the work I might be called upon to do, as that no excuse might be found for cruelty of any sort.'[42] Bullen went from neglect and indifference, without friends or family, to becoming the youngest member of a shipboard crew that served as the fathers, brothers, and friends he lacked. While rooted in Bullen's own struggle for identity, his framing of this first-voyage process is a more subtle account than most of the ways a seafaring community could adopt its youngest members.

Walter Runciman also recounted being rescued by the crew when his captain blackened his eyes in a fit of temper. The sailors berated the captain and took Runciman to live with them in the forecastle. In that case, however, there was no way to reconcile the conflict. Although he admired the seafarers he was working with, Runciman had aspirations for training and advancement, and could not limit himself to life as an ordinary sailor. Nor could he face being subservient to that captain again. Instead, he took the first opportunity to leave the ship, and sign on as an apprentice in the North Sea trades.[43] He had learned enough during that first voyage to realise that there were hierarchies within seamanship, and that it was not enough for an ambitious boy to run away to sea – he had to know which sea, which ship, and which kind of seafaring would offer him the best way forward.

Authors remembered being overwhelmed, but also inspired, by their ships, and even experienced seafarers could be thrown back into first-voyage fear and disorientation when they stepped on a vessel different from those they were used to. John Bain, after years of coastal seafaring, boarded an Australia-bound clipper and 'felt for the first twenty-four hours as if I had never been on board a ship before.'[44] The masts of his old vessels, he thought, would barely have been long enough to turn sideways and serve as yards on this ship. If they were sometimes intimidated, however, sailors turned the scale and complexity of a vessel into a point of pride, especially when they could brag about it with their peers. William Crutchley encountered apprentices in port who would 'take rank' from some attribute that their vessel supposedly had over others, often a particular sail arrangement that they would insist was superior. Crutchley called this 'ship worship.'[45]

Herbert Lightoller embraced this culture as soon as he went to sea in the late 1880s. Lightoller realised that his ship *Primrose Hill* was unusual in having skysails, small sails at the top of the two-hundred-foot masts. The skysails made the ship stand out in port like an old-time clipper, thought Lightoller, and earned bragging rights among fellow apprentices on shore: 'I learned exactly how to throw out my chest as I described my ship as a "three skysail-yarder."'[46] That pride in belonging to a ship, and even a willingness to fight in defence of any slight to its reputation, appears in a number of memoirs by apprentices, and points to their adoption of an honour code around gentlemanly loyalty. It also seems to have happened almost immediately when they joined the vessel, amid the peer pressure of joining a group of boys.

Many authors went into a great deal of detail about how they acquired their technical skills, and we will discuss this in chapter 4. They also, however, couched the experiences of their first voyages as being less about skill and more about character and rites of passage. Charles Dixon's testimony about his first time aloft, as a sixteen-year-old ship's boy in 1889, stands for many. Dixon described the challenges of climbing, of finding hand-holds and safe ways around obstacles and dangerous angles. He remembered the dislocation of perspective, as the ship looked suddenly small. While he did not discuss fear as such, he admitted he had been 'weak and shaky,' yet determined to 'keep going.' Back on deck, Dixon's crucial feeling was that 'I had been initiated.'[47] He recalled exactly the difference that hour aloft had made to his sense of self, and of belonging to the crew, the ship, and the craft of seafaring.

Pride in surviving, while also beginning to earn the right to call themselves sailors, emerges from many memoirs. Some authors report a catalogue of hardships, dangers, and soul-searching, freely admitting their initial dislocation. The mental impact of going to sea resulted from extreme new experiences for which first-voyagers had no realistic reference points, despite all that reading of classic novels. It was – is – hard to believe the angles of roll that ships can reach without capsizing, or the wave heights and wind speeds that can be safely endured. Youngsters in their first rough night at sea had no way to differentiate common working conditions from imminent disaster. Bill Adams described his exhausted, befuddled state during a first-voyage storm, when he spent hours helplessly expecting the ship to founder.[48]

Indeed, many authors claimed that they nearly abandoned the sea after their first voyage. John Wilson's testimony has a number of common elements.[49] First was fear of being seen, by the people back home, as a failed seafarer: 'the first voyage was nearly the last, and would have been if I durst have faced ridicule.' Wilson came from a mining background, and dreaded the contempt of the men he had grown up with: it was, he wrote, not a 'love for the sea' or 'any excess of boldness,' but simple 'moral cowardice.' Wilson's second reaction was to acquire some confidence and proficiency in seafaring skills as soon as possible, and this self-help narrative is also a feature in seafarers' recollections. In Wilson's case, it involved waiting until dark before practicing climbing the rigging and rowing a boat. Although this added to the risks he was taking, Wilson felt it reduced the chances of embarrassing himself until he reached a certain level of competence.

Most common of all Wilson's reflections on his first voyage was how quickly he forgot its hardships. He describes bargaining with himself that he would leave the sea if he was spared long enough to reach shore. Running into Hartlepool in a storm, the vessel was watched by crowds on the quay who expected a disaster, but it reached the harbour thanks to the captain's skill. Faith in his captain, and disdain for the pilots who had failed to come out to their aid, rekindled Wilson's sense of becoming a seafarer, and no sooner had the danger passed than he forgot his doubts.

The formative value, and shock, of first voyages was reinforced by their length. Many of our authors sailed on deep-water ships that spent months at sea. Their transition to work was very different from that of boys on shore, who typically had a hybrid life for years after they started employment, remaining resident with parents while spending their days with workmates. Authors liked to think that long voyages let them grow up faster, but being away from home did not necessarily turn boys into men at an accelerated pace. Indeed, a seafaring adolescence might have been more extended than the learning period of a boy doing a simple job on shore, because of the complexity and range of experiences that had to be faced. Nonetheless, surviving a first voyage was a powerful reinforcement to our authors' sense of themselves as seafarers, even if they were still seafaring boys rather than seafaring men.

⁂

Most of our authors recalled their childhood dreams, and their boyish fears and mistakes during early voyages, without embarrassment. If a passionate interest in the romanticised anachronism of seafaring had worried their parents, the men themselves, looking back across their years at sea, drew a different lesson, valuing the adventurous mindsets that had started them on the right path toward maritime manhood. A boy going to sea was not making a rational calculation, but taking a leap of faith founded on centuries of inherited mythology. Memoir-writers embraced that process by emphasising, rather than suppressing, the contrasts between childhood visions and working realities. If they later became ships' officers and men of reason and science, that did not mean they had to censor their initial motivations, and indeed they recalled fondly the risk-seeking boys they had once been. Book-reviewers got the point: one argued that any young reader 'scared by the more fearsome aspects' of a maritime tale was not the sort of boy wanted at sea anyway.[50]

Ironically, our authors' efforts to explain the route from seafaring boyhood to manhood contributed to a broader cultural tendency to infantilise life and work at sea. While seafaring memoirs were widely reviewed in newspapers and literary journals, critics often assumed their target audience was the boy contemplating a career at sea, even if some adults might also read them with pleasure. In any sample of reviews, phrases like 'a boy's book,' for 'every true boy,' and 'will delight the boys' crop up repeatedly.[51] Sea-writing in general was pigeonholed as juvenile by the late nineteenth century, as classics like *Robinson Crusoe* became perceived as children's literature, and newcomers like *Treasure Island* were considered that from the outset. Seafaring memoir-writers faced the assumption that sea stories were for children, and their own focus on the boys they had once been reinforced that message, eclipsing their accounts of growing into seafaring manhood.

It is also important that so much of our authors' inspiration was rooted in a distant and imagined past, and in the age-old tradition of running away to sea. Scholars have noted that a good deal of literature for boys more generally was distanced in time and place from their contemporary lives, making it easy to construct mythical standards that did not have to engage too closely with the grubbier realities of the present.[52] Perhaps this did not matter much when a boy left school to work in an office or a factory. But sea apprentices in the early twentieth century were still trained in sail, despite shipowners knowing that their future would be in steamships. It was easy for those boys to regard themselves as inheritors of ancient ways, while fearing that their industry had somehow passed its peak and would never recapture its glory days of adventure and discovery. They doubted if the seafaring men of their own era could be a match for the proper sailors of a century before, although they took comfort in the idea that they were still superior to the new steamship crews. All this seems a backward, even reactionary, mindset to be adopted by those entering an industry already dominated by new technology, business models, and working practices. It had persistent implications for the ways in which our authors defined themselves and the seafarers around them.

2

Seafaring Men

When memoir-writers looked back at their fellow seafarers, they were remembering not only co-workers, but men who were a constant presence in their lives, on and off duty. Over the years, those men had taken on a deeper significance as the last sailing-ship mariners, and for most authors as symbols of a better kind of seafaring manhood. Descriptions of seafarers emerge from a complicated time-warping: they are usually older men's recollections of the sailors they encountered as boys, seen through the lens of subsequent careers that took authors into very different kinds of maritime work. And given that most authors were always destined to be officers, they also wrote about seafarers through the assumptions of Britain's class and occupational distinctions.

Maritime memoirs often focus on working-class bodies and middle-class minds, part of a broader tendency in our period.[1] Authors paid great attention to the physicality of the men in the forecastle, confirming and perpetuating stereotypes about their outlandish clothing, hair, tattoos, and muscles. When they wrote of the higher ranks on board, they often prioritised character, knowledge, and skill. This was never simple, though. As well as sailors' bodies, many writers acknowledged quick wits and nautical knowledge. In addition, they remembered aspiring to the bodily vigour of seafarers, and those who became officers did not see this as a contradiction with their later selves.

Authors also remembered the remarkable diversity of the seafaring men they met, in nationality, ethnicity, age, education, and shipboard roles, as well as the myriad character variations that fascinated young sailors. Some extreme personalities seemed to confirm seafarers as wild men heedless of social convention. Memoir-writers were caught between celebrating the individualism of seafarers and trying to categorise them into types, and most authors repeated nationalist and racist prejudices even while praising individuals of many origins. Merchant ships had long been cosmopolitan workplaces, but that became more controversial with the solidification of the nation state and new imperialism of the nineteenth century, and with fears about the number of foreign sailors working on British ships. In addition, scholars have recognised the entanglement of racial and national prejudices with those relating to gender and sexuality.[2] Our authors promulgated a widely-believed hierarchy, at the top of which were white British Able Seamen with faultless seafaring skills. Everyone else occupied lower rungs, and some very low indeed. Yet all were seamen, and the representations we have of them reveal the complex interactions of masculinity, race, nationality, and class in this era.

PICTURING PROPER SAILORS

Memoir-writers often described in detail the physical appearance of their crewmates at the start of a voyage. This was an easy way to introduce them to readers, but it also fed the wider visual imaginary of flamboyance and eccentricity around sailing-ship mariners. Reviewers of sea novels poked fun at the tendency for crews to be 'a set of middle-aged, hairy-chested, whiskered shell-backs,' described by authors who 'liked men with beards and whiskers.'[3] Memoirs did nothing to refute this image, and James Barker's description of 'Long John Trevellyan' can represent many others. Even among 'the strangest looking fellows I had ever seen,' wrote Barker of his early days at sea, Trevellyan stood out: 'His raven black hair was thick and curly, his complexion clear as that of a child. Tattooed full across his deep chest was a square-rigged ship under a cloud of canvas. His biceps were enormous, and he could lift a six hundred pound kedge anchor and heave it over a ship's bulwarks. This handsome, good-natured fellow was about thirty years old, and every inch of him a sailor.'[4]

We cannot know whether Trevellyan really looked like that, or whether he existed at all. Barker admitted that his memories of individuals had become 'mingled' during his many years as a sea captain, and such descriptions are likely an amalgam of the seamen that authors remembered, and generic representations absorbed over time.[5] Barker's picture is still revealing, though. Alongside Trevellyan's dramatic presence are hints of the simple, gentle-giant character that is also common in these portrayals, and Barker rooted Trevellyan's physical prowess in his identity as a seafarer, both in his choice of tattoo and in his mastery of the ship's work.

Trevellyan's tattoo leads us to another common point made by our authors: sailing-ship crews constructed and performed their own images. The men Liam O'Flaherty recalled seeing at the London docks in 1918 appeared 'extraordinary' in their clothes and mannerisms, rooted in 'a conscious desire to look romantic and piratical.' As well as their tattoos, he invoked their brightly-coloured and ornamental shoes, belts, and handkerchiefs, their 'waddling' gait on 'widespread legs,' and their 'burlesque scowls.' Importantly, O'Flaherty saw a sharp contrast between them and the stokehold crews from the steamships. Those new seafarers usually wore an ordinary suit on shore, looked more like dock labourers or coal-heavers than traditional sailors, and were generally 'less bizarre.'[6]

Still, it was that extravagant appearance that appealed to most authors. Walter Dexter even used the title of his memoir to invoke a metaphorical merging of man with ship; the sailor's hair was rope-yarn, his fingers were marline spikes, and his blood was tar. The men Dexter had encountered on his first voyage in 1888 were, in his memory, exactly what his childhood reading led him to expect.[7] Authors who had been apprentices contrasted their own brass-buttoned formality before the voyage with their wind-swept and storm-battered appearance at sea. They liked the idea that they looked like men out of time. Rex Clements's ship, toward the end of a lengthy voyage in 1904, hailed a passing steamer to ask for drinking water. Rowing a boat over to collect it, Clements realised that he and his fellows were in a poor state: 'a wilder and more piratical boat's crew never boarded a peaceful merchantman.' Far from being embarrassed, Clements revelled in the way the men carried themselves, 'lean, brown and sunburnt – bare-footed and half-naked to boot.' He played up the idea that they were a throwback to the age of buccaneers as they returned to their ship with 'treasures' in the form of fresh water, tobacco, and old newspapers, looking and feeling very different from the crew of the steamer.[8]

Clements's comment about his 'half-naked' shipmates, behaving as throwbacks to a more primitive seafaring masculinity, raises another important point. Art historians and literature scholars have long debated the portrayal of working men at the turn of the nineteenth and twentieth centuries. Well-studied examples include the sea-painting of Henry Scott Tuke, and the numerous descriptions of soldiers bathing that appeared in early writing about the Great War.[9] Painters and writers focused on the physiques of men and boys in a complicated mix of motives. Some were expressing their own sexuality through the male nude; others sought to represent working men as more healthy and natural than the decadent middle classes; others still were attempting a revival of what they saw as classical ways of seeing and behaving, after the rigid constraints of the Victorian era.

Discussion of ship-board nudity is actually very rare, but a few authors highlighted it in relation to a ritual that occurred during the first tropical downpour of a voyage. According to Frank Symondson, Clements himself, and Bill Adams, this would provoke the mass washing of clothes, bedding, and bodies after weeks during which it had been too cold to remove clothing and too damp to dry anything. The deck would suddenly be full of naked sailors spreading out their laundry to wash in the rain, and then be dried when the sun returned soon after. Similar scenes ensued if a ship had run low on fresh water in the tropics, and the crew took the opportunity to fill tanks with rainwater, as well as washing their clothes and bodies.

Symondson, one of our earliest writers, made only the briefest comment on these scenes, just asserting that they would appear 'ludicrous' to any landsman, among many eccentricities of seafaring life that he represented. Although he notes that the crew 'stripped,' Symondson does not even state explicitly that they were naked.[10] Perhaps, writing in the 1870s, Symondson felt a limiting sense of propriety around discussing nudity, and certainly did not dwell on the point. In contrast, Clements and Adams, writing in the 1920s and 1930s, went into more detail, and made their point more forcibly: Adams used 'stark-naked' twice in one sentence, for example, and emphasised that all the sailors and apprentices, though not the officers, participated.[11] Far from thinking the scene ludicrous, Clements and Adams convey a sense of exuberant carnival, of letting off steam and boosting morale. By the time they were writing, those authors could equate naked sailors with the vision of pre-industrial, elemental manhood that they wanted to impress upon their readers.

Some authors picked out memorable individuals in an effort to capture the fusion of physical prowess, strength of character, and other-worldliness that they saw in their early crews. Clifford Fenton, who went to sea as an apprentice in 1901, remembered a man called Jenkins as huge and imposing, with remarkably long arms. Jenkins volunteered to do an unusual rigging job in a storm, 'looking not unlike a gorilla,' and showing great nerve. Jenkins also used his physique to stand up for his rights as a sailor; refusing to be searched for alcohol, he simply held the ship's mate at (very long) arm's length until the mate backed down.[12] Fenton's comments show the difficulty some authors had in portraying their shipmates, using Jenkins's body as a comic device that played into prejudices about the ape-like working classes, yet also conveying a powerful statement of an ordinary seafarer's dignity.

Authors were especially fascinated by the appearance, and then the character, of the oldest sailors they encountered. Such men invariably emerge from memoirs as weathered, grey, and grim-faced, but also as sharp and perceptive. The wise old shellback was a blend of myth and memory recycled across autobiography and sea fiction alike. There are clear parallels here with the way images of aging army veterans became a positive symbol of military manhood late in the nineteenth century, and an intergenerational guide to youngsters looking to serve their country.[13]

Admiration for the oldest seafarers is common across our time period, and became self-perpetuating. Henry Moffat, who went to sea in the 1860s, wrote of 'Old Jack,' a seaman allegedly more than seventy years old, who was a voice of caution during disputes with officers, and was nicknamed 'Sinbad.'[14] Fred Farmer reckoned that more than half of his shipmates on *Katardin* in the 1890s were 'old men, belonging to a dead and forgotten past.' Five, he believed, were more than sixty years of age, and could yarn about the classic clipper ships from a time when steamers were 'a thing of the future'; such men gave authors a sense of inheritance and continuity. Farmer was impressed by their wisdom and knowledge, and how they seemed instantly familiar with any new vessel they joined; he described one old sailor as having a look that 'searched your soul with clear keen eyes.'[15] William Jones wrote that there were several 'older seamen' in his 1905 crew, 'veterans of the clipper-ships of an era when "wooden ships and iron men" won the admiration of the world.'[16]

Of course, the men Jones wrote about were Moffat's contemporaries. Generation after generation, the oldest seafarers served as symbols of a heroic age that was always just past. By the time they came to write, many authors were the same age as the old shellbacks they remembered. Instead of a comfortable retirement crafting their memoirs, though, the shellbacks had been working aloft in the seas around Cape Horn. Unsurprisingly, a sense of wonder and even envy creeps into many narratives. Some authors adopted the 'shellback' label for themselves: Walter Runciman, wealthy shipowner and soon to be a baron, hailed his fellow 'old shellback' Robert Ramsay in a foreword to the latter's memoir in 1930.[17]

The vague chronology in depictions of older seamen, as well as uncertainty about their ages, also suggests a striking degree of intergenerational mythologizing. Authors portrayed the transformation of the sailing ship from elegant wooden clipper to hulking steel cargo-hauler as a fall from grace, for ships and men alike. Old shellbacks were living proof that something had survived from one era to the next: their working lives had changed radically, yet they maintained the seafaring identity observed, and then claimed, by our authors.

HIERARCHIES OF SEAMEN

Many of our authors claimed they were writing to reveal the hidden and mysterious world of the maritime workplace, and they often sought to explain the system of ranks and occupations on merchant ships. The largest single group of men on a sailing ship were Able Seamen (known as ABs), with a smaller number of lower-ranked Ordinary Seamen (OSs). ABs were required to handle sails, ropes, and the wheel ('hand, reef, and steer' in the jargon), but there was no agreed standard for those competencies, and no certificate for having achieved them. An OS could make the transition to AB by experience rather than formal qualifications. ABs' wages were higher, of course, so sailors (and the boarding-house keepers who tried to find them work) often had an incentive to claim that rating.

However, Frank Symondson believed in the 1870s that few inexperienced seamen took the risk of claiming the higher rate. This was not because they feared officers, but rather their crewmates, who would punish them for causing the ship to be short of proper seamen.[18] Among OSs, there were men who aspired to be seafarers, and who looked down on the 'farmers' and 'hobos' who were sometimes hired in that rating to make up numbers.

Clifford Fenton recalled that real sailors took great pride in what he called 'sailorizing,' a complex set of skilled tasks involving ropes, rigging, and sails; if officers wanted to punish capable seamen, they took them away from these jobs and assigned them cleaning and other menial work that should have been done by the 'farmers.'[19]

For all the apparent simplicity of ranks and roles, sailing-ship crews created their own complicated and subtle hierarchies among the ABs and OSs in the early days of a voyage. Certain kinds of seafaring experience carried great weight. Recalling his time as an OS in the 1850s, John Wilson listed symbolic points on deep-water voyages that represented rites of passage: 'the man who had been across the line and around the Cape considered himself one of the elite of the trade, and looked down with contempt upon the man who had simply served in the coasting trade.' The 'line' was the Equator; the 'Cape,' usually Cape Horn. Wilson had a keen sense of inferiority over this, and after gaining some experience in the North Sea trades resolved to 'rise to the higher grade' by making voyages to the East. Indeed, Wilson was so conscious of the 'pride of caste' that he continued signing on as an OS, fearing that his crewmates would not accept him as an AB until he had experience on the deep-water routes.[20]

Sometimes these distinctions seem non-sensical, but were keenly felt. Frank Bullen spent the first half of his memoir recounting voyages across the Atlantic and around the West Indies, full of hardship, danger, and transformative experiences. But he only began to consider himself a proper sailor when he joined a ship heading for India. He predicted that he would cross the Equator four times, round the Cape of Good Hope twice, and return 'looking down from a lofty height of superiority upon other sea-boys who had never sailed to the "Suthard."'[21]

Walter Runciman pushed back against this prevailing view. His first experience was on a long voyage around the bottom of Africa and across the Pacific to South America. While he thought the crew showed no end of courage, he returned to his native Northumberland convinced that he would get a better training in the North Sea collier brigs. Working in shallow water, against contrary winds and currents, meant that young sailors were 'quickly drilled into the superb mysteries of seamanship unknown to the southern-going man.' Still, Runciman knew that most sailors looked down on 'mere Baltic men and colliers.'[22]

Wilson, Bullen, and Runciman were writing about the third quarter of the nineteenth century, when sailing ships remained common in many trades, and debates about preferred career paths were still meaningful. By late-century, with sail pushed to the geographical margins, voyages in the southern oceans became an increasing proportion of the surviving sail routes. If rounding Cape Horn had long been a key measure of the proper sailor, for the final generation of sailing-ship mariners it became a cult. Not only were they the last men of their kind, they believed they had to keep passing the toughest test. At the very beginning of his memoir, James Barker noted how many years he had been at sea, and how many in command, but he mostly wanted to stress his forty-one voyages around Cape Horn.[23]

Some authors were surprised to find that not all seafarers were OSs, ABs, or officers, and they became fascinated by sailmakers, carpenters, and boatswains (bosuns), often referred to as the ship's 'tradesmen.' Apprentices felt particular debts to these men for the training and mentoring they often provided. As a mark of respect, they were known by occupational titles rather than their own names; carpenters were always 'Chips,' for example, sailmakers usually just 'Sails.' Tradesmen's work combined many masculine tropes, mixing traditional craft skills, inventiveness, and ingenuity, and also a respected understanding of seafaring and the needs of a ship. They were skilled users of specialised tools, able to create parts for the ship at short notice and out of whatever material happened to be available; they often commanded higher wages.[24]

Bosuns had formal responsibility for all the ship's fittings, and served as foremen when a group of sailors had to work on repairs or maintenance outside of their usual duties. Authors remembered the bosun's locker, a treasure trove of everything from tools, rope, and spare fittings to needles, thread, and paintbrushes. Boys were often tasked with keeping it in order, because in an emergency the boy – of little use for anything else – would be sent running to find the necessary equipment.[25] Carpenters had similar status: Frank Bullen thought they represented some of the best traits of seamen in general, both for their technical skills and their independence. They decided for themselves what work was needed on the ship, and did not have to be ordered about by officers: they were 'silent, thoughtful and strong men who study the requirements of their ship as a great surgeon studies his patients.'[26]

Sailmakers too had an aura of traditional seafaring craft skill that seemed to represent a continuity running deep into the past. However, unlike carpentry, sail-making was supposed to be something that any seafarer could do at some level. Such was the wear on sails even in normal conditions, and the total loss of many during gales, that a ship needed multiple sets, as well as spare canvas that could be sewn into still more replacements. Although sewing and working with fabrics was often coded as women's work, there seems to have been little sense of this among seafarers. Sail-making was evidently regarded as an industrial form of textile work rather than a domestic one, but even mending clothes was a normal and acceptable activity for seafarers. Henry Moffat, whose 1910 memoir bemoaned what he regarded as the declining skills of seafarers since his first voyages in the 1860s, thought that every sailor had once been a tradesman to some extent, with the ability to perform key crafts. Moffat's symbol of this was his 'ditty bag,' in which he had kept a small kit of tools for working with rope and canvas, and which he thought few men now carried.[27]

Attitudes toward crew members became more complicated the further their roles were from traditional ship-handling. The steward on a sailing ship was primarily the captain's servant, and while he lived in some comfort relative to those before the mast, few sailors would contemplate the role because of its apparent subservience. Frank Symondson noted that the steward on his ship was known as the 'flunkey,' and that his work was considered 'menial and effeminate.'[28] When Frank Bullen recalled his brief spell as a boy steward, he called it 'the toilsome routine of housemaid's duties,' and was by no means alone in feminising both the job and those who did it.[29]

Boy sailors realised early that they should distance themselves from such work if they wanted to earn the respect of the proper sailors. It was common for younger, weaker sailors to act as 'Peggy,' carrying food from the galley for the crew and doing cleaning duties.[30] This menial domestic work, assigned a girl's name, sent multiple signals about how unmanly it was. Although stewards became a large proportion of the passenger-liner workforce in the early twentieth century, men in those occupations continued to find their masculinity being questioned. Such prejudice was a long-standing continuity rooted in the age of sail, despite radical changes in the nature of the work itself. In time, the new liner crews often resisted discrimination by creating more fluid and tolerant spaces for gender and sexuality in their departments.[31] That only became possible when they were employed in numbers, however, and the isolated stewards and cooks on sailing ships had no such collective strength.

Cooks feature in almost all maritime memoirs, although they were often represented less as individual seafarers and more as symbols of wider issues onboard ship. Cooks were the butt of seafarers' complaints and hostility about poor food, and also because they were spared the rigours of night-time watches on deck. The resentment was mutual. Cooks often worked long days in difficult conditions. They were expected to make extra efforts for Sunday meals on the one day of the week when seafarers traditionally did only essential work.[32] Like stewards, their work was considered more appropriate for women. In addition, many cooks were of African origin, and it is hard to unpack at this distance whether authors were prejudiced against individual cooks because of their ethnicity or their occupation; their status on board could be driven by a very complicated mixture of forces. The next section discusses these men in more detail, in the context of the broader diversity of the sailing-ship crew, and the implications that had for our authors' representation of their shipmates.

THE COSMOPOLITAN FORECASTLE

The shipping industry has a centuries-old reputation for workforce diversity in terms of nationality, race, and ethnicity. Ships often had to replace lost, sick, or deserting sailors at their next port of call, seafaring skills were transferrable internationally, and the seafarer's self-image embraced adventurous transience. Even if ships left port with a full complement of their own local sailors, they would return, months or years later, with a far more mixed crew. In addition, some shipping companies actively recruited sailors overseas. In the eighteenth century, the British East India Company hired seafarers in Asia and returned them there at the end of a round-trip voyage, trying to prevent Asian mariners settling in Britain. Some seafarers found ways to escape these restrictions. Even in the early nineteenth century, independent seamen of Asian, and also African, origin were already sufficiently numerous, and their lives difficult enough, to attract violent prejudice, public concern, and official enquiries.[33]

In the late nineteenth century, steamship companies working in Asia and Africa adapted that old system to their new workforce, and the best research we have on race and ethnicity in British shipping focuses on the steamship era.[34] Indeed, the steamship was a driver and symbol of imperial expansion and racial differentiation. White British officers commanded crews that were segregated by race and employment. Sailors in the deck crew were usually white; trimmers and firemen in the stoke-hold, who shovelled coal and maintained fires in extreme conditions, were Asian or African, depending on where the company operated. Shipowners created condescending stereotypes around Asian and African seafarers, representing them as docile, sober, and obedient workers who could tolerate high temperatures and poor living conditions, although such mythology rarely benefitted the men themselves. These seafarers were employed on contracts that restricted them to particular ships and routes, known as 'Asiatic Articles' in the case of Indian seafarers. By the time our authors were writing in the early twentieth century, travelogues and memoirs about steamship travel in the East were common, and the reading public had long-established impressions of Asian workers.

What about our authors' crews, in the last sailing ships? There, racial and national demarcations were if anything more complex, and ethnic minority seafarers were employed as individuals rather than as entire departments or sections of the crew. Unlike some American vessels earlier in the century, British ships did not have enough Black seafarers to employ so-called chequerboard crews, with racially-segregated teams of sailors.[35] Neither did Asiatic Articles apply, because those contracts forbade voyages in high latitudes, thereby excluding the Cape Horn route in which later sailing ships specialised.[36] Sailing-ship officers were white and British, to be sure, and that was usually true of the largest single group of seafarers. As sail declined, the rest became a diverse mixture of men who together made up a very unusual workforce for their time. Apart from texts about colonial or frontier societies, seafaring memoirs are one of the few British sources from the late nineteenth and early twentieth centuries that describe racial, national, and ethnic relations in the workplace. In addition, sailing-ship mariners all signed the same contract, regardless of race or nationality, and there was no formal workplace segregation.

This did not mean, of course, that sailing ships were havens of equality. Our memoir-writers were all white, and brought up in a culture that had appropriated Darwinian evolutionary ideas to locate men like them at the highest rung of any hierarchy. Their sense of entitlement combined race, nationality, and seafaring heritage, and assumed superiority over white sailors from other countries, let alone men of different skin colour. Although there are fundamental differences between prejudices based on race and those focused on nationality, white British seafarers did not necessarily regard all their white crewmates more highly than Black sailors; southern European seafarers, for example, often received more criticism in memoirs than Black seamen. Some memoir-writers seemed fascinated by the multi-ethnic crews they worked in, and devoted considerable space to representing this to their readers, but usually in detached, almost anthropological ways. As the leading scholar of race and seafaring argues, events and testimony at local and individual level cast doubt on monolithic theories of identity, and reveal 'a surprising variety of responses.'[37]

Most sailors of African or Caribbean heritage appearing in our memoirs were cooks. This is a broadly accurate reflection of the later British sailing-ship workforce, but it raises immediate complexities. Historians have noted that an unusual proportion of Black British pugilists and boxing champions across the nineteenth century had worked as cooks at sea, perhaps an indication of the violence they could face and their desire to stand up for themselves.[38] Cooks had unusual power for Black men in this era, controlling their own space, even if it was just a cramped and dangerous galley, and determining what sailors should eat. That power, though, came from doing what most sailors considered unmanly work.

John Bain's depiction of his ship's cook can stand for many examples of condescension to Black seafarers. The crew believed that the cook's professed Christianity was insincere, and berated him for cowardice and hypocrisy. The cook's nickname was 'Sambo,' and Bain had him speaking in a pidgin dialect, whereas most of the other sailors in his memoir spoke standard English.[39] When authors represented the speech of foreign, minority, or lower-class sailors phonetically, they must have known that writers for centuries had used dialects to poke fun at servants and yokels, and that they would inevitably invoke condescending humour.[40] They were also infantilising their Black crewmates as naive or easily led, or as displaying the kind of insolence associated with boys – 'saucy' had long been a common description more generally.[41]

Authors who seem more respectful toward Black seafarers were usually patronising their strength and confidence as if they were the 'noble savages' of eugenic pseudoscience, or were honorary whites. John Mason described an African-American sailor called Wallace as 'a white man in every respect, except in colour – a hard-working, good-tempered steady man.'[42] Many invoked the racist trope that Black men had an inflated sense of their own status. Henry Moffat praised his ship's cook, but thought 'he had such big ideas of his own importance and dignity that he would not listen to a reprimand from anyone.'[43]

A few authors wrote of Black seafarers in less common ways, often when those men had been a particular help to their younger, vulnerable selves. Some of this testimony reads very strangely to us now, because authors could express affection for individuals while using all the racist language of their day. Frank Bullen, for example, repeatedly expressed his gratitude to a young sailor called Jem, who looked after him through seasickness and depression in the difficult early days of a voyage. With every mention, though, Bullen reminded his readers that Jem was Black, using now taboo terms.[44] Bullen encountered more Black seafarers doing a wider variety of jobs than most of our authors, because he worked on voyages in the West Indies, and he wrote respectfully about them. In the norms of the time, however, Bullen felt the need to emphasise to his audience that these men were good sailors and loyal shipmates, despite the expectations that readers probably had based on these seafarers' colour.

Robert Ramsay recalled a Black cook called Joe Blair as 'a thorough sailor, and a perfect specimen of manhood.' Blair was far from subservient, and beat crew members who called him by racist epithets. He also came to Ramsay's aid more than once.[45] Frank Symondson described Millington, his ship's cook, as dressing in an elaborate manner, with a topcoat and patent shoes along with his carefully trimmed moustache. While Symondson is partly feeding a common trope about the extravagant clothing favoured by Black sailors, he had no doubt that cooks faced hard work and abuse, and thought a man in that position might want to set himself apart from his job by every means possible.[46]

Attitudes towards Black seafarers were part of a much broader range of stereotypes and prejudices applied to the plethora of ethnicities and nationalities encountered working at sea. British memoir-writers always rated their white countrymen as the world's best seafarers. Northern Europeans came next, then southern Europeans, then everyone else. The northerners were collectively known as 'Dutchmen,' the southerners as 'Dagoes.'[47] These stereotypes can be found across the chronology of our memoirs. Frank Symondson's account of his 1870s voyage as an apprentice highlighted the perception that southern European sailors were cowardly and ill-disciplined. He claimed a ship would be in trouble if there was a majority of 'the lowest of foreign seamen – namely Turks, Greeks, Italians and Spaniards,' who lacked 'that brightest of jewels, "British fair-play."'[48] Later memoirs consistently echoed that worldview.

If that was the underlying frame, however, the labels often became stretched when writing about particular crewmates. Authors who had relied on the kindliness of older sailors held a lingering sense of loyalty, and remembered individual seamen who defied the national prejudices. Those who had been officers for many years must have understood that the crude categorisation of sailors into national groups made no sense. Equally, they all knew that the national profile of seafarers working on British ships had long been a controversial political issue, and that their opinions would be read against that familiar background.

Rex Clements pondered those arguments when describing his first crew in 1903. He did not pretend to be recording his impressions at the time, but compared the men to his later crews, and editorialised the whole encounter in nationalist terms. His first crew was above average, he thought, partly because the leading ABs were an Englishman ('a sailor every inch of him') and an Irishman. There was also a New Englander, a Finn, and a Norwegian, all good seamen. Importantly, though, Clements could see beyond some stereotypes. One of the other Britishers and a German were slow workers. Lopez the Spaniard was old and inefficient, but 'very willing,' an unusual nuance for a nationality that many memoir-writers wrote off as lazy. Clements made the ritual claim that it would have been better to have an all-British crew, but also thought that 'a bad Britisher is very bad indeed,' and certainly inferior to the Nordics.[49]

Positive assumptions about Nordic seamen were deep-rooted, and indeed, the idea of a Viking maritime heritage had long been appropriated into Britain's own sense of its seafaring character.[50] William Jones believed that northern Europeans had an inherited seafaring ability rooted in the heroic past: 'most of the Scandinavians and Germans in our crews were prime seamen, with that inborn understanding of the sea and ships which comes from centuries of tradition, and is the heritage of a seagoing race.'[51] Bill Adams recalled how impressed he had been by a huge Norwegian 'who might have voyaged with Leif Ericsson.' However, Adams also admired Nordic sailors for the power of their emotional responses, which he thought few British seafarers would have revealed. After a tense funeral in rough seas, Adams reported his crew dispersing quickly back to their posts, except for 'a giant Finn' who 'began to curse the sea. He shook his huge fists at it. He waved his great arms, yelled, screeched, screamed curses.'[52] At the same time, however, seafarers across our time period were cautious about Finnish sailors, who for all their physical presence and seafaring ability were supposed to have supernatural beliefs that interfered with the weather.[53] Many of our authors embraced that Victorian need to classify men, nations, and races by applying all manner of pseudo-scientific indicators and categories.

Authors keen to eulogise the last generation of British sailing-ship mariners could easily compare those men with their foreign counterparts, because they all worked on the same ships. Our authors rarely explained to readers why their own time in sail, apparently part of Britain's heroic maritime heritage, was actually a much more complex, globalised amalgam of mobility and migration, and that without its multi-national workforce the British sail sector would have vanished long before it did. Instead, they persisted in depicting a hierarchy of nationality and seafaring competence that ultimately undervalued the men themselves.

SAILING-SHIP MEN

As will already be clear, most of our authors were keen to represent sailing-ship mariners as idiosyncratic men, easily recognisable and distinguishable from workers on shore as well as from steamship crews. Such judgements, in a major British industry at the turn of the nineteenth and twentieth centuries, could not fail to become entwined in questions of class boundaries, consciousness, and belonging. The fact that most of our authors had been officers, and that many had been destined for those ranks from the beginning of their careers, means that we can never ignore the distances between them and the seafarers they worked with, and later commanded. Specifically, then, where did our authors locate maritime manhood within the complexities of Britain's class and occupational hierarchies?

This question is made more problematic by the timelines involved. The last sailing-ship mariners were arguably still pre-industrial workers, maintaining long-standing occupational skills and customs into the age of steam and steel.

In that sense they were like agricultural workers or miners, whose relationships with employers predated large-scale industrial capitalism, but whose jobs persisted, and in some cases grew in importance in the new era.[54] Such workers had resisted efforts to turn them into a proletariat during the industrial revolution, determined to retain their own identities centred on craft and tradition, separate from the new factory and mill operatives.[55] As a result, there was never a single working-class identity or consciousness. In addition, much of the historical evidence comes from polemical, partisan writing in febrile political circumstances.

This was certainly the case in debates about the character of the British seafarer in the later decades of the nineteenth century. A series of parliamentary enquiries into safety and working conditions at sea heard conflicting evidence. Seafarers were represented as hard-working, brave men indifferent to danger and discomfort, or as cowardly fair-weather sailors who failed to turn out in difficult conditions. British sailors abandoned the sail sector because of the parsimony and greed of shipowners; alternatively, the drunken incompetence of British seamen forced employers to resort to foreigners. Gradually, legislation and regulation improved health, welfare, and safety, but the life-saving technicalities of load-lines and victualling scales never captured the public imagination like debates over seafarers' character and morality.[56]

Unsurprisingly then, our earlier authors saw seafarers through Victorian narratives about drink, temperance, religion, and the moral improvement of the labouring classes. John Bain and William Lord wrote their memoirs in the 1890s from similar perspectives. Both praised sober and responsible men they had encountered, but Bain thought that overall the notorious drinking habits of many British sailors were driving shipping companies to employ foreign seamen.[57] Lord began his book with a plea for readers to be sympathetic to seafarers, but saw the drinking habits of so many men as the root of the industry's problems. Lord thought the poor reputation of waterfront districts revolved round 'Jack's folly and short-sightedness,' and that seamen lapsed into apathy when they could have taken better care of their own situation.[58] Both authors attributed their personal advancements to sobriety, hard work, and surrounding themselves with like-minded seafarers. Neither wrote in terms of class or social division, nor did they draw much distinction between sailing-ship and steamship crews. Morality, character, and self-help were their key distinctions.

Our later authors, writing from the 1920s onwards, were much more likely to idealise the sailing-ship mariner. Sometimes, they wanted to represent him in favourable contrast to what they regarded as the militant, even revolutionary, working classes of the early to middle twentieth century. There are probably two factors here. First was the career pattern of authors themselves, who by the time they retired had often been officers on large steamships. There, they commanded crews, sometimes hundreds strong, in a regimented industrial workplace far removed from the sailing ship. Second, the Russian Revolution, global wars, and the Depression meant that none of our middle-class authors could feel entirely secure in their social and economic authority.

With hindsight, some thought that signs of decay had already been creeping into the seafaring workforce before the Great War. Albert Bestic's testimony is a useful example. Bestic first went to sea in 1908, but did not write his memoir until 1958. He thought his first shipmates were 'a good crowd, sailing-ship men,' as if those were synonymous. To Bestic, proper sailors were almost bred for the trade and lived outside petty concerns. They were 'men of the sea who performed their arduous work by instinct rather than by a sense of duty.' Bestic drew a sharp contrast with those who went to sea without such ideals, such as a stowaway called Kemp who appears throughout Bestic's memoir personifying a debased minority. Kemp had grown up in the slums, claimed Bestic, where 'bluff and lying' were his approach to work and authority.[59] For Bestic, Kemp's lack of a moral code was also an absence of the manly responsibility demanded of a proper sailor, which could transcend the new class conflicts of the industrial age.

Other authors promoted the idea that the old sailing-ship men had a higher moral purpose. Bill Adams, looking back from the 1930s, drew some revealing, if unlikely, parallels. Steering the ship that he loved, and being at one with the vessel and the sea, was like a soldier's sense of fighting a righteous cause, a priest's commitment to his vocation, or a tailor's contentment in finely-cut cloth. For Adams, this calm but determined sense of manly mission could only come from sail, and the steamship's mechanised distancing of man from traditional craft destroyed it: 'there is no calling like the sailor's was – today the steamers have our sea.'[60]

Some authors thought that the character of old-time seafarers had lessons not just for the steamship men and the slum-dwellers, but for their supposed social betters as well. Charles Dixon, one of the few authors who wrote of lengthy service as a captain in sail, took pride in his ability to manage sailors, but also thought the men themselves were maligned in the popular imagination. Looking back from the 1930s, Dixon repeated the trope that some sailors could be lazy and troublesome, but also argued that 'a great deal of arrant nonsense' had been written about the 'crudeness and savagery' of sail. Most striking, though, were some of Dixon's comparisons. Sailing-ship men, he thought, were 'superior to the crew of many a fancy city office – in looks, in manliness, and in intelligence.' He had also heard 'more obscene talk and unhealthy discussions' in gentlemen's clubs than he ever heard at sea. Another rare element in Dixon's testimony was his willingness to criticise some shipowners of the 1890s, among whom there had been 'a lot of mean, selfish, hard-hearted men,' not least the 'fat old millionaires of Liverpool' who opposed reform of working conditions.[61] Dixon was taking advantage of the time-distancing powers of memoir to assert his own independence of mind, as a ship's captain of the old school who could claim to know his men as well as he knew his employers, and to compare their morals and character across conventional class lines.

The extent to which our authors saw seafarers as individuals is important. A denial of distinctiveness and diversity within the working-classes was common to polemical scaremongering about urban degeneration, with many accounts of workers as a homogonous, deplorable mass.[62] Such lumping is rare in descriptions of sailing-ship mariners. Most writers celebrated the particularity of the men they remembered from their early days at sea, seeing them not just as individuals, but as individualists. In part, this may have been a device to reinforce their regret about the passing of sailing ships and a more colourful, flamboyant breed of seafarer. But it also complicates the class status of our authors, and their sense of having been able to stand alongside seafarers and know them as working men rather than just as an anonymous forecastle crowd. At least, it seemed important to their own seafaring identity to believe they had done that, and to persuade their readers that was the case.

Authors also walked a fine line between celebrating sailors as individual men who were superior to any industrial mass, and insisting on the discipline and obedience to authority that they regarded as central to life under sail. John Mason worked as an Ordinary, and then Able Seaman, moving back and forth between sail and steam, and was already thirty when he qualified as a master mariner. So when he wrote that 'the sea was a hard school, with no place for weaklings or misfits of any kind,' Mason was positioning himself in a definition of seafaring manhood derived from his early work. He wanted to pay tribute to the sailing-ship mariners of the 1880s, and felt they were being forgotten by the time he wrote his memoir forty years later. Crucially, though, this sober, diligent type of seafarer was by no means subservient to overbearing officers. In an early conversation with his bullying captain, Mason objected to the captain's claim that he owned his crew 'body and soul': surely, insisted Mason, a real seafaring man had to at least call his soul his own, whatever hardships his body might have to suffer in the work of the ship.[63]

James Bisset was also troubled by the competing masculinities that he had to negotiate in his own career. While proud to belong in the ranks of adventurous lads who had run away to sea, he knew with hindsight that too much of that trouble-seeking mentality posed a disruptive challenge on board. Bisset, who started as an apprentice in 1898 and went on to captain large passenger liners, thought that working in sail was 'a grand adventure and a useful start to a seaman's career.' It became clear, though, that he meant it was a good foundation for a career like his. Men who chose to spend all their lives in sail were a different matter. To Bisset, they were likely to be 'of a roving disposition,' escaping the 'restrictions of a home life'; men, in other words, who rejected the responsible breadwinning masculinity of the respectable classes in the early twentieth century. Bisset also tied seafaring manliness to discipline and obedience on board. He thought some of the early seafarers he encountered lacked 'the manliness to defy authority openly, or the greater manliness required to obey authority cheerfully.' Bisset thought them the antithesis of proper sailors, even the most transient and dissolute of whom would, when sobered up at sea, turn out for their watch 'manfully and cheerfully.'[64]

How to square these overlapping circles? Ultimately, authors invoked the sailing-ship mariner as a conservative influence, whose eccentricities and independence were those of an idealised English past, and the antithesis of any radicalised urban mass. Authors argued that such seamen were endangered by the rise of steam, to be sure, but also by other innovations, including those designed to help them. Henry Moffat, one of our earlier authors, sat his officers' exams in the years of Samuel Plimsoll's agitation against overloading and other dangerous shipping practices. He then worked through the British state's subsequent efforts to improve shipping safety and conditions between the 1870s and 1890s. Moffat took an extreme and unusual position against these reforms, but in a revealing way that paid tribute to his vision of the proper sailor. Seamen were being infantilised and emasculated, Moffat argued, and so wrapped in protection as to lose their free spirit and working identity: 'the grandmotherly protection of the Board of Trade has disgusted them and they have all left.'[65] Moffat believed that self-respecting old-style sailors had abandoned the sea for proper manly work on the American frontier or in Britain's colonies.

Madden Jardine deliberated the conservatism of seafarers more than most, even trying to map attitudes to seafaring onto the party politics of his time as an apprentice in the 1880s, the era of Tories, Liberal 'Radicals,' and Irish Home Rule. He had his hero, an AB called Hesketh, deliver extended soliloquies on the period's bewildering rate of change. Hesketh had some surprising views, not least an acceptance of steamships. Importantly, though, Hesketh only came to 'tolerate' steamers for conservative reasons – some of his own shipmates had made the move to working on them, and he felt he had to respect their decisions. Equally, he thought steamers would not exist unless they ought to, a characteristic seafarer's nod to fate and ineffable forces. Hesketh's fellow 'Tory sea lawyer,' another AB called St Ives, offered a bleak assessment of the likely fate of Britain's maritime empire, which was no longer in the hands of seafaring men like him and his forebears.[66]

All this was, of course, rather convenient for most of our authors, seeking a model for stalwart working men who knew their place in an orderly middle-class society, and who were respectful of the ships' officers that so many memoir-writers had become. Old-style sailors, in this view, had a sense of ancient rights and responsibilities, which rooted their relations with officers in a mix of traditional customs and personal ties, rather than class-consciousness. This resonates with broader patterns of local, individual relations between employees and employers in small workplaces, and the few voices we have from the sailing-ship forecastle do not diverge much from that.[67] As we will see in the chapters that follow, they too depict ship-board disagreements as arguments over tradition, custom, and personality, rather than the systemic industrial disputes of the new era.

*

Memoir-writers had no doubt that sailing-ship mariners represented an older and better kind of manhood. Exactly how they should define that masculinity was often less clear-cut, however. Walter Dexter, for example, thought that the forecastle crews he encountered 'had very definite ideas of what constituted a man, and this manhood test was for them the deciding factor' in assessing fellow sailors and people on shore.[68] What that was, though, Dexter did not say – we have to extrapolate from the rest of his memoir the usual amalgam of ideas about courage, hardiness, independence, strength, recklessness, and loyalty. Melbourne Garahan boiled this down to a vision of the seafarer's rough masculinity: 'he is a strong man doing a strong man's work, has a strong stomach to deal with strong food and strong drink, and naturally likes his language strong too.'[69] Beyond the stereotypes, however, he too fell short of a prescription for characterising the industry's workforce.

In the following chapters we will dig deeper, therefore, into all those indicators of seafaring masculinity that our authors mention without necessarily offering conclusions. Their testimony was complicated by their own need to claim a seafaring identity despite having left the sailing ship and moved into the dubious world of steamships. Our authors had to reconcile difficult tensions, and believed that the classic British sailor had played his role in the heroic past and could be commemorated for that, while new seafaring men, still trained in a hard school, would make the transition to leadership in steam. Men, in other words, like them.

3

Shipmates and Others

Seafaring required cooperation, teamwork, and collective responsibility. Memoir-writers paid a great deal of attention to these group dynamics, not least because deep-water sailing-ship crews were often formed from scratch at the beginning of every voyage. Strangers with no knowledge of one another's skills or experiences had to collaborate immediately to deal with routine work, life-threatening situations, and day-by-day living alike. Authors offer rich descriptions of the way sailors built camaraderie and even a kind of family from such unpromising beginnings, as all the characteristics of seafaring men revealed in the last chapter were tested by the challenges of lengthy voyages.

Having to work and live together limited sailors' self-determination and individualism in exchange for comradeship and fraternity, and that reconciliation is important to the picture of seafaring men that our authors conveyed to their readers. The occupational, domestic, and private sides of life and character were played out in the same cramped spaces. At best, being at sea moulded the crew into a close unit, and we have ample testimony of men risking their own comfort and safety for their fellows. On other voyages, there were tensions between competitive, prejudiced, or recalcitrant individuals who had few ways to avoid one another. The idea of the 'shipmate' emerges from memoirs, as a measure of loyalty to the crew, but also as a standard against which some men were held wanting.

Hierarchies and demarcations on board made these relationships more complex still. Teenage sailors in trainee roles formed their own fraternity, almost as an extension of school, but their presence also created an intergenerational dynamic. Seafarers and boys were of an age to be fathers and sons, or older and younger brothers. Crews often policed their own disputes, reluctant to involve officers, and believing in codes of 'fair dealing,' 'fair shares,' or a 'fair fight,' but whether those rules were really fair troubled some of our authors. Officers in turn had to decide when to leave seafarers to handle their own business, and when to impose what they believed to be traditional shipboard discipline. The ship at sea was a very personal society, in which almost all issues had to be resolved on the spot by the individuals present – for all its bureaucratic capacity, the Board of Trade was a long way off. If the state provided a growing regulatory and contractual framework in the late nineteenth century, our authors thought that custom and character offered more immediate solutions for these isolated communities of men and boys.

THE RULES OF THE WATCH

Life and work on a sailing ship was a mixture of rules, conventions, traditions, and choices. The sociologist Erving Goffman thought ships were 'total institutions,' in which groups of men lived and worked apart from mainstream society, yet were controlled and managed by those whose authority was sanctioned by the state.[1] It also suited shipowners to define their vessels as remote workplaces, where captains took absolute responsibility, and officers and crews had to shoulder the blame for accidents and disasters.[2] Seafaring autobiography – like that of male writers more generally – has a tendency to focus on places of labour, on colleagues and workmates, and on work itself, as fundamental elements in male identity.[3] But ships were domestic as well as working spaces, and ship-board organisation had implications beyond any narrow attention to work. We need a brief survey of these structures before discussing the wider implications for how seafarers lived within them.

The fundamental unit of organisation on a sailing ship was the watch, and many authors took pains to describe to readers how this worked, intrigued by the mix of cohesion and division that it created. On British merchant ships, the day was divided into five watches lasting four hours each, and two 'dog watches' in the late afternoon which lasted two hours each. Half the crew worked in each watch while the other half rested. The dog watches created an odd number of watches, so that sailors switched their daytime and night-time working pattern from one day to the next. It was therefore necessary to divide the crew into two groups at the start of the voyage. Confusingly, these were also called watches, a port watch led by the first mate and a starboard watch led by the second mate. Each watch (group of seafarers) worked a watch (unit of time) before handing over to the other. Table 3.1 sets out the pattern over two days at sea.

This pattern ensured that there were always seafarers on deck to steer, maintain lookout, adjust the sails and rigging, and respond to any emergencies. It seems ironic that seafarers who saw themselves free from the clock-obsessed discipline of jobs on shore nonetheless worked in a regime of such rigid time-keeping. However, ship-board time did not correlate with wages quite in the way that clocking in for a factory shift did. Seafarers were paid by the day, to be sure, but envisaged their employment across the voyage, not watch-by-watch. They saw the watch pattern, and other shipboard routines, as a traditional mechanism rooted in the needs of the ship, rather than an emasculating control over a man's time for the benefit of a factory-owner; as the historian Eric Sager puts it, this was 'a workplace hierarchy with a pervasive egalitarianism.'[4] Seafarers expected officers to respect their off-duty watches, and only call all hands on deck when that was essential to the safety of the ship.

Dividing the crew into port and starboard watches was one of the early set-pieces of a voyage. Looking back, authors thought their early officers had shown an uncanny ability to identify the best seafarers almost at first sight.[5] The mate would pick a man to serve in his watch, then the second mate picked one for his, and so on. As William Jones put it when recalling his days as a second mate, 'I picked a few prime seamen, and some who would obviously be malingerers, but I had no other choice.'[6] It worked the other way too. Memoir-writers remembered trepidation or relief at being selected for one or another watch, based on their impressions of the officers. New apprentices were chosen last, reminding them of their place. For all that authors believed in the judgement of officers, though, the system encouraged superficiality; men who just looked the part gained status, unless they subsequently proved to be very poor sailors.

Table 3.1 The daily pattern of watches

	Time	Day 1	Day 2
First watch	8pm – midnight	Port watch on duty	Starboard watch on duty
Middle watch	midnight – 4am	Starboard	Port
Morning watch	4am – 8am	Port	Starboard
Forenoon watch	8am – noon	Starboard	Port
Afternoon watch	noon – 4pm	Port	Starboard
First dog watch	4pm – 6pm	Starboard	Port
Second dog watch	6pm – 8pm	Port	Starboard

Watch selection fixed who would be working together for the duration of the voyage. Although chosen by officers, the men in each watch then took ownership of the grouping, creating an immediate peer pressure. Fred Farmer, who worked as an Ordinary Seaman in the 1890s, described how a watch made clear to officers that they were a unit. If the call came for the resting watch to deal with an emergency, the men waited in the forecastle until all were ready, then went on deck as one. Farmer also thought that men constantly judged the contribution of their watchmates: 'when pulling on a rope, every man knows to an ounce the amount of energy that each is giving to the ship.'[7]

This peer surveillance discouraged shirking, but it could also be used against officers. John Keane recalled a watch that could flawlessly act out the great effort of hauling at a rope without moving the rope at all, just to antagonise an officer who was insisting that they tighten a rope that was 'already as tight as a harp string.'[8] According to William Crutchley, on dark nights a group of seamen might agree to work sails and ropes in absolute silence, forcing the mates to move around the ship checking what was being done; in normal circumstances, the sounds sailors made were enough for the mates to know from a distance.[9]

Rivalry between watches appears in memoirs across our time period. Albert Bestic, one of the last of our authors to go to sea, thought that watches acted as if separated by 'a subconscious wall. Each watch considers itself better than the other.'[10] Back in the 1860s, William Lord had sensed a 'kind of indefinable feeling' separating the watches as soon as they were selected. Lord reported a pitched battle between the watches when his ship was berthed in a Spanish port, following a build-up of stresses and too much drink. Importantly, though, Lord expressed no loyalty to his own watchmates, and took himself off to a quiet part of the ship: 'I had no interest in their quarrels, and did not see why I should be mixed up in them.'[11] Although an Able Seaman rather than an officer-apprentice, Lord was already constructing an identity for himself as a responsible sailor who might one day be promoted, even if that meant losing face with his more belligerent crewmates. His testimony is a reminder that some of our authors faced important decisions about the kind of masculinity they wanted to adopt and perform.

The watch system created some theatrical moments. Mustering the whole crew on deck at the turn of each watch made sure all the seafarers were safely accounted for, but it also emphasised the officers' control over the men. It could therefore be a flashpoint for seafarers who wanted to push back against what they saw as an insult to their independence as working men. Looking back on his apprenticeship in the 1880s, Madden Jardine recalled the absence from a muster of a sailor called Keely, who had to be fetched from the forecastle, all the while blaming his crewmates for not wakening him. Jardine subsequently discovered that Keely had been late deliberately, after telling the crew that mustering was a 'played-out lime-juice habit that grows on ye if ye don't watch it.'[12] It was, thought Keely, more appropriate to schoolboys than adult seafarers.

The early-evening dog watches had significance beyond their practical purpose in alternating daily work patterns. Authors recalled the dog watches as a hybrid time, when much of the ship's work was suspended to enable the crew to eat and engage in storytelling, music, and hobbies. This was a traditional use of time that sailors prized, but officers were careful not to let seafarers' sense of independence get out of hand. Fred Farmer recalled that his ship's mate would make a great show of issuing orders just before the start of the dog watch, but these seemingly crucial tasks would normally just take a few minutes, and were recognised as a symbolic act to remind the crew of the mate's authority before they were free of him for a short while.[13]

Sailing-ship customs defined space as well as time, and the key division was between the forward and rear parts of the ship. Spatial separations were so ingrained that these were used as short-hand for the men who occupied them.

The Ordinary and Able Seamen lived in the forecastle at the bow, so were known as the 'men before the mast' or the 'forecastle crew'; officers had cabins in the stern, and were often called the 'afterguard.' Other seafarers occupied spaces in the middle of the ship, befitting their awkward liminal relationship between the two extremes. Apprentices usually lived in a structure on deck known as the half-deck, which sometimes also accommodated the bosun's locker. Cooks, stewards, and ships' boys had accommodation in various places, but often in or near the stern so that officers could easily give them orders, and to maintain a sense of distance from the crew.

Some ship-board practices could be points of conflict, but also of negotiation, between officers and crews. Seafarers were not supposed to talk while on watch except to answer questions from officers, confirm their orders, or report threats and dangers to the vessel. This was partly a safety measure. Officers gave orders verbally or by whistle, and time was kept by striking the ship's bell, so seafarers needed to be listening for all those signals. However, silence was also a long-established rule in workplaces designed to create an atmosphere of discipline, and even of menace. Talking could therefore become a pressure point for a crew determined to test or undermine their officers' authority. Bill Adams recalled a crew that was never far from mutiny on the long voyage from Oregon back to Europe at the turn of the century. Eventually, they came to an accommodation with the captain that they would do their work if allowed to talk and smoke as they wished. Adams, then a senior apprentice who had internalised a strong sense of ship-board order and propriety, was unimpressed, and thought 'the ship was like a madhouse with their noise.'[14]

For all the traditions and conventions, every crew was a unique group of men, and the dynamics among the crew, and between the crew and the officers, had to be formed anew during each voyage. Although their early experiences were separated by forty years, John Bain and Henry Hughes both believed that most discipline and order was self-imposed by the seamen. Bain wrote of a process of settling into the voyage, as men took responsibility for their assigned tasks, knowing their place in relation to the others, and satisfied with their roles. Sailors had to take orders, but they could in turn give orders to boys and cooks. Their collective purpose became the safe navigation of the vessel.[15] Hughes reported that seafarers soon identified the most senior man in the forecastle, and appointed him as the 'father' of the crew; this man had 'the onerous duty of keeping the house in order and order in the house.'[16] Both authors' recollections are arguably rather rosy, and there are many examples of more fractious crews, even in their own memoirs. Still, they make a useful statement of a conservative, officer-class vision of how crew cohesion should feed into the working of the ship, if everyone slotted into their places. And importantly, that included the officers, who should respect the crew's space in the forecastle and leave them to manage their own business.

As these nuances suggest, the watch system created complex distinctions. Seafarers could claim great independence and privilege in their own space and time, but had to accept that officers could call them on deck at any moment. A man might be subservient to a bullying captain, yet dominant over his watch-mates. If the system demanded them-and-us thinking, there were always tensions within both sides, and individuals who bridged the divides. Mentally and physically, too, the watch system strained some sailors more than others, and watch cohesion could be fragile when men were exhausted, ill, lazy, or simply bored after a long voyage.

Whatever the strains, though, a crew was supposed to stand as one until the very last moment. Only when a ship was irretrievably lost would officers signal the suspension of that culture and order 'every man for himself.' That formal equation of seafarer individualism with the loss of the ship is a revealing symbol of assumptions about duty and discipline, ingrained in officers' worldviews but also, as we will see in later chapters, shared by seafarers who chose to stay with their shipmates in times of crisis.[17]

FRATERNITY

The fact that most of our authors had become officers by the time they wrote their memoirs presents a challenge to interpreting their descriptions of shipboard friendships. Apprentices, intending to be officers from the beginning, were always at some distance from the crew, even if they had a good deal of contact with them during their training. As they became second mates, then mates, and then captains, men could not readily form close connections onboard ship without risking their status and authority. When most authors wrote of their own friendships, they harkened back to early days at sea, when they sailed with other youngsters. Recalling those voyages also let them write of mentoring by older sailors. Seafaring memoirs therefore resonate with the wider findings of research into remembered masculine relationships, namely that men are on safer ground discussing past, lost, and idealised friendships, through which they can more readily express their feelings.[18]

As in most workplaces, new sailors had to earn their place. Socialising employees was a long-established aspect of working life everywhere, of course, especially in relation to inducting apprentices, and industrialisation provoked much discussion about society and culture on the shopfloor.[19] This was more complex still at sea, with the mix of new sailors working as ships' boys, OSs, or officer apprentices. All were assigned ample hard work, and sailors also played practical jokes on them, gave them boring, unpleasant tasks, and poked fun at their appearance and habits, all to test their character. Memoirs include tales of wild goose chases, when crews conspired to have apprentices running all over the ship in search of mythical pieces of equipment or spaces, such as the 'key of the keelson,' or the 'fog locker.'[20] Charles Stevens reported that on his first voyage the sailors told him fearsome tales of the ceremonies he would be put through when crossing the Equator; on edge for days, he was finally put out of his misery by being told they had already crossed the line, and that Neptune had been 'too busy.'[21] Manly acceptance of such treatment was part of gaining recognition by the crew, and those who stood on their dignity could find themselves ridiculed.

As we will see, there were cases where such initiations were the beginning of more systematic bullying. For the most part, though, the usual survivor's bias of memoirs obscures the negatives, and authors wrote approvingly of fraternal seafaring traditions that they would in turn impose on others. When John Patterson arrived on board with a trunk of books in 1880, for example, the crew gave him a succession of nicknames that questioned the manliness of fresh-faced boys with a reading habit: 'the queer 'un,' 'the maid,' and 'the bookshop.' But Patterson claimed that because he learned his job, the men regarded him with amusement rather than hostility. Some asked him to write letters to their sweethearts for them.[22] Later that decade, Frank Worsley put up with being called 'a bairn' during his first voyage, and was rewarded by two sailors who watched out for him and taught him technical skills. The true dynamic of that relationship is unclear, however. The two men continued to wind Worsley up, calling him 'sir' and asking his opinion about everything, as if he were a well-trained pet rather than a shipmate.[23]

Many memoirs suggest that seafarers did not need to gain the acceptance of the whole crew, so long as they could relate to one particular friend, sharing confidences and watching each other's backs in case of trouble. The words for this varied. Some used 'companion,' others used 'chum.'[24] Bill Adams recalled his shipmates bonding together during the battle to round Cape Horn in 1897. Once safely past, he thought that 'the Horn had bound us all in comradeship. We knew each other now. Men chummed in pairs.' Adams's own chum on this voyage was an older apprentice called Glynn, although Adams was initially deferential to Glynn's seniority. On his next voyage, Adams and a new apprentice became chums from the outset. According to Adams, Paddy was a 'lad with thick curly black hair and very deep blue eyes that looked right into mine. And, seeing him, I knew at once I'd found a chum. Later he told me that he had felt the same, the moment he saw me.'[25]

Uniquely in our memoirs, Adams described these friendships as 'love.' Discussing the chum phenomenon, he wrote that 'love as you may your comrades, there must be one best loved.' He and Paddy discussed trying to stay on the same ship despite the normally high rates of crew turnover: 'we'd stick together, he and I, through all our days at sea.' Adams wrote that his fellow apprentices recognised and respected such friendships, and they were gentle and supportive of Adams when Paddy was lost overboard.[26]

Adams's language is hard for us to interpret now after a century in which human relationships have been increasingly defined in sexual terms. Adams does not tell us whether there was a sexual element to the chum relationship, although elsewhere in his memoir he is open about his own pursuit of women on shore, and he describes how Paddy was a promiscuous visitor to brothels in Oregon. Adams's testimony seems to fit with other writing about Aristotelian ideal friendships between equals, which was important in Victorian school stories, and then in late-nineteenth-century debates about same-sex comradeship and love.[27]

Especially after Oscar Wilde's trial and imprisonment in 1895, men who had sexual relationships with other men were increasingly stigmatised and criminalised. In turn, men who valued loving, non-sexual friendships feared being denounced as homosexuals amid that broader social polarisation.[28]

Reticence and caution were natural responses, in life and in writing. By the 1920s, though, memoirs and novels about the Great War reminded the public that noble, manly, but non-sexual love for comrades could be important in dangerous environments, where men had to live and work far from the normal world of women and family.[29] Seafarers, Adams seems to be arguing, had always known that. Wherever Adams might have located himself within the diversity of human sexualities, he wanted to stress to his readers the unusual emotional power of seafaring companionship.

Friendships sometimes appear in memoirs as a statement of shared manly values, and often in opposition to the behaviour of other crew members. When John Mason was an AB in the 1880s, he befriended a sailor called Cockney Charlie, who was sober, restrained in his language, and proud of his ship. The two discussed the seafaring merits of their officers and crew, and their ship's sailing capabilities. Throughout his memoir, Mason rarely claimed to be the only proper seaman on board any given ship, rather presenting himself as part of a small group of superior men.[30] Although some memoir-writers give the impression of standing apart from everyone else throughout their careers, Mason highlighted fellowship with like-minded seamen – even if they were few in number – as an important element of his own seafaring identity.

John Keane, at sea in the 1870s, also described building a small fraternity at the expense of the rest of the crew. One of only two experienced British sailors on a ship with violent officers, Keane thought that the other sailor, Jimmy, was 'one of the most desperate characters I ever met,' but the two men nonetheless built a working partnership based on their nationality and seafaring ability. They made clear that they were essential to the voyage, deflecting the officers' attention away from them and toward the inexperienced foreign sailors.[31] That mutual strength in numbers, even if the numbers were small, appears in many memoirs, and when men lacked even one friend, they felt it keenly. Pryce Mitchell wrote that the loneliness of being the only boy on one of his early voyages stayed with him for years, a revealing reflection from an author who otherwise trumpeted his independence and self-determination. All the same, when Mitchell did have peers, that did not rule out competition. Finding himself junior to his new ship's other OS, Mitchell immediately started working harder: 'I intended to lead in my rating.'[32]

One of the great barriers to lasting seafarer friendships was the high turnover of crews with each new voyage. Apprentices had an advantage here, often staying on the same ship throughout their four-year terms, and could maintain connections better than most. Hans de Mierre told how his apprentices on *Arno* in 1908 became a spirited crowd that could make a lot of noise during the dog watches, and also on shore when apprentices from different ships exchanged stories about their experiences. He thought the 'unselfish comradeship' among apprentices was one of the great compensations for hardships at sea, although he acknowledged that few bothered to analyse such thoughts: 'they were just jolly young sailors.' A less common element is de Mierre's testimony that his group included 'two or three from the fo'c's'le who were so young that they were more at ease with us than with the old shellbacks.'[33] The idea that youth could trump class and role distinctions in that way is unusual in memoirs, although some of those boundaries do seem to be more porous in later testimony, like de Mierre's. Overall, it is much more common in memoirs to find apprentices sneaking into the forecastle to listen to the crew yarning than to have any sailor wanting to spend time with apprentices.

If the men before the mast tried to stay together from one voyage to the next, they were often thwarted. Although seafarers liked the idea that they were free to take their own decisions, they ran out of money quickly on shore and had to join any ship that wanted a crewman, regardless of its reputation, route, or cargo. Attempting to sign on in pairs only reduced their options. In the early 1890s, Walter Dexter wanted to sail from Liverpool to Australia with 'one of my old chums' who had just failed his second mate's exam and needed more sea experience. Only after weeks in port, loans from family, and a move to London did the pair manage to find a ship that needed two sailors with their ratings and experience.[34]

Dexter's testimony is unusual, and most seafarers had no choice but to abandon friendships for new opportunities. When Fred Farmer deserted his vessel in Canada, he claimed that he regretted attachments left behind. However, he wanted the higher wages he could probably demand on an American ship, and to see more of the world rather than return straight to England.[35] Arthur Mason, in a similar situation, analysed more deeply the nature of seafarer friendships. He was initially upset and even offended when his fellow deserter, a sailor he called Liverpool Jack, left him with a perfunctory goodbye on shore. On reflection, though, Mason thought a degree of fatalism, or a childish trust in the future, made seafarers confident that they might well meet again – indeed, it was a compliment to their comradeship that they could walk in and out of each other's lives with such little fuss. Mason's perspective on this is rare, because he claimed to have often encountered the same men on other voyages.[36] Most authors found the opposite, with crews an ever-shifting cast of strangers. Some variation on 'I never saw him again' is the most common way in all these memoirs of ending the description of a particular individual.

Authors thought seafarers were well adapted to transient friendships, and could maintain companionable relations despite, or perhaps because of, knowing very little about the private lives of their shipmates. John Sutherland observed an unspoken convention that sailors asked few questions, leaving it to each individual to decide what to reveal. He thought it was common to be on good terms with shipmates for extended periods without ever knowing if they were married, or where they came from.[37] For Herbert Lightoller, however, the same process often produced rather more knowledge. While a man might seem to reveal very little in any conversation, voyages were so long that 'whether he likes it or not,' his life-story would gradually become apparent to his shipmates. In the end, 'each man knows the other better than he knows himself.'[38]

Intergenerational ties were important on ships that employed everyone from fourteen-year-olds to old shellbacks in their seventies. Whereas the chum phenomenon seems to have applied to those of similar age, connections across a generation gap were seen more in terms of mentoring or even parenting. Authors often remembered older seafarers as fatherly figures in their lives, but sometimes just as competent adults on voyages where those seemed lacking. These relationships could have edgy moments, though, as authors tried to unpick the complexities of age, class, rank, nationality, and experience that made those men so fascinating, yet also created substantial divides between them.

Madden Jardine and Clifford Fenton both benefited from the mentoring of foreign seafarers, but remembered incidents from their apprenticeships that revealed underlying prejudices and tensions. When his ship was being unloaded in Rio de Janeiro in the early 1880s, Jardine's crew got into a racially-aggravated fight with the cargo handlers. He was restrained from getting involved by the ship's Danish carpenter, a man whose counsel and friendship he had repeatedly valued. Jardine, 'in the mad excitement of the moment,' delivered a rant about how a 'square-headed Dutchman' should not try to give orders to 'an English lad.' The carpenter, in heavily accented English, pointed out that he had loved him like a father, at which point Jardine became 'a heap of stripling humiliation, all the fire of nationality and caste washed clean out of me.'[39]

Two decades later, Fenton was taught sailoring by a foreign AB, the Chilean 'Holy Joe' Casternas, and 'used to cultivate Joe's acquaintance a good deal.' One day, though, Joe told a story about cutting off a cruel mate's ear, which seems to have triggered all Fenton's inherited fears about Latin sailors, knives, and brutality. Terrified, Fenton moved to another part of the ship for the rest of the watch.[40] Both Jardine and Fenton reveal a muddle of attitudes to race and nationality that made no sense in relation to the fatherly foreigners who were training them to be sailors. Their immediate reversions to type in moments of fear and crisis exposed the rather thin layer of tolerance that kept multi-generational, multi-ethnic crews working together, until the moment came when it failed.

Respect for those old shellbacks was at the heart of many relationships between crew members, with similar accounts separated by decades. John Wilson reported that he and 'a Russian Finn, named Abraham,' were 'drawn together by a mental gravitation' in the late 1850s. There was 'a wide difference' in their ages, and Abraham did the talking, telling Wilson of his seafaring experiences as they walked the deck during night watches. This took place during a difficult voyage under an inept captain, so Wilson's need for a reliable older presence was understandable; he characterises Abraham as having 'a great kind heart in your weather-beaten and storm-scarred body,' serving as 'an inspiration towards a nobler manhood.'[41]

At sea in the 1880s, John Patterson thought much the same of a sailor he called 'Old Shells,' who had 'a deep, fatherly, manly kindness, continuous and shorn of all nonsense.' Patterson's memoir more generally seems to be a quest for paternal support and advice, and he used the word 'fatherly' many times in describing the older men he encountered. Before he went to sea, he sought the views of seafarers and fishers encountered in Scarborough. When told by 'divers big-booted men in sou'westers that a boy could not go to sea until he was twelve or fourteen years of age,' he accepted this, while resisting the same instructions from his own father. 'Old Shells' proved to be a constant presence, as the two served on the same ship several times, and Patterson reported being traumatised by the older man's death following a sailortown fight.[42] By the time he wrote his memoir, Patterson was a published poet and novelist, with a cultivated style and transparently literary characters. Even so, Old Shells fits the broader representation of father-figure mentors at sea, and most authors claimed to have depended on such men in their early years.

For all that they reported firm friendships, our authors' testimonies also make clear how temporary and contingent that fraternity was. Bill Adams's idea of comradely love is an unusual expression, and it is much more common to find seafarers connecting for short-term, pragmatic purposes, whether to resist bullies or learn trades. Competition was never far away, nor were the realities of power and authority on board, and few links between seafarers seem to have survived the end of the voyage. This does not mean that rhetoric about the brotherhood of seafarers was overblown, however. Being able to establish strong ties with even a few crew-members in the course of a voyage points to a resilient workforce that had made a virtue of its transience, and which, as our authors often commented, had learned to prioritise essentials.

TENSION AND VIOLENCE

Authors were conflicted when they had to explain tensions among sailors, especially those not rooted in what they regarded as healthy competition between watches. Discovering that some ship-board communities were full of argument and even violence challenged one of the more common representations of seafarers in memoirs – that they were easily led astray onshore, but lived purer, more noble lives at sea. Some authors invoked occupational pride, blaming disagreements on a minority of disruptive, work-shy sailors who had no loyalty to the craft of seafaring. In addition, violence was, and remains, a common indicator of social class; middle-class authors absorbed visions of a brutal underclass from fiction and early sociology, while they themselves adopted more ritualistic forms, inculcated through the supposedly character-forming physical punishments of the public schools.[43] As that suggests, most memoir-writers addressed violence and conflict in two contexts. On the one hand, they wrote of the tensions between sailors, and recalled their own youthful fights and arguments. On the other, many described how officers – including themselves as they rose in rank – used violence to impose discipline. We will return to that second form in more detail in chapter 5.

Many authors argued that truly disruptive sailors were in a small minority. John Bain, for example, thought diligent work could hold most of a crew together, however eccentric some of its individuals, while a few men stayed on the margins causing trouble. He remembered one deep-sea crew of thirty-six as being made up of 'good fellows, queer chaps and bad characters'; after coming through their first storm, though, there were only 'three or four incorrigible rascals.'[44] However, such clean distinctions became harder to justify as authors realised the nuances and complexities of living and working at sea. The arc of the voyage was important. Authors describe seafarers going through phases, sometimes working hard, at other times refusing to leave their bunks regardless of the impact on the rest of their watch. Attitudes and behaviours shifted when men became ill and exhausted after a long period at sea. Troublemaking men often had allies who respected their resistance to officers' authority, although sympathy could wear thin after prolonged periods of extra work.

Authors often focused on a single seafarer as a device for revealing attitudes towards disruptive sailors. Madden Jardine's character Keely regularly appears making extravagant claims about his own seamanship, and denigrating the skills of mates and sailors alike. On the rare occasion when he could be found working, Keely was a capable seaman, and knew how to do enough to avoid serious trouble from the officers. He was an astute observer of, and participant in, the power relations on board, reserving his worst scorn for a sailor even less popular than he was, and thus deflecting the crew's anger. If Keely had no friends on board, he had few real enemies either, and most of the crew seem to have tolerated him most of the time. Only in the later phases of a lengthy voyage did the crew lose patience with Keely's carefully cultivated aches and pains. Finally, in one of the last set-pieces of Jardine's memoir, Keely was kidnapped by boarding-house crimps when the ship was in Oregon, and no one made any attempt to help him.[45] Jardine was reminding his readers that in seafaring, many problems simply went away at the next port.

Memoir-writers were struck by the way crews could swing from sympathy to hostility, especially if they felt that a man was taking advantage of them as shipmates. Sailors could also be embarrassed by displays of sentiment that turned out to be misplaced. Albert Bestic described a man called Kemp, whom he regarded as a degenerate product of the slums, shirking work and putting the ship in danger. One day, Kemp could not be found, the men suspected he had gone overboard, and they began to question whether he had really been so bad. When Kemp suddenly reappeared, having been hiding from the hard work his crewmates were enduring, they turned on him, infuriated as much by their own gullibility as by his behaviour. To Bestic, men like Kemp defied the supposed ennobling effects of being at sea: 'even the mighty sea failed to alter his crooked outlook, let alone mould his nature into that of the average sailing-ship man.'[46]

Authors reported some seafarers trying to distance themselves from their malingering crewmates by appealing to the officers for respect as proper sailors. John Mason recounted his crew's plea for more food when handling cargo in an American port after a long voyage across the Pacific in the 1880s. One of the crew directed a long speech at the captain, reminding him that they were 'quiet men' who wanted no trouble, and who had served him well on the outward journey. During a storm, the sailor claimed, 'we proved ourselves to be supermen,' not least because they were short-handed thanks to the captain's decision to employ some useless 'hobos' to make up crew numbers.[47] If some of the rhetorical drama of this incident seems implausible, it serves to set out Mason's own vision of a class of sober and capable sailors, who were all the more impressive for having to work alongside the scum of the waterfront.

Most memoirs include occasions when ship-board arguments slipped over into physical violence. Given our authors' disproportionate emphasis on their early years at sea, it is no surprise that they often discussed violence through their own experiences as boys and young sailors. Harsh physical and psychological chastisements were common in education and child-raising during this period, and almost all young seafarers would have witnessed, and probably experienced, the beating of boys their age in various situations before they went to sea. Historians have identified a long-standing public consensus in favour of corporal punishments for boys, often as a means of moulding manly character. Schools also inculcated efforts to make rough manliness more respectable through ideas like the 'fair fight,' while adventure stories and popular culture promoted norms like using fists rather than knives, or refraining from hitting a man while he was on the ground.[48]

Accordingly, several of our authors claimed that violence had been a formative part of their adventurous, risk-taking childhoods, and that it had prepared them for life at sea. William Crutchley reported being beaten in school, and again when he was a ship's apprentice in the 1860s, and seemed sanguine at having moved from one kind of ritual punishment to another. It is no accident that boys were beaten using particular means, whether canes in school or rope-ends on ships, to emphasise the tradition being invoked and to distance the adult from the process. Crutchley himself looked back on this as a powerful driver of character building, and regretted what he called the 'sickly sentimentality' of those opposed to corporal punishment.[49]

The early chapters of Arthur Mason's memoir recount an 1880s childhood in Northern Ireland that was seeped in violence. Regularly beaten by his father, his schoolmasters, and other boys, Mason fought them all in turn as he grew older and stronger. Still, he discovered a more structured violence during his early voyages. He wrote of his first Cape Horn voyage that, 'I learned to fight on board that ship, for there were some tough men in the forecastle.'[50] What Mason meant was that he grew out of the raging rebellious violence of his childhood to absorb more tactical and scientific approaches, biding his time, learning to box, and seeking allies.

Many authors recounted fights among apprentices. James Barker, who became a pugilistic martinet as a captain, recalled his fellow apprentices regularly fighting each other 'for the sake of excitement,' and turning out bruised for their next watch.[51] There is little to distinguish between such accounts and tales of public school boys fighting for honour. Bertram Hayes, for example, recalled a senior apprentice who put on airs and tried to dominate the other boys, until one of them fought back – inevitably, in Hayes's recollection the two became firm friends thereafter.[52] Probably this code was so pervasive that our authors really believed it had resolved their problems, but of course we lack testimony from those who persistently lost 'fair fights.'

Some writers tried to explain the limits of ship-board violence involving younger sailors. While both officers and older seafarers clearly felt able to chastise boy sailors, in other circumstances they thought youngsters needed protection. Fred Farmer reported that the youngest seafarers would be hit with belts or similar implements, but that they should not be struck with a 'closed fist.' Revealingly, he made this distinction in relation to a popular young sailor called Jack, rather than the kind of recalcitrant youth that we might expect. Jack was 'something of a pet,' and 'all healthy minded men admire a display of spirit in a youngster.'[53] If that spirit slipped into insolence, the crew had no problem punishing Jack, but within the unwritten code that maintained that violence as a ritual.

Boundaries were not always so neat and readily explained, however. Probably the most extreme event in Farmer's memoir is a fight between two seamen, Henrick and Jimmy, over a sick young Norwegian called Alex. When Jimmy struck the blind and defenceless Alex, accusing him of malingering,

Henrick responded by trying to tear Jimmy's throat out with his teeth, an act of such ferocity that even the crew were astonished. As soon as the fighting sailors were separated by their crewmates, Henrick went back to looking after Alex, 'cooing to the boy as a mother over a sick child.' Farmer thought there was something bizarre and primitive about both extremes of emotion: Henrick was displaying 'a pity for the boy which was far more terrible than his mad frenzy.'[54]

Most memoirs are like Farmer's, recounting some violent scenes, but as exceptions rather than the norm. Few authors claimed to have perpetrated much violence, although Robert Ramsay reported fighting other sailors throughout his career. Initially, he claimed to have beaten those who bullied or insulted him as a youngster, arguing that self-defence should be part of any boy's training. He continued fighting as an officer, both to discipline insubordinate sailors, and, less commonly, when he fell out with his superiors. Ramsay even spent time in an Australian jail because of a dispute with his ship's captain; after his release, he got another ship home and fought the second mate.[55] While he admitted to having a drinking problem by then, Ramsay's battling approach predated his alcoholism, and he expressed none of the regret for fighting that he claimed to have for drinking by the time he wrote his memoir.

It is no surprise that our authors included depictions of ship-board tensions and violence. Sailing ships employed many younger-than-average men doing risky work in confined conditions, and doing a job known for – and proud of – extremes of masculinity. The evidence for young men being perpetrators of a disproportionate share of violence across many nations and long time periods has been well-established by scholars.[56] At the same time, working on a British deep-water sailing ship was nothing like the lawless world that men faced in the American West, for example, however much seafarers liked to see themselves as adventurers and frontiersmen. Most of the discussion of violence in memoirs has a ritual air, and authors seem to have believed it was channelled into constructive character-building, reinforcing rather than undermining crew cohesion. They stressed the mitigating effects of shipboard structures, which constrained extreme behaviour through a range of institutional, fraternal, and communal norms.

*

The 'total institution' of the sailing ship was indeed a strange society, but arguably rather different from most of the situations that attract that label. Seafarers were not actually at sea to be punished or kept separate from society, as if they were in a prison or asylum, yet the effect on their character was still profound.[57] Memoir-writers wanted to depict crews having positive, affirming relationships among themselves that reinforced a wider sense of being free men who could roam the world in a fraternity of proper sailors. Part of that agency was an acceptance of structures that regulated work and life at sea, but also a sophisticated understanding of how men could negotiate and manipulate those conditions. While the physical and mental violence of old-fashioned, rough masculinity comes across in many memoirs, so do brotherly and fatherly relationships that were much gentler, even if they too depended on respecting the power of the stronger men on board.

Whatever its strengths and attractions, though, some authors concluded that sailing-ship society was limited and eccentric. Long voyages in difficult conditions with small crews may have created strong bonds of necessity between groups of men, but left little that would survive the dispersal of the men at the next port. John Bain realised what he had been missing when he served as an officer on emigrant ships to Australia. Those vessels really were communities in microcosm, and small towns afloat; interacting with the passengers had 'a civilising effect on a man who has spent most of his years away from the society of friends.'[58] For all that he wrote kindly of some of his shipmates, Bain did not regard them as enough for a man's social fulfilment. The more reflective of our authors realised with hindsight that living and working in sailing ships had been a dead end, however formative it was, and however nostalgic they were to become about it.

4

Becoming

Seafaring memoirs are full of transitions, and our authors wrote that their early years at sea had been a three-fold process of becoming something new. They were growing from boys to men, surrounded by adult male role models who combined great diversity with a narrower set of expected, even stereotyped, attributes. They were becoming seamen, as they grew in strength and skills from dogsbody first-voyagers to effective maritime workers. Finally, most were building an officer identity as they observed the behaviour of captains and mates, and hoped to take the Board of Trade exams. These three elements were never separate, and authors sometimes struggled to convey their progress in this combination of formal training, informal mentoring, learning by example, and absorption of skills and character.

As this chapter and the next will demonstrate, rank, work, craft, age, and masculinity interacted in intricate ways. Those who went to sea as apprentices were expected to display a respectable, officerly version of manhood, but they could be tempted to emulate the exciting, rougher manliness of the seamen before the mast. This was made more complex by a genuine pride in the time-honoured skills they learned from the ABs. In addition, ships' officers sent confusing messages, often being men of science, leadership, superstition, and violence all at once. While it was normal for any boy to go through phases of insecurity and rebellion, young sailors had an unusually wide range of models and issues to confront.

Looking back, authors were conflicted about how much they had needed to be taught, and what they owed to intrinsic characteristics. Some claimed to be more natural seafarers than others, but all recognised that sail-, rope-, and ship-handling skills could only be acquired by close observation and instruction. They also accepted that officer exams prioritised seamanship and navigation, and there seemed to be no shame in admitting that those had to be learned formally. When it came to attributes like confidence and leadership, however, many authors preferred to see themselves as self-taught, or as having those qualities innately. For all their certification and training, being a ship's officer was part of a broader cult of amateurism, which valued a manly character above any book learning, and expected that character to combine internal strength with public performance. Maintaining a long-standing, craft-focused culture in a professionalising occupation coloured the early years of many seafaring officers' careers, and some of our authors were still working through its implications decades later.

BOYS TO MEN

For many authors, going to sea and becoming a man had been inextricably tangled from the beginning. Bertram Hayes recalled that the shipowner Henry Fernie 'promised to make a man of me' when signing indentures in 1880, and that phrase permeates memoirs as an industry cliché.[1] For James Bisset, being at sea could literally build a man, turning a tiny boy into the mighty physical specimens we met in chapter 2. When a former schoolmate returned from a voyage, Bisset found him 'bronzed, fit and well, much bigger than before,' and Bisset himself was allowed to go to sea when his doctor concluded that it would 'make a man of him.' He could chart this using his own body – only 4 feet 2 inches tall when he first went to sea in 1898 at the age of fifteen, Bisset was a more imposing 5 feet 8 inches when he finished his apprenticeship and qualified as second mate five years later.[2]

Many authors shared this same broad view. James Barker thought that early years at sea 'made men of blubbering schoolboys, and towards the closing days of apprenticeship there were *sailors* in the half-deck, husky, shaven headed brutes, strong as colts.'[3] Similarly, for Alan Villiers, sailing ships cast a spell over the boys who sailed in them: 'And the spell is this – that it makes them men. Who does not want to be a man?'[4] Villiers was a philosopher of seafaring, Barker a disciplinary martinet and unsentimental businessman, yet they shared that sense of the sailing ship as a tool for making a particular kind of man.

Nonetheless, authors could be vague about what they meant by growing into manhood. Their indicators often boil down to little more than a superficial focus on the male body, its physique and presence. Elsewhere in their books, they offered more complex ideas of manly mindsets and worldviews, but when they had to express themselves in brief, authors usually fell back on simple appearance. They also took it for granted that a relatively short passage of time should, given the right raw material, make a huge difference, and that this would be clear in relation to others. Those reaching the later stages of their apprenticeships compared themselves with new arrivals, and this boosted their confidence while sometimes provoking mixed feelings.

William Jones, for example, 'pitied the poor little devils' who joined his ship, but gained a sense of his own achievements at the same time: 'a man of eighteen years can look down from a great height of experience on mere boys of fifteen.'[5] When Hans de Mierre was in the final weeks of his apprenticeship, he met a first voyager from another ship on shore in Australia. The youngster was already playing the part, 'the peak of his cap cocked over one eye, puffing a big pipe,' but he reacted 'almost with awe' to de Mierre.[6] Arthur Rostron thought the older apprentices on his first voyage seemed 'rather wonderful fellows to me and I drank in all they said of what they had done and seen.'[7] Just as they had looked up to the sailors they met on shore as children, our authors felt privileged to be acknowledged by apprentices who were only a year or two older, and remembered those inspiring conversations decades later.

On the other hand, being recognised as a seafaring man proved more difficult when boy sailors went home on leave. Walter Runciman had a particular need to demonstrate his transition from boy to man, because his parents had repeatedly told him that he was too young, small, and fragile to be a sailor. A captain had finally agreed to take him on (inevitably, to 'make a man of him'), and Runciman returned from his first voyage believing he 'was growing quickly into manhood.' His family had different ideas. His mother was quick to rebuke him for his acquired 'forecastle manners' at the dinner table, and he noticed that younger relatives and the local farm people expected him to adopt the singing and storytelling persona of a sailor on shore. The educated adults of his own circle seemed unimpressed, and believed that he was still too young to be working at sea.[8]

As Runciman's testimony suggests, going from boyhood to manhood, and from first-voyager to experienced seafarer, has to be seen through different lenses. On shore between voyages, young sailors felt they had to maintain a performance for the benefit of parents and elders who often had no understanding of their experiences, but who did have deep-rooted assumptions about life and work at sea from popular culture. James Bisset knew his father still questioned his decision to go to sea, so made sure his stories were positive, to the point where he came to believe his own mythology.[9] Pride and self-respect overcame doubt and insecurity, as boys saw themselves becoming independent men, sometimes cemented by the scepticism they encountered.

That identity was fragile to begin with, though, and boy sailors were keen to return to sea, and get back on a path to manhood among men who understood them. If part of this was about seafaring skills and knowledge, it was also about a different pace of manly transition. Manliness had to be recognised and affirmed by a group of one's peers or those in a shared occupation. This usually had to take place away from the domestic sphere.[10] Importantly, it would happen on different timelines. Families would continue to regard their sons as boys throughout years of home-visits. At sea, however, the boy was surrounded by men who had the measure of his courage, skills, and qualities as a shipmate; in their ranks, he had the prospect of being accepted as a man much sooner than his boyish appearance on shore would suggest.

For all that, physical presence was always a major element in being accepted as a seafaring man. Arthur Mason reported that the crew of his second ship defined him as a man in large part because he looked like one; his first voyage, followed by a period working on shore, had built his strength and nimbleness. He now described himself as 'five feet ten, sinewy, quick of eye and hand, nimble upon my feet, and deep-chested.'[11] Likewise, John Bain, although still in his teens, had years of experience in coastal vessels when he joined his first large deep-water ship. While taken aback by the scale of everything, he knew enough to play the part: 'so well did I affect the *role* of an old hand that I passed the scrutiny of the "forecastle," who never suspected that I was a "greenhorn."'[12]

Ships' officers recruiting crews were often able to pick from a large pool of potential sailors, and were not always concerned about the seafaring ability of those chosen. They prioritised physical strength and stamina, which they assessed by the superficial appearance of the men, and could afford to reject anyone who looked young or weak. Indeed, officers often subcontracted the whole process to boarding-house keepers. Small wonder that memoir-writers remained sensitive about the shallowness of it all, when it seemed to them they had grown so quickly into manhood.

By the time he finished his apprenticeship in the mid-1860s, Walter Runciman was in his late teens, a capable sailor, and also 'tall and well set up.' But he still 'carried the looks of a boy, and found it hard to get any captain to take me as a full-blooded hand.'[13] Only when his most recent captain spoke up for him did the others put aside their first visual impressions and take Runciman on as an adult seafarer. Henry Moffat also struggled to get jobs because of his 'youthful appearance' after several voyages, and even after time spent gold-prospecting in Australia. He still had officers doubting his age after ten years at sea.[14] Others remembered provoking their peers by calling them 'boy' and 'lad' at precisely the point when they thought they might have escaped those labels. When Melbourne Garahan and his fellow apprentices were taking turns to serve as third mate, each barracked the others with complaints about useless boy sailors. Garahan portrays this as healthy banter, but it was close to the bone.[15]

As this testimony suggests, our authors had many ways of expressing their transition to manhood, but often struggled to overcome their elders' assumptions about physical appearance and presence. Boys would have preferred to be judged on seafaring skill and character sooner than they were, especially those who still looked boyish into their twenties. But they could never separate that multitude of factors in their writing, just as they had been bombarded at the time with overlapping, and sometimes conflicting, ideas about what it meant to be a seafaring man. The rest of this chapter teases out those distinctions, and how they added up to a new, multifaceted identity.

APPRENTICES AND OTHERS

As noted in the Introduction, around half of our authors initially went to sea as ships' boys or Ordinary Seamen, while the others were officer-apprentices. Both groups could become officers with the right experience and passing of exams, but the apprenticeship route came to dominate entry to officer careers by late-century. Apprentices normally needed the financial support of their parents to pay a 'premium' indenture fee to the shipping company, and this made it hard for poorer boys to take that path. Sail apprenticeships became 'conspicuously modelled on the public-school system,' strengthening the creation of a social as well as a professional elite.[16] It was also difficult for OSs and ABs to save enough funds to spend time at navigation school, which was a virtual necessity for passing the exams. Jack Randell, for example, reported that he could never afford to pay for enough shore training at one time to qualify for his certificates, and spent almost a decade at sea before passing as a second mate.[17] His better-connected contemporaries managed it in half that time.

The system's growing overtones of middle-class privilege caused our later authors a deal of soul-searching. They thought dependence on parental funds sat awkwardly with the adventurous trope of running away to sea, and wondered if it was really the proper way to attain seafaring manhood. When Leslie Morton signed up as an OS in 1910, his father 'rescued' him by paying the shipowner a premium and converting him into an apprentice. Although this intervention put Morton on an easier track to his career as an officer, he claimed to have felt indignant and humiliated at the time.[18]

Some writers thought the prestige of the apprentice route was ironic, given the hardships of sea-life. When William Crutchley looked back on his apprenticeship in the 1860s, he recalled that seafarers mocked the idea of 'gentlemen's sons that pay to go to sea,' and agreed that 'such a custom certainly seems humorous.'[19] John Keane, another early author who had been to a prestigious school, referred to seagoing apprentices as 'young gentlemen,' and believed that the training ships *Worcester* and *Conway* produced the right kind: 'they have such an open, manly, English public-school boy style about them.' Although inclined to be 'a little uppish' at first, this was a good fault, thought Keane, because it made clear their separation from the sailors.[20] Some apprentices certainly thought they were members of an elite club. Arthur Rostron found three other '*Conway* boys' on his first ship in 1885, and commented on the 'bond' that immediately existed between them all.[21]

Such patterns became stronger over time. On his first voyage in 1901, Melbourne Garahan, a *Worcester* graduate, found to his 'astonishment and indignation' that the officers picked apprentices for their watches in the same way that they chose sailors, with disparaging and sarcastic remarks about their appearance and lack of seafaring skills.[22] Bill Adams encountered a mutinous crew who ridiculed the apprentices' efforts to sail the ship: '"look at the damn bridge ornymints!" they jeered, making great fun of us who each, some day, would be an officer.'[23] Clifford Fenton thought that boys who ignored the harsh conditions and showed willing at the start of the voyage would be accepted, while those who tried to behave like future captains were punished by sailors and officers alike, and he made sure he was on the right side of that line.[24]

The sense that apprentices were entitled objects of contempt encouraged some authors to seek another route. Walter Dexter claimed his story was different because he was a 'freelance'; although he started as an apprentice in 1888, he 'early broke these bonds and gave way to the "wanderlust."' He decided that deserting, and then joining another ship as an ordinary sailor, would enable him to take control of his own destiny as a free man. He could choose his ships and routes, rather than be tied to the company that held his indentures. More than that, he thought he would have more social freedom on the ship itself, no longer stuck with an apprentice's awkward liminal status between the officers and the crew. Dexter maintained this thread throughout his memoir. After six years at sea, he went for the unusual 'Only Mate' certificate, a harder qualification than the second mate's ticket, and claimed that his greater variety of seafaring experience enabled him to pass easily.[25] Crucially, Dexter was not rejecting the ideal of becoming an officer, but rather asserting that he had found a better way to attain it.

Pryce Mitchell also worked his way up from being an OS in the late 1870s, in a deliberate act of independence from his family's connections. Mitchell was related to major shipowners, and rejected offers to find him a good apprenticeship. Revealingly, though, he took this principle only so far. Having worked as an OS and AB on a succession of voyages, Mitchell found himself blocked from taking his exam for second mate because of his record of desertion. At that point he had no hesitation in asking relations to pull strings, and he also accepted help in securing a job with a prestigious steamship firm. Mitchell seems to have believed that becoming a seafarer was something he had to achieve without the taint of social privilege, but that he could be more pragmatic about how he became an officer. In addition, he never rebelled against his family, included them in all the celebrations of certificates and promotions, and claimed that his key motivation in becoming a liner captain was to provide for his mother after his father's death.[26]

Mitchell's account is a complicated mix of aspiration to manly self-determination, while retaining the obligations and privileges of a well-connected middle-class family. Other authors took the apprenticeship route, but found ways to push the boundaries, balancing their class and professional respectability with the piratical inspirations of their boyhoods. They were claiming that such impulses showed them to have been the right kind of adventurous youths, even if in the end they settled down to responsible manhood. The apprentices' half-deck was a microcosm of seafaring society but also an outlier, tangled in class-based perceptions of how boys should behave. Many episodes read like public-school memoirs, an important form of middle-class life-writing more generally.[27] The older apprentices were the senior prefects wielding manly authority over juniors; there were practical jokes, a sense of honour rooted in gentlemanly ideas, and above all an obsession with food. Apprentices built their fraternity, and also established a rough equality, by sharing out the food parcels they brought from home, or that were sent to them by their families.[28] It went beyond that, though, into peer pressure to steal food from the ship's stores, which they justified by their belief in the unsporting parsimony of shipowners.[29]

In light of the status expectations surrounding apprentices, punishment was unlikely to be severe: boys, everyone agreed, would be boys. Herbert Lightoller, who went to sea as an apprentice in 1888, recalled that 'sneaking food was no crime, it was a religion.' He and his peers conceived this as a battle of wills with the cooks and stewards rather than directly with the officers, a convenient fiction that excused their behaviour. When caught and reported to the captain, they were punished with extra duties, but always assumed that the officers were 'inwardly amused' by these exploits.[30]

Lightoller's wider testimony suggests that apprentices knew which lines they could cross. Having been rescued from a shipwreck and put ashore in Australia, Lightoller enjoyed the local hospitality for three months, despite his shipping company demanding that he make his way home as soon as possible. When he did return to work, he could have been in considerable trouble, but found that captains were often charmed by a young man who showed initiative, and he talked his way into jobs with entertaining stories of his adventurous, unconventional exploits.[31] As in most professional lives, gaining the social capital to learn which rules really mattered was crucial to the career path of a merchant officer.

Some of our officer-writers remained uncertain, decades later, about their social and professional advancement, and perhaps especially those who began work as ships' boys or OSs. Edgar Britten, who went on to be commodore of the Cunard White Star Line, constructed an image of his career that had him going to sea younger than he did.[32] He claimed that whenever he saw a sailing ship in later life he remembered his first voyage, and pictured his old captain helping a 'little boy' understand some technical manual of seafaring. But according to his officer certificates, Britten was just short of eighteen when he first worked at sea, spending five years before the mast. Britten claimed to have been 'barely twenty-two' when he sailed as first mate, although in reality he was nearly twenty-five. He quickly gained his master mariner's certificate, however, and made his big step up to working on Cunard steamships.

This was an impressive rise from an unlikely starting point, but Britten seemed embarrassed by taking longer than his peers might have done by the apprentice route. More than once, Britten mentions his irritation at having had to start at the very bottom of the hierarchy, worried that those early steps had taken him too long to be truly worthy. The distortion of his age is perhaps a compensation for that. It also seems to be a nostalgic muddling of his working career and his first ever sea voyage, as a six-year-old child with his mother. Looking back on a successful career by any definition, Britten still felt more comfortable with the illusion that he had been that classic boy sailor, glossing over the time he 'wasted' at school and in his first office job.

Although apprenticeships conferred many advantages, and were clearly favoured by middle-class parents at the end of the nineteenth century, it is revealing that many of our authors doubted whether they represented the right track to seafaring manhood. Anxieties over the alternative ways of gaining sea experience prior to becoming an officer permeated many aspects of our authors' careers, and the ways in which they wanted to represent themselves in their memoirs.

LEARNING TO BE SEAFARERS

Memoir-writers devoted much space to the immense technical complexity of work on a sailing ship. Sailors had to learn the names of every rope, sail, mast, yard, and fitting, as well as the language of orders and actions. Many did this without being able to read, or to understand much English. They then had to work with all those things, developing great skill and dexterity, not least because they were often handling them in the cold, wet, and dark. Yet educated observers could be puzzled by the mindsets that sometimes accompanied such proficiency. Alan Moore, a writer and critic who reviewed many of the maritime memoirs of the 1930s, thought there was an unbridgeable gap between those who went to sea in search of philosophies and states of mind, and those for whom the craft of seamanship was an end in itself. The strangeness of many seafarers, so knowledgeable yet so limited, seemed rooted in a cult of practicality that was suspicious of broader meanings.[33]

Our authors had no doubt that the sailor's craft – the physical and mental work of the 'proper sailor' – was fundamental to maritime manhood, and a constant challenge to aspiring seafarers. New sailors all had to learn the seaman's skills, regardless of whether they were ships' boys, OSs, or apprentices, or indeed whether they already had aspirations to become officers. This was not unusual to shipping, and most industries had a training and testing process for boys, holding them at a closely-defined level until they were permitted to take on men's jobs. Boys rarely moved up until they had 'served their time,' even if they might have been competent to do so earlier. Seafaring comes across in most memoirs as a cult of practical craft-learning, a process of trial, error, and eventual competence. It depended on a community of mutual reliance, with intergenerational instruction and guidance, and was central to occupational identity. Exactly how that worked varied with the willingness and ability of the crew to pass on their skills, the extent to which officers took an interest, and the attitudes of the trainees.

Most memoir-writers remembered initial days and weeks at sea spent doing menial work. We saw earlier that OSs were often despised as 'farmers' or 'hobos,' and were only accepted as seafarers after they had learned some rope or sail work. Apprentices found something similar, and reported that they were constantly watched and tested at first. Many authors argued that a willingness to take on hard work in the early days at sea was a key indicator of a would-be sailor's prospects; character could overcome ignorance, and had to shine through despite initial appearances. Fred Farmer, for example, was one of two OSs working on his ship in the 1890s; he called the other man 'Dutchy.' Although very slow to learn any useful skills, Dutchy 'was a willing worker and never complained,' so was spared any 'rough handling.' Farmer himself relied on a sailor called Jim to teach him seamanship, but thought that the most important aspect of this was gaining self-confidence, which Farmer believed was 'the foundation of a rapid rise in ability as a sailor.'[34]

Officers watched young sailors in their first weeks at sea, deciding when to assign progressively harder tasks to them. Leslie Morton resented his first week of 'menial jobs,' but he recognised with hindsight that the second mate was checking to see whether he was prone to seasickness before sending him up into the rigging, and waiting until the vessel was in stable sailing conditions before putting him at the wheel.[35] Madden Jardine's early days at sea were also carefully observed by the officers, as much for his morale as his physical safety. The captain lectured him on the role of the officer apprentice, which gave the seasick Jardine a 'glow of enthusiasm.' A few nights later, however, the second mate ordered Jardine to stay in a safe part of the afterdeck, because 'small people often disappear on dirty nights at sea.'[36] Jardine conceded that the order was welcome, but wanted to prove his courage and ability. Similarly, Walter Runciman reported being kept below for the early days of his first voyage because the sea was so rough, which hurt his dignity.[37]

Such surveillance had the unfortunate effect of provoking risky behaviour in some boys, when they practiced new skills out of sight of officers to avoid embarrassment. The only danger Charles Stevens reported during his first voyage came when he tried to handle a rowing boat unsupervised and got into difficulties.[38] Other authors, though, took a larger gamble, figuring that risk-taking in plain sight would build their reputations among officers and crew alike. Robert Ramsay reported running about aloft as a boy sailor, taking such extreme chances that the officers punished him for his recklessness. But he calculated that this would win the acclaim of the sailors, showing that he had the makings of a proper seafaring man, and that the officers would secretly approve.[39] Frank Worsley performed similar acrobatics against all advice, although he claimed it was simple 'animal spirits' and the 'joy of living' that drove him; indeed, this is consistent with Worsley's relentlessly positive memoir, couched as much as an adventure story as the beginnings of a sea career.[40]

Both OSs and apprentices learned their seafaring skills from the Able Seamen. ABs taught rope and sail work, and bewildering technical language. There would also be an AB at the wheel whenever an apprentice was given a turn at steering. The idea that apprentices would be taught practical seamanship by the forecastle crew raised tricky issues around class, rank, and status.

Some authors thought this was a natural transmission of skills from one generation to another. William Jones reported that he 'found those hardened old shellbacks – many of them unable to read or write – always willing to teach a boy, patiently, what they had learned in the years of long experience.'[41]

For others, learning to be seafarers meant getting close to men who were looked down upon by the ship's officers, and even by senior apprentices. Bill Adams owed much of his training to an AB called Tom Swift, who was, in Adams's telling, an unpleasant individual when in the company of his fellow seafarers, talking of all the 'women he had known the world across, his every other word a swear word.' Adams was therefore surprised to find that Swift shared his appreciation for a fine sunrise, and this opened a new connection between them, despite knowing that it was 'against the rules for apprentices to fraternize with common sailors.' Adams and Swift were both transgressing normal behaviours. Swift conformed to a more respectable code of masculinity with Adams, with no swearing or talk of women. Adams's peers sneered at him for being friendly with someone they regarded as 'no better than a pimp.'[42] We cannot know how Swift's crewmates viewed his training of the apprentice, or what Swift himself thought. Authors like Adams, though, looked back on such relationships with a sense of bravado, impressed by their own willingness to cross lines and push boundaries in pursuit of learning their craft.

As they moved through their time at sea, apprentices started training each other. This was an important way to inculcate knowledge, because apprentices liked to appear more proficient than they actually were, and teaching a new hand helped them mould their self-image as a seasoned sailor. James Bisset remembered passing on sea lore to the ship's new apprentice, keen to demonstrate 'from my vast experience … the right sailor's way of doing things.' Bisset's testimony mixes teenage confidence and adult self-deprecation, capturing the gulf that young sailors felt opening up, very quickly, between them and people who had never been to sea: 'as I was now sixteen and he was only fifteen, I felt that he had everything to learn.'[43]

Authors remembered a sense of pride and power when they began to be trusted with important sailorly tasks. Albert Bestic was on lookout one day when he reported a steamer ahead, and the officer on deck ordered the man at the wheel to change course.[44] Although all the decisions were taken by the officer, Bestic enjoyed the illusion that his call from the top of the mast had led directly to the ship's manoeuvre, in contrast to a young sailor's usual feeling that he had no say in anything that happened to him, let alone the ship.

Leslie Morton recalled how his first watches at the wheel made him feel part of the long historical continuity of famous seafarers – he cited Nelson, Cook, and Ulysses – and proud that he was doing important seaman's work at a young age.[45] Although mastering technical skills was crucial, that additional layer of belonging to a crew of men, and being part of the seafaring heritage behind that, was important to those seeking a career at sea, even if they did not always articulate it as clearly as Morton did. It is also no accident that Morton identified specifically with captains and admirals: seafaring and command had become intertwined in his sense of self.

As he progressed through his apprenticeship, Herbert Lightoller realised that his officers had devised milestones in skills and status based on the layout of their ship's sails. We saw earlier that Lightoller's ship *Primrose Hill* carried skysails high on its masts; these could only be reached by shinning up the wire backstays that braced the mast itself. This hair-raising manoeuvre was assigned to first-voyage apprentices, sometimes as a punishment for misdemeanours, but apparently as a general toughening and training exercise. By the time he reached the fourth year of his term, however, Lightoller was 'promoted' to working no higher than the royal sails, while the new first-voyagers became the 'skysail yarders.'[46] Using the name of a sail in this way reveals how intimately trainee sailors identified with nautical language and practice. It also suggests how opaque that culture might be to outsiders.

A few authors, revealingly, took a very different view of gaining their seafaring craft. Frank Symondson, who left the sea after one voyage, thought that being an apprentice was 'a farce.' One of our earliest authors, Symondson's 1876 memoir was an exposé of life in sailing ships, published at a time of controversy over safety and conditions at sea, and national soul-searching about whether Britain's maritime power was being undermined by a shortage of willing recruits. He thought that first-voyage apprentices simply did the work of common sailors – expecting to be trained in navigation, they found themselves sweeping the decks as cheap labour. Symondson claimed that proper cadet training ships were the answer, because on those ships the boys lived aft, did no manual work, and were formally taught seamanship.[47] His concern was about class and status as much as seafaring training, but it is telling that those things had become so mixed even in Symondson's day.

Seafaring skill, self-image, and an ability to gain the approval of sceptical officers all came together in authors' memories of key moments in their formative years at sea. Clifford Fenton dated a turning-point on his road to manhood precisely, to an unusual conversation with his captain. As a small, fifteen-year-old apprentice, Fenton was steering his ship successfully, despite struggling with the large, heavy wheel. The captain quizzed him on his navigational knowledge, and was surprised to find that Fenton had already acquired a good deal of it during a spell at nautical school. In his memoir, Fenton wrote openly about wishing the captain had been his father, a replacement for the real father he had not known. That hero-worship, combined with being able to impress the captain with his seafaring ability, did not provoke the most obvious conclusion, however, that he had proved himself as a sailor. Instead, Fenton wrote that 'when I went away from the wheel that day I most certainly was not a boy; I was a man.'[48] That conceptual leap reveals the entanglement of youth, seafaring, manliness, and the desire to belong that drove the emotional as well as the occupational development of our authors.

BUILDING AN OFFICER IDENTITY

We have already seen that making fun of apprentices offered some crews an outlet for dissatisfaction without the risk of confronting real officers. In turn, most officers felt apprentices had to learn to look after themselves, so they rarely intervened to protect them from banter and humiliation. If apprentices found this difficult at the time, however, they took comfort from knowing that they ultimately belonged with the officers, and that nothing actually dangerous would be allowed to happen to them. John Sutherland recalled the approach of his first captain, Jock Muir: 'although he was hard on us himself, it was Heaven help anyone else on board who as much as looked sideways at us.'[49]

How did former officers look back on their relationships with apprentices? John Bain, a captain in both sail and steam between the 1860s and 1880s, gave an unusually thoughtful account of this. He focused on the need for apprentices to know their eventual place: 'While they had to learn to perform the laborious work of a sailor, their ultimate destination was to command others. It is a great matter to teach them that they belong aft.' He claimed he had always had 'a nice set of lads' on board his ships, and that teaching them navigation 'kept one's heart young.'[50]

Bain also discussed at length one unusual case, when, as first mate, he tried to support an apprentice called Andrew who was being bullied by the captain. Bain did not stand up against the captain, but rather acted as a mentor to the young sailor: 'I made more of a companion of him than I used to with boys,' Bain recalled, partly to counteract the captain's undermining influence, but also because of Andrew's 'attractive character.' Bain's use of 'companion' here is uncommon, as is his listing of Andrew's qualities in such detail. Andrew seemed to have the 'blood of some old Viking,' and put himself forward unselfishly to do the ship's work. In the end, though, Bain admitted that he could not prevent Andrew's complete demoralisation, and had to watch him give up his apprenticeship.[51] Bain seemed to offer Andrew's case as a reminder that even if mates and apprentices became close, they were both subject to the authority of captains, something that Bain himself, in the end, had to agree with.

Charles Dixon, who worked his way up from ship's boy to captain in the 1890s, recalled taking a paternalist, and sometimes exasperated, attitude toward his own apprentices as he tried to instil officerly qualities. When three apprentices deserted in New Caledonia, Dixon initially tried to persuade them to behave like gentlemen and turn themselves in. He even sent a telegram to one of them, stating that, 'I don't want to use my authority in the matter, but leave it to your own good sense.' That apprentice, Dixon wrote, did not return, but moved to Australia and did well for himself. Perhaps Dixon secretly admired the boy's style; his testimony seems more concerned with appeasing the 'good British families' whose sons were under his charge.[52] The reality was, too, that shipping companies had no problem recruiting apprentices, and any vacant berth would be filled immediately upon return to a British port.

As their time went on, training in navigation became the key indicator of whether apprentices were being prepared for their officer exams. There was a great mystique around navigation, and some of our authors thought their early captains had combined modern science with ancient wisdom. Rex Clements recalled his Captain West stressing the 'importance of learning to know the face of the sky and sea and studying the ways of birds and fishes.' As well as instruments, West seemed to rely on an oral culture of 'proverbs and scraps of doggerel easily memorised' to convey to the apprentices how they should respond to changing conditions. Clements believed that his captain's dead reckoning and folklore would be anathema to the 'modern liner-officer,' but that in the right hands it made for an uncanny ability to take a ship safely through narrow waters and heavy seas. Captain West did keep up with what he regarded as useful innovations, however, and believed in Maury's work on the most efficient sailing routes.[53] Maury's routes were the product of analysing sailing-ship logs, compiled by skilled and diligent ships' captains, so West was making use of the cumulative knowledge of men like himself. As well as describing a formidable formative influence on his career, Clements was acknowledging the passing of an older form of seafaring knowledge. It was one that he respected, but could not follow as he moved to steam and the demands of shipping companies and timetables.

Would-be officers knew they had to study scientific navigation to pass the second-mate exams, but some struggled to fit this into their self-image as carefree young seafarers, to say nothing of their sense that book-learning was a suspect topic for proper sailors. Bill Adams thought that no one really bothered with navigation training until the last weeks of their term.[54] Others wrote of cramming lessons into as short a period as possible, happy to be seen not to take this too seriously, at least in comparison with the practical seamanship they really valued. Pryce Mitchell made an unusual admission about navigation school, that the greatest benefit was 'mingling with men of the officer class and listening to their ideas ... from the officers' point of view.'[55] Mitchell was hardly ignorant of the mercantile and professional middle-classes, given his family ties to shipowners. He nonetheless seemed to feel a gap in his knowledge, a lack of exposure to ships' officers in situations where they might talk as equals.

Taking the exams to qualify as second mate was an important set piece in many memoirs, and a symbolic moment for looking forward and back. Young sailors returned to the classroom, memorising mathematics and astronomy at a nautical training school. They then had to sit written tests in a large room with rows of desks, usually in one of the Board of Trade's Mercantile Marine Offices. Questions they could have answered instantly on the deck of their ship seemed incomprehensible: John Bain recalled being reduced to 'imbecility.'[56] When they passed, though, they felt their life choices had been validated, and that remaining a 'boy' all those years had been worthwhile.

How they passed was also important to some authors. Not trying too hard, and giving an impression of cool, effortless achievement was another manly attribute that some constructed for themselves. When Herbert Lightoller passed the exam for second mate in Calcutta in 1892, he claimed to be surprised by his own success, and amazed that his ship's best theoretical navigator had failed on the first day of the tests. But Lightoller had taken care to absorb the necessary knowledge, even if he insisted that it was then forgotten until the next examination. He also made sure to acquire ample and varied sea experience, and recognised that passing exams at the first attempt was crucial to rapid promotion. Failure might mean another year of sea time, falling behind one's peers. Lightoller looked back with some pride in his ability to manoeuvre through both the hiring processes of shipping companies and the certification systems of the state, while mysteriously overtaking more conventional young men who seemed to be following all the rules.[57]

William Lord discussed passing as second mate in some detail, and like many others wrote of the lightness and joy he experienced as he left the exam room. Unusually, though, he depicted his success as a joint effort with a friend of his, who had gone for first mate at the same time: 'My friend was waiting outside, and it was with the heartiest of mutual good wishes that we congratulated each other upon our success. Let no University graduate smile at the pride of two young sailors.'[58] The two men found their next ship together, as first and second mate. That friend personifies Lord's acceptance into the world of the ship's officer, which he regarded as a fellowship of men, for all the extreme individuality and isolation that officers might have to endure on any given ship and voyage. Lord also seems to be stressing that it was a fellowship open to those who worked their way up, without the class privileges of shore professions. In addition, by the time he wrote his memoir in the 1890s, Lord would have been conscious that more officers were training as apprentices, rather than starting as ship's boys as he had done in the 1860s.

Many of our authors had what appeared to be a seamless rise through the ranks, but of course this is an artifact of the genre, as most memoirs were written by successful men. Some were proud to have taken risks to bypass what they saw as career bottlenecks, and we lack testimony from those whose risk-taking did not pay off. Working on a voyage to West Africa early in the twentieth century, for example, Jack Randell realised that dangerous cargo-handling conditions off the coast, and a hostile disease environment on shore, killed so many officers that survivors could expect speedy promotion. He made an unorthodox move to working dredgers in Lagos harbour, earned double his usual salary, and was soon a captain.[59] Randell believed he had gained prestige for both his courage and his physical resilience, reinforcing the manly virtues that underpinned perceptions of a ship's officer, both among his peers and potential employers. The next chapter discusses in more detail the sense of adventurous manhood which so many of our authors saw at the heart of seafaring in general, and becoming a ship's officer in particular.

*

At the end of chapter 1, we saw how reviewers classified sea-writing as children's literature in the early twentieth century, completing an ironic circle of the romantic delusions of boy sailors. But the growing and learning that those boys experienced in their early years at sea suggest another, deeper connection between boyhood, youth, and seafaring. They were rushing to create a model character for themselves, rooted in maritime traditions and mindsets, and one that tried to find a route forward by looking back.

Perhaps because their younger selves became so many new things so quickly, our authors were also sensitive to continuities, and conscious that much of what they learned from their captains and the old shellbacks was a deeply conservative vision of seafaring skill, manhood, and command. Whatever the compromises they faced and made in their later careers, they were proud to remember how their mental and physical transformations as young sailors had entwined adolescent exuberance with what they saw as the ancient moral compass of the seafarer.

By the 1920s, that mindset was increasingly associated with Joseph Conrad's writings. When Virginia Woolf published her elegy to Conrad a week after his death in 1924, she focused on the way that the 'vast and implacable integrity' conveyed in his writing was at the heart of his appeal to young readers. Loyalty, honesty, courage, and dignity were still aspirations for the young as well as clichés for the cynical.[60] Conrad had been clear about this himself. Suspecting that more aesthetic writers thought him a cold fish, Conrad argued that maintaining self-control and refusing to give way to extreme emotions was the 'first condition of good service' for both a seafarer and a writer: 'you can't, in sound morals, condemn a man for taking care of his own integrity.'[61]

Albert Bestic, who wrote his memoir in 1958, offers a case in point. He recalled facing an imminent shipwreck back at the turn of the century. One of his fellow apprentices welcomed the possibility of abandoning ship, arguing that they were close to shore, and would probably be sent home in comfort on a steamer. Bestic thought this was a betrayal of his seafarer's creed, and was determined to stay with his ship if at all possible, however much that made him appear to be a 'sentimental fool.'[62] Growing from boyish idealism into the worldview of a seafaring man and a ship's officer was a complicated transition on many levels, but some of our authors looked back hoping that they had kept that youthful character in a world that might no longer value it, or them.

5

Men of Rank

If memoir-writers portrayed seafaring as a masculine occupation in the age of sail, they thought of the work and character of ships' officers even more strongly in those terms. Our authors believed that effective officers, and especially successful captains, had to lead, and even dominate, their crews. Unmanly traits such as emotional weakness, cowardice, and capriciousness seemed especially shocking when encountered in officers. By the late nineteenth century, however, the interaction of masculinity, class, and professionalisation was complicating such perceptions. New officers – including most of the men who became our authors – were increasingly likely to come from the middle classes. These men had to command seafarers who represented a rougher kind of manhood. Sailors might be physically stronger than their officers, had often spent more time at sea, and prized their mix of independence and fraternal watch cohesion. How then did authors convey to their readers such competing identities, as officers worked to establish authority over men who were, by some indicators, more manly than them?

Officer culture included a strong performative element. Captains and mates emerge from memoirs as men acting and living their parts. Often, we read set-piece displays of courage and determination. Authors remembered how their early officers had maintained a mystique, keeping their distance from the crew, yet giving the impression of being an all-seeing presence. With that detachment, however, came the well-known loneliness of command, which tested self-worth. Nor were the officer ranks monolithic. Authors described tensions between captains and mates, especially when the latter felt deprived of promotion, or when captains were showing the strain of great responsibility. Our authors' own experiences varied widely. Some wrote about their early officers through the lens of their own long careers as captains; a few never reached command, and always viewed officers from below. All accounts are distorted by the aspirations, successes, and failures of those involved. Overall, then, ships' officers emerge from maritime memoirs as an unusual occupational group, and a challenge to some common impressions of Victorian and Edwardian middle-class masculinity.[1]

PERFORMANCE, EXPERIENCE, AND KNOWLEDGE

Command, like other indicators of masculinity, was a state of mind for the individual, but also something to be displayed for the benefit of others. Most authors believed that officers had to demonstrate, as well as simply possess, a set of key characteristics, although some felt that constantly performing that role could push them into overconfidence. Officers set a tone with their first orders while the ship was still in port, trying to establish authority over men who arrived drunk and ill-prepared for the voyage. Once at sea, they claimed power over the ocean and the elements. Driving ships fast through rough seas, and striking a fine line between assurance and recklessness, built the reputation of a cool and effective officer. The exploits and foibles of individuals became well-known on the seafarers' grapevine, and everyone, however junior, judged the officers, sometimes against fundamentalist standards. Similar testimony exists across decades. Bill Adams and his fellow apprentices in the late 1890s took an early dislike to a new second mate who, in their view, had no pride in their ship.[2] And as Pryce Mitchell recalled of his early days at sea in the 1870s, 'we boys had our ideals': while they watched one captain 'with awe as he stood like a bronze god' in a storm, they had no respect for officers who failed to live up to their values.[3]

Authors often looked further into the past when trying to define successful officers. Tales of legendary clipper-ship captains were part of the occupational genealogy of the late age of sail, but they sometimes offered contradictory lessons. John Mason, for example, thought captains had to resist celebrity, because fame contaminated seafaring and command alike. He told of two men from the generation before he went to sea in the 1880s, both with the common Victorian nickname 'Bully,' but of very different temperament. Bully Martin was Mason's perfect captain, a 'silent, tenacious man, with an iron constitution, iron nerve and iron will,' who never became enamoured of his own importance. Bully Forbes was 'second to none' as a seaman and a navigator, but had a foolish vanity and pride; after he wrecked the famous *Schomberg* off Australia, he was, according to Mason, a broken man.[4] By referencing captains from recent history, Mason reinforced a vision of manly leadership that he could then take forward through the officers he encountered personally, and to his own commands.

Melbourne Garahan and Frank Worsley offered similar characterisations of merchant captains at the turn of the century. They thought there were two kinds. One was, in Worsley's words, 'a splendid seaman but rough, uncouth and almost illiterate,' and knew nothing beyond his profession. The other was 'intelligent, educated and generally a gentleman.' Although a more capable navigator, the latter was no better a seafarer overall. Worsley noted that the more refined type was usually to be found in the smarter shipping lines, suggesting that class divisions were already evident.[5] Garahan thought the great liner firms employed officers of a class similar to those in the Royal Navy, which was a compliment in his eyes; sailing ships and tramp steamers, however, were still captained by 'old school, hard-case biscuit-eating old stiffs.' Garahan had little to say about seamanship in making that distinction. He focused rather on character: the new men had proved during the Great War that reforming the officer classes had not come at any expense in 'bravery, daring, heroism or efficiency.'[6] Garahan left the sea after serving an apprenticeship, while Worsley had a long career as an officer and adventurer, but they reached the same conclusion about the British class system being manifest in the professionalisation of merchant officers.

Many authors put the capacity for measuring and taking risks at the heart of a captain's character. Memoirs include numerous examples of captains carrying the maximum possible sail in the interest of a faster voyage, and leaving little room for error or changing conditions. On the face of it, discussing this posed a dilemma for our authors, who might not have wanted to portray their own profession as reckless, but there are many accounts nonetheless. It is clear that captains felt some peer pressure, and knew how powerful and far-reaching seafarers' yarning culture was. Walter Runciman, looking back from the 1920s on a career spanning more than half a century, believed that having one's ship dismasted through carrying a heavy press of canvas 'carried great glory with it'; other captains would visit the ship at its next port to admire the damage and the repairs, and the circumstances would be widely discussed in the maritime community.[7] Assuming, of course, that the ship made it to port at all.

Herbert Lightoller's recollections of Captain 'Jock' Sutherland encapsulate the pressures masters imposed on themselves and their crews, and also the respect they could sometimes command from their juniors. Lightoller claimed that apprentices gained prestige by serving under Sutherland, who was 'one of the greatest crackers-on out of Liverpool' in the 1890s, and who built the legend that he would never be passed by another ship as long as he had more sails at his disposal. Lightoller appreciated the sensory excitement – driving a great ship at extreme angles in a gale 'used to thrill us boys to the bone.' Sutherland's luck ran out when racing another ship at night, but Lightoller had nothing but praise and sympathy for his captain. As always in Lightoller's memoir, we have to wonder if twenty years of pondering the fate of *Titanic* made him determined to show the complexity of events at sea, and the unfairness of second-guessing actions taken in good faith. Lightoller described sea conditions that changed almost inexorably over hours, and thought fine officers could take a sequence of justifiable decisions that still ended in disaster.[8] While he recalled some incompetent officers in his memoir, Lightoller rejected as simplistic any assumption that losing a ship was itself a mark of poor seamanship or leadership.

This was a long-standing view. Writing in 1897, John Bain had also been keen to explain that even the best seafarers could be shipwrecked. Early in his memoir, he reported the loss of one of his former captains, hailing him as an inspiring skipper, with the ideals and seamanship of a true sailor. Later in his career, Bain had further reason to reflect on recklessness and responsibility when he became a Board of Trade accident investigator. By then, he thought that ships' officers were 'clever, intelligent and sober,' and 'as steady a body of men as can be found in any profession in the world.' He still claimed great sympathy for masters who had accidents, reflecting on the 'innumerable perils' he had encountered despite careful navigation. However, Bain conceded that some were overconfident, often neglecting the basic checks of position or depth of water that might have saved them.[9] The tone of Bain's memoir is unfailingly positive about officers, to the point that this criticism stands out.

Captains also took risks in port, encouraged by the presence of an audience and, in particular, their fellow captains. Rex Clements's Captain West was on shore in South Africa when a storm blew up. All the other captains decided to spend the night in town, but West ordered his four apprentices to row him back to their ship, anchored in the bay. This took them four hours of hard work, with the boat having to be bailed out constantly. Far from complaining, Clements thought 'it was a wonderful feat of boatmanship on the old man's part,' and the apprentices claimed to have been 'cock o' the walk' for the rest of the time they were in port.[10] When it worked, therefore, this kind of theatrical courage and skill fitted the self-image of captains and also the aspirations of would-be officers like Clements.

Henry Hughes was unconvinced. Although his memoir relates to a brief time at sea as a boy in the 1890s, Hughes was a naval officer during the Great War, and acquired an extensive knowledge of maritime history and practice before he wrote his memoir in the 1930s. He thought cracking-on was a 'foolhardy practice' rooted in the mythology of the old clippers, and irrelevant to vessels carrying low-value goods with little economic urgency. Hughes was also puzzled by captains who refused to head for port to repair weather damage, and by the even stranger acquiescence of crews in this.[11] Walter Dexter recalled a captain who favoured slightly slower voyages in exchange for conserving the ship's fittings and keeping his crews healthier and safer, but conceded that such men were rare. Dexter argued that cracking-on was partly motivated by fear of gaining a reputation for being cautious and slow; such officers struggled to find work, and preferred to please their owners with fast passages.[12]

Presence was key to an officer's performance, in complicated ways. Some captains exerted great power without being seen on deck very often. The mates ran the ship, yet it was always clear that they did so with the captain's authority, and that he somehow knew everything that happened on board. John Bain recalled one early captain as a 'perfect aristocrat' who presided over the vessel with dignified detachment: 'it was entirely beneath his notice to take any cognisance of the ship's affairs.' Dressing formally for dinner, he received reports from the first mate, but otherwise expected the ship to be run without his involvement, and was 'certainly the grandest swell I ever sailed under.'[13] Other captains went to the opposite extreme. Arthur Mason recalled a captain, dying of consumption, who lashed himself to the rail and issued orders throughout several watches, bringing the ship through an Atlantic storm. For Mason, 'My opinion of the men who command ships was formed then and there. I realised, as I do now, how little the world knows of these men, or of what they have given to Progress.'[14]

Captains who failed to play their expected parts alienated and demoralised their crews. This was difficult ground for writers who had been captains themselves, and who believed in unquestioning obedience. Memoirs usually suggest that failing captains lacked manly attributes like self-control, and early authors, brought up in the era of temperance agitation, often blamed drink. Charles Protheroe, who wrote in 1903 of voyages in the 1880s, had to work for a succession of drunk, bullying captains with extreme mood swings. Over time, Protheroe thought merchant shipping reforms had been a good influence, curtailing the worst excesses of rogue captains who now feared being taken to court on shore.[15]

James Barker recalled that his first voyage as an apprentice in 1889 might have been his last if the drunk captain had been allowed to interfere when the mates were overseeing a critical manoeuvre to keep the vessel away from rocks. One of the sailors disarmed the captain, knocked him out, and stowed him in his cabin, all actions that Barker would have condemned as mutinous on his own ship.[16] Indeed, much of Barker's book is a justification of his own strict, and sometimes violent, disciplinarian approach to command. But Barker had supreme confidence in his own abilities, and even he wanted to explain to his audience that a captain who could not live up to the role might have to be removed.

If not drink, cowardice. Albert Bestic, one of our later authors who went to sea in 1908, wrote of a captain who became obsessed with the risk of damaging sails, masts, and rigging, and refused to carry even normal amounts of sail in case of sudden gales. After weeks of slow progress, food was running low and tensions on board were rising. The crew began to question the captain's character and manliness, and finally confronted him on deck. Asserting their own courage and work ethic relative to the captain's failures, the sailors promised to work 'all hands' whenever there was the slightest danger. According to Bestic, the captain called their bluff and lost – he ordered full sail, the gale never came, the ship made good progress, and the crew did indeed turn out to work without hesitation.[17]

Most authors discussed such cases because they considered them rare rather than typical. Positive accounts of ships' officers are far more common. Seamen had to admit that their officers knew every seafaring task on board, however much they might have grumbled about the abilities and application of individuals. All officers on British sailing ships had worked at sea for at least four years before gaining even their second mate's certificate.[18] Importantly for a physical occupation that required bodily strength and capability, all officers had climbed a tall mast or worked at the end of a long yard, and seafarers knew it. At the same time, experienced seafarers had good reason to believe that they were just as capable as their officers at many aspects of handling the ship, not least because they had trained generations of apprentices along the way.

Crucially, though, the same was not true of navigation, which became the key element in the occupational mystique that separated officers from crews.[19] Most of our authors stressed that only officers had the training and equipment to determine the ship's position at sea, and to understand the log that recorded that position over time. In addition, officers did not share those findings with the crew. Leslie Morton, who went to sea in 1911, recalled that 'it was always kept a great secret by the after guard in sailing ships just where the ship was.'[20] Authors thought that keeping the crew ignorant of the ship's location was an important statement of officers' power. Indeed, some reported captains who kept even their junior officers oblivious to the ship's whereabouts. William Crutchley recalled his time as a second mate back in the 1860s, sailing on ships where 'it would have been little short of sacrilege' to ask to look at a chart: the captain would have interpreted that as a challenge to his command.[21] An alternative explanation, especially in earlier periods, is that some captains were insecure about their own navigational skills, so this ensured they were never in a position to be questioned.[22]

William Jones was ambivalent about the effects on seafarers of such ignorance. He recalled his captain once asking a mutinous sailor to point in the direction of the nearest port and state how far away it was, knowing that the man's floundering efforts would unnerve the crew and bring them back in order. More paternalistically, Jones thought unfamiliarity with navigation might reassure the crew, because it enhanced their respect for the officers, and in turn spared them the responsibility of command.[23] Not knowing their location at sea, Jones seems to be arguing, was important to knowing their place on the ship.

Surely, though, restricting knowledge like this infantilised seafarers, and challenged an important element of their self-image – they could hardly have manly freedom and independence if they did not know where they were. A strong element of tradition seems to have made it acceptable for sailors to be kept in the dark about their location in normal times, but that would be undermined when officers sought to exploit their knowledge in ways that sailors considered oppressive. The grand bargain between officers and crews that enabled ships to function was rooted in maritime tradition, yet constantly tested and strained, whether by the individual characters on board, the conditions in which they worked, or the changing dynamics of the industry.

DISCIPLINE, VIOLENCE, AND MENACE

Much of the performance of being a ship's officer was about maintaining discipline, an amorphous concept that memoir-writers agreed was central to life and work at sea. Authors who offered any rationale usually focused on the safety of the vessel. Sea and wind conditions changed so quickly, they argued, that ships could be lost unless the crew obeyed officers' instructions immediately, and such readiness required a constant level of disciplinary observance. Men were giving up their individual autonomy in the interests of keeping the ship and their shipmates safe. At the same time, some memoir-writers contended that formal discipline was rarely necessary on board because seafarers had a strong sense of duty, if not to their officers, then certainly to the ship and each other. Duty, of course, was a strong Victorian indicator of manliness, a way of squaring the sometimes awkward circle in which free men had to obey orders. It had also become the foundation of the cult of Nelson, whose signal at the Battle of Trafalgar – 'England expects that every man will do his duty' – had embedded the word in national mythology by the early twentieth century.[24]

Authors reported that officers, and especially captains, had many subtle tools and traditions at their disposal to help make discipline seem natural and effortless. Captains used the spatial traditions of the ship to assert and reinforce their authority over sailors. Generally, captains remained aft, sending the mates to issue instructions and requiring the crew to come to them. The afterdeck was an important location of a captain's power, not only at the rear of the vessel but also elevated above the main deck. When a captain wanted to reward, threaten, or intimidate his crew, he would order them aft, out of their space and toward his, and literally talk down to them.

Occasionally, a captain would go further, and bring the crew into the mess room or main cabin beneath the afterdeck. On many ships, this was a well-furnished, even luxurious, space. James Bisset recalled being 'struck dumb with wonder' the first time he saw the polished maple panelling, red velvet upholstery, and shining brass-work of the saloon on *County of Pembroke* at the turn of the century.[25] While such a space gave captains some physical comfort compared with the crew quarters, domesticity was not its purpose. It was intended to emphasise the power and status of the shipowners and their representative, the captain. The fittings were often hard and masculine. There was usually a large table, but no sailor would ever have a meal at it. If the men before the mast did enter the room, it was to stand near the door, while the captain issued orders from behind that table. Even when they were there legitimately, it made them nervous. Charles Dixon was impressed by the sudden change in Chips the carpenter, an experienced, confident seaman reduced to childlike embarrassment 'sitting there in the old man's cabin' while the captain bandaged his injured finger.[26]

Madden Jardine witnessed his first captain's use of this space when some of the crew refused work in Rio de Janeiro in the early 1880s. After giving the sailors some time to contemplate going to jail on shore – 'the tyranny of suspense,' Jardine called it – the captain judged that they would probably back down. He had them called into the main cabin one by one, where he went through a performance of writing their names in the ship's log, then ordering them to report to the mate and carry on their duties 'as men and sailors.' Jardine alone saw that the captain was not writing in the log at all, but on a separate sheet of paper placed on top; as soon as the men left, the captain tore up that sheet, leaving no formal record of the incident. Jardine was left to ponder the complexities of a man playing the part of 'a typical deep-water martinet.'[27]

James Barker claimed to have done something similar to refute a rumour that he had buried an injured sailor at sea before the man had died. Sitting at the head of the mess table, with his revolver and the ship's logbook before him, he played on the discomfort of the men in an unfamiliar space. Writing a statement in the log, Barker brought his second mate and apprentices up to sign it one by one, building a momentum that the crew could not resist: all signed the log, even if they could only mark a cross. Such was Barker's confidence that he included in his memoir the view of his disgruntled first mate, who condemned Barker's actions as 'all pantomime,' which of course is exactly what they were.[28] But Barker knew very well the power of theatre and props, and his memoir is open about his reputation for wielding firearms and punching insubordinate sailors earlier in his career. If the violence of that performance was only implied, it had its foundations in reality.

Authors thought such subtle dominance was clever, but not always sufficient. They reported that many officers shouted, swore, and intimidated their watches into harder work. Sometimes they went further. Many former captains' memoirs make no secret of the violence they inflicted on seafarers, and they evidently expected their readers to agree that this was a legitimate and necessary facet of command, especially in the face of dangerous situations at sea. Such violence was part of a wider amalgam of toughness and manly identity, but also assumptions about class and social order.

It is important to stress, though, that ships' officers operated within legal constraints in the late nineteenth century. Memoir-writers are clear that officers would hit and kick sailors who were insubordinate or refusing to work, or who had threatened them first. Persistently recalcitrant sailors might be locked up in irons. But there is little unprovoked or extreme violence by officers in these accounts, and legendary maritime punishments like flogging were just that – tales told in yarning sessions by old shellbacks who had never experienced them. Everyone knew of sailors who had taken violent officers to court at the next landfall, and most officers were careful to ensure that they would be able to cite self-defence, or the safety of the vessel, if they ever appeared before a judge.[29] It is also telling that authors singled out American rather than British sailing ships as having the worst reputation for routine violence, and there was even a sensationalist sub-genre of publishing about the US merchant marine.[30] Authors mostly represented violence on British ships as individual rather than institutional, and as punishment for specific offences rather than a daily means of managing seafarers.

The early days of a voyage were crucial in setting these parameters. Walter Dexter thought that 'men and officers tried each other out,' pushing to see where the limits were. Officers might engage in 'a little brutality' at the start, hoping that this would send a message and lead to a peaceful voyage. Usually, sailors who thought they could 'tame' their officers were disappointed. Even so, Dexter feared that the distance between officers and sailors, ingrained from the start through the apprenticeship system, made misunderstandings (and therefore confrontation) more likely, because 'it tended to breed a class of officers who could not enter into the psychology of the sailors.'[31] Fred Farmer, one of the few authors who worked as an Ordinary Seaman, described feeling that he had to stand up against a bullying second mate early in a voyage, or else be a victim throughout.[32]

Farmer also recalled a time when his good-natured captain, driven to drink by a slow passage across the Atlantic, began cursing a seaman called Tom who was hauling a rope. The rest of the crew found this difficult to watch, because both Tom and the captain were respected as good sailors. Fortunately, Tom did not give in to provocation, the captain could not find an excuse to strike him, and the moment passed. In addition to the captain's drinking, Farmer makes the spatial dimension clear. It was the close proximity of the two men on the main deck that muddied the usual separation between them and made a physical confrontation more likely. The encounter would not have been nearly as ominous if the captain had stayed on the afterdeck and cursed Tom from there.[33]

As that suggests, some memoir-writers had thought seriously about the limits of ship-board violence, and in particular the point where men would push back against what they perceived to be bullying by officers, or a violation of unwritten codes around 'a fair fight.' Even seafarers who accepted violence as a tool of command objected when officers targeted weak crew members. John Wilson characterised a captain and a second mate as bullies who should be resisted, and risked a beating himself by standing up to them. Wilson thought this was a lesson in crew cohesion; younger seafarers needed help from more confident crewmates if they were to be protected from bullying.[34]

Authors recalled some soul-searching as they resolved their own use of violence and menace, especially in the context of their changing roles on board. During his first voyage as mate in 1893, Arthur Rostron heard that sailors had vowed to stab him, so he carried a revolver everywhere and was never close to a sailor unarmed. He believed this would deter any threat: 'I suppose they became aware of my preparedness.' On the way home, Rostron had his 'last stand up fight with a sailor,' when a man became impertinent and refused to back down. Rostron thought he had to 'knock some respect into the fellow' or lose all discipline on the vessel. Furthermore, 'a fight like that seldom left bad blood, so long as it was a clean scrap.'[35] After that ritual statement of the old ways, though, the future for Rostron was in the modern managerial discipline of the steamship, not in what he regarded as the timeless brutality of sail. It is telling of the sensationalism that leaches into some of this writing, though, that for all his concern about guns and knives, the only violence Rostron actually faced was an ordinary fistfight.

Indeed, several authors stressed that violence was mostly a thing of the past, and romanticised it as part of the colourful, pugilistic behaviours of officers 'in the rough sailing-ship days.'[36] William Lord acknowledged that his early officers had liked using their fists, but that was because their crews had been 'rebellious spirits.'[37] Clifford Fenton agreed, believing officers far from land were in a difficult position, having no authority but their own, and often facing seamen who saw their ship-board status tied up in resistance to authority.[38] Some writers sought the middle ground. James Bisset took boxing lessons while studying for his second mate exams, believing it useful for an officer to know the 'scientific way of taking care of himself in case of need.'[39] That telling phrase located controlled violence in a modern portfolio of technical skills, rather than depicting it as a hangover from more primitive times – Bisset included it in the same page as the list of mathematical, navigation, and seamanship attributes that he needed to acquire.

Some very different authors could reach similar conclusions about an officer's role as leader of men. Arthur Mason went from being an ordinary seafarer to an officer in the 1890s before leaving the sea. When he became a mate, Mason learned and used the sailors' real names, rather than 'some manufactured names with an oath.' He claimed a management philosophy rooted in a vision of masculinity that required close working with subordinates for mutual respect: 'to choose a man you have got to know him, and he should be treated like a man, once you put him to work.'[40]

Bertram Hayes made much the same argument, urging officers to 'treat those under you as men and not as cogs in the machine.'[41] By the time Hayes wrote his memoir he was commodore of the White Star Line, and his account shows little sentimentality about seafarers, but he nonetheless wanted to convey that ideal to his readers. Pryce Mitchell remembered one captain who did not make his crew do the constant extra work that some officers thought was necessary to maintain discipline ('to keep the devil out of their minds,' as Charles Protheroe put it). Such respect for the core craft of proper sailors made that captain Mitchell's ideal – 'a master of men as well as of seamanship and navigation.'[42] All these authors had visions of discipline rooted in a masculinity that expected seafarers to take a manly pride in their jobs, and to be led by officers who respected them for that in turn.

Albert Bestic painted an optimistic picture of relations between a ship's mate and crew at the end of a voyage around 1910. Although seafarers normally left their ships without ceremony, on this occasion they lined up to shake hands with the mate. According to Bestic, the German sailor who was the crew's spokesman hailed 'a goot mate' and 'a fine sailormans,' and wanted to 'say goot-by.' Revealingly, Bestic thought that the mate's positive response to this showed that he was 'but a man among men, united to them by the bond of servitude to a mighty and exacting mistress, the sea.'[43] There is a great deal of contrary testimony in memoirs, and Bestic's sense of seafarers being all men together is self-serving. Nonetheless, it depicts a class-bridging masculine ideal that many authors wanted to believe was possible in a sailing ship, where officers and crews still knew each other's work.

THE CHAINS OF COMMAND

Memoir-writers often recalled that becoming an officer had not been quite what they anticipated. They remembered their pride at qualifying to be a second mate, and their excitement when they secured their first job at that rank. Once on board, though, they found their status almost as dubious as it had been when they were first voyagers. William Crutchley wrote of the timeless sailor habit of blaming the second mate, 'who has been held responsible for everything that has gone wrong from the time of the Ark.'[44] Such conventions created dilemmas for young officers over conflicting kinds of manly behaviour – standing up for oneself on the one hand, and obeying superiors on the other. Walter Dexter remembered new second mates who forgot themselves, joking with the crew and the apprentices, and then having to overcompensate with harsh words and actions to re-establish their status. This upset the watch, because no one knew where they stood. Remembering his own elevation to second mate, Dexter was sarcastic and self-deprecating: he had now reached the dizzy heights of having 'milk in my tea and coffee,' and being called 'Mister.'[45]

James Bisset recalled complicated pressures when he was a new second mate in 1903. Both his superiors took out their personal resentments on him. His captain was a fine seaman who had worked on the classic clipper ships, and felt that being in charge of a slow cargo vessel was a step down. The mate had a master's certificate, but Bisset believed he had never moved beyond his original mindset from the coasting trades, and he could not get a command. Both men had hoped the shipowner would appoint an older, experienced second mate, rather than the ambitious young Bisset. Still, Bisset conceded that once he had proved himself capable of doing the work, the officers came to accept him.[46]

Authors report a great range of such examples, with complicated, shifting dynamics working on all the officers. Age or seniority were not reliable predictors of rank in any given case. A lucky and determined captain who had the confidence of shipowners might find himself one of the youngest men on board, giving orders not only to old shellbacks, but to mates with much more experience than he had. As ever, the self-selecting bias of memoir-writers is important. Fast-climbing officers who enjoyed long careers were doubtless more likely to publish their memoirs than disappointed men who were stuck as mates for voyage after voyage.

The loneliness of command was already a cliché when our authors went to sea. Captains felt the need to maintain distances from their crews and even – sometimes especially – from their officers. This posed challenges. Too much distance, and a captain could suffer extreme isolation and also be so remote from his crew that they were not reminded frequently enough of his presence. Too little, and the captain might find his decision-making impaired by personal attachments and antagonisms, and his authority diluted by familiarity. For all that seafarers of all ranks cultivated the image of the self-reliant man comfortable in his own company, the reality of work and life at sea was co-operative and collaborative. Every young sailor spent years working, living, eating, sleeping, and socialising with a group of boys and men. When he became a junior officer, he moved into his own cabin, but his watches were spent in constant interaction with seafarers, and his captain could demand his presence at any time. Only when he became a captain himself did he suddenly lack both peers and superiors.

This is why fictional accounts of captains' friendships at sea are often located in odd circumstances outside the vessel's chain of command, perhaps the best known being Conrad's *The Secret Sharer*. Conrad himself was in a ship-board friendship years later, when he sailed as a guest on a Q-ship in the Great War. John Sutherland, the captain of that vessel, told of many hours walking arm-in-arm, in deep conversation, around the deck of his ship with Conrad.[47] Although this points to the easy intimacy that men with shared rank and experience could strike up during a sea voyage, it also emphasises how rare it was for a captain like Sutherland to have such a confidant on board.

Authors reported a great variety of relationships between mates and captains, which often hinged on whether the captain trusted his subordinates to do their jobs. Again, the captain's character seems more important in authors' minds than his seafaring abilities. When William Lord was a second mate in the 1860s, he sailed with an unpredictable captain who demoralised his officers by creeping about the ship at night trying to catch any slackness. Later, as a first mate, Lord encountered a young captain who lacked such insecurities. The two worked 'harmoniously,' and 'a friendship such as ours was, forms one of the compensations of sea life.' Lord thought this captain was assured in his own self, and 'was a man, in the best sense of the word,' because he 'studied the interests of those around him.'[48] However, Lord made clear that this instance was unique in his experience. Albert Bestic also cited the theory that captains had to be seen to demonstrate great trust in their officers, and only realised subsequently how hard it could be to sit in his cabin hoping such trust was justified. The line between leadership and interference was thin, and captains who crossed it alienated the mates and unnerved their crews.[49]

Fraught relations between captains and mates are common in memoirs. Walter Runciman recalled a tense set of relationships during his first voyage in 1861, praising the self-denial of the second mate, who kept the peace with his captain despite some provocation. The second mate was a skilled and experienced man who had served in distinguished ships, and even captained a schooner before suffering a breakdown and taking to drink. Runciman did not understand how such a man could endure the captain's pomposity, but came to realise that the second mate had nothing to prove, and 'had good sense enough not to flourish his style in the eyes of his chief.' On another ship, Runciman thought that both the captain and the second mate managed their relationship with tact. While the second mate boasted of his superior knowledge of the North Sea, the captain took no offence, and did not embarrass his officer when the ship moved through the Channel and beyond the second mate's comfort zone.[50]

Charles Dixon offers a rare example of an author reflecting on his time as a captain, and admitting to having made a poor decision in the appointment of his first mate. It is worth quoting in full because it encapsulates a number of issues: 'I made a bad mistake when I shipped that mate, but he would have fooled anybody, I think. He was a fine big specimen physically, had a nice way with him, and meant well, but he was never meant to wield authority, and he was rather stupid.'[51] Dixon had to confront the reality that an officer could have the necessary certificates, look the part, behave well, and yet lack the presence and authority considered necessary to manage a sailing-ship crew. Revealingly, Dixon's focus was entirely on officerly character: he makes no comment about the hapless mate's seamanship, which appears to have been unproblematic.

If relationships with their officers and crews would inevitably be awkward, some captains nonetheless tried to recreate some kind of family life on board, with themselves wielding the paternal authority. One common way to do this was to take an interest in the education and development of the ship's apprentices. Rex Clements thought his old Captain West was rather transparent about it. Having been in command for decades but with no sons of his own, the apprentices became 'his boys,' and while West never let slip his 'masterful manner,' Clements believed he was 'almost fatherly' during the evening navigation classes.[52]

Other captains went further, taking their wives and children to sea with them. Such captains made a strong statement that they wielded greater patriarchal power than anyone else on board, as men as well as a captains. Memoir-writers were conflicted, and reported that seafarers often pushed back, alleging that a wife's influence actually made the captain less manly. Frank Symondson, who went to sea in 1872, thought his first captain's wife was 'an amiable person,' but that sailors believed her presence meant a slower passage – the captain allegedly would not risk carrying much sail because of the 'anxieties of his wife.'[53] Four decades later, Leslie Morton recalled sailor gossip about a vessel called *Gwydyr Castle.* The captain's wife was supposedly 'a formidable person' who ran the ship, giving the captain his instructions.[54] Similarly, Pryce Mitchell remembered a ship in Calcutta where the captain's wife yelled orders at the apprentices, who in turn became known around the port as the 'Mother's darlings.'[55] Gender role reversals in marriages are a long-established comic device, and sailors enjoyed the idea of hen-pecked captains. Equally, apprentices taking orders from women reinforced a wider mockery of their privileged entitlement, and the sense that all those aft were a more domestic kind of man than the rough fraternity of the forecastle.

Writers who had taken their own wives to sea with them rarely offered any explanation. As if anticipating readers' concerns about dangers, captains usually wrote about wives and children in terms of their resilience; indeed, they are often only mentioned at points in the narrative when they are being commended for their courage. Doubtless they were brave, but it is also clear that they are being depicted in ways that reinforce authors' assumptions about gender roles and responsibilities. In particular, captains kept their wives and children below deck for extended periods. Most risk arose from working at sea rather than just being at sea, and wives and children who stayed below during rough weather were much safer than the crew on deck and in the rigging. Unfortunately, this damaged their physical and mental health, not least because they were left imagining the worst of what was happening above.

Elizabeth Wayth, who sailed with her father and mother in the 1860s and 1870s, gives us some rare testimony, recalling the anxiety of enforced stays below deck in near-darkness. As Wayth makes clear, women knew a great deal about seafaring, and were well aware of the danger facing the crew and the ship, but were rarely allowed to do anything about it. When their ship went to the rescue of a foundering vessel, Wayth and her mother confronted a new worry for the safety of the men who had to row the ship's boat. So many of the crew came from their own town, that 'if anything happened there would be the sore hearts and reproachful eyes of mothers, wives and sweethearts to greet us, even if we ourselves reached home safely.' In that immediate case, however, the boat returned safely, and Wayth's father finally let the women do something practical by helping nurse the injured from the other vessel.[56] All of those involved were clearly well aware of the gendered constraints upon them, but remained within them nonetheless.

James Barker also kept his wife Mary and their children below deck for extended periods during the difficult 1905 voyage of *British Isles*. Barker, as always in his memoir, was performing the role of the dominant captain, and by extension the masterful husband. He knew that his wife was not happy at sea:

'on more than one occasion I had heard her declare that she loathed it and hoped that none of her sons would ever become enamoured of it as I was.' Indeed, Mary had probably suffered from depression and seasickness on previous voyages. Barker referred to separation from her mother and relations casting 'a spell of sadness over her which I was at a loss to dispel,' and which resulted in her lying in her bunk 'for weeks on end.' On another voyage she was 'so weakened by prolonged inability to partake of nourishment' that Barker made plans to put her ashore. However, he kept taking her to sea on successive voyages, and reported being 'tranquil and secure in mind at the pleasing prospects of my family being with me again.' When Mary reported disturbing dreams on the eve of sailing, Barker tried to 'laugh her fears away,' telling her of 'sailing under blue skies,' and of 'a healthful life for the children.' Looking forward to the voyage himself, Barker 'was not inclined to dwell on any feminine fears.'[57]

Unusually, we have some testimony from Mary herself, in the fragment of a letter home that she wrote during the voyage but never sent: Barker still had it three decades later when compiling his memoir and it is reproduced in his book. In three short matter-of-fact paragraphs, Mary reported her seasickness, the chaos in her cabin as everything was flung about during a gale, food so 'terrible' that she wondered if the steward was trying to poison them, the misery of the ship's apprentices, and her own 'dread' at facing the seas round Cape Horn. She concluded, 'It seems ages since I saw a woman. I'm tired of seeing only men.' Barker was impressed by this letter, commenting, 'What portentous words!' Revealingly, though, he went no further in addressing the troubling range of issues Mary's letter opened up, and moved his narrative back to the safer ground of writing about his crew and apprentices.[58] Having his wife and children at sea was supposed to reinforce the paternal image of the captain, especially in his own mind, and not to challenge those fundamentals.

⁕

The idea that ship-board authority and command were intimately connected to masculine attributes comes across in most memoirs, albeit in conflicting ways. Independence of thought and action were important in a manly approach to life, but so were obedience to authority and following orders for the good of the ship. Inevitably, tensions emerged at the boundaries of those forces, especially when officers seemed unable to live up to the standards expected of them. Some authors thought captains had to be literally the masters of all the challenges facing the ship, or else fatally undermine the confidence of the crew. In everything from navigation to treating diseases and injuries, thought Frank Symondson, 'Jack puts his faith in the "cap'en."'[59]

Despite the increasing capture of higher ranks by the professionalising middle-classes later in the nineteenth century, our authors tended to play down class distinctions on board, preferring the idea that officers wielded a traditional form of authority, rooted in seafaring ability and personal character, which predated new forms of industrial relations. This continuing mix of ancient and modern thinking, attributed by our authors to ships' officers, tests assumptions about managerial manliness that have emerged from studying the factory or the office. If bosses on shore began to distance themselves from dangerous workplaces, sailing-ship officers remained exposed. Factory and office managers compensated for their white collars by taking up new sports, hunting, or joining volunteer military units to demonstrate their continuing physical masculinity; captains and mates in sail had no need for that. Even at sea, though, the navigating officers on giant liners were beginning to look detached from traditional seafaring masculinity by the early twentieth century. As we will see in the final chapter, this caused some soul-searching among our authors as they moved to steam.

6

Elements, Beliefs, and Wonders

Extreme conditions at sea could have an overwhelming impact on the senses, and maritime authors struggled to convey the onslaught that seafarers felt in their bodies, minds, and – some said – their souls. Some writers concluded that those who had not been there could never imagine it, and those who had needed no reminding.[1] Other authors stressed that seafaring could be surprisingly dull, and that being becalmed for weeks in tropical heat tested sailors' mental strength just as severely as the intense action of storms. One way or another, as the scholar Robert Foulke puts it, 'living at this interface always holds out the possibility of extraordinary experience.'[2]

In addition, our authors were fascinated by the way seafarers attributed events and phenomena to supernatural forces, maritime folklore, and half-remembered Bible stories that scandalised more orthodox believers. Seafarers were notorious in nineteenth-century commentary for being both superstitious and godless, rejecting organised religion and especially the clergymen who promoted it, while yarning about spirits, fate, and pagan sea deities. Sailors' spirituality could be a challenge to authority and discipline because it was a powerful individual connection between a man and whatever higher power he chose to invoke. A common sailor might be less deferential toward his officers if he thought he had God, or Neptune, or the ghosts of long-drowned shipmates at his elbow every time he climbed the rigging.

Authors faced dilemmas in representing extreme events. Their self-image as hard-headed men of the sea made them hesitate over descriptive flourishes, not least because they knew that sea fiction had long used storms, shipwrecks, and ghost stories as staple narrative and plot devices. They took a genuine pride, however, in having travelled to places never seen by non-seafarers, and in the wonders that they encountered there. Some invoked a scientific fascination, dressing their descriptions in marine biology or meteorology, and taking on another indicator of manliness as believers in science and reason. As ever, we have the question of audience expectations. Readers were already attuned to the idea that seafaring was full of mystery and mythology, so authors could increase the apparent authenticity of their work by including such tales, and there was a danger that the process became self-fulfilling. This may also help to explain the broad continuity of memoirs over time: although there is some sense that earlier authors devoted more space to superstition, faith, and dramatic experience, they remained persistent features throughout.

For the purposes of this book, the question of how men express emotions and discuss profound experiences is itself an important indicator of masculinity. Some maritime authors claimed an emotional connection with the sea even before they were seafarers; others came to realise the power of waves and weather only when working in storms. Others still found themselves entangled in the reactions of the ship itself to the stresses of the ocean, in the sounds of the rigging and timbers, or the wild movement of pitching and rolling. If some authors claimed a reluctance to believe supernatural explanations for events at sea, they told those stories nonetheless, arguing that they had to do justice to the superstitious old shellbacks. The sea confronted men with forces they could not control, yet the act of facing those challenges, and living to tell the tale through their yarning camaraderie, confirmed rather than undermined their sense of seafaring manhood. The results are often weird, uncanny mixtures of custom and science, modernity and mysticism, told by men struggling to translate one world to another.

AT ONE WITH THE SEA

Authors often wrote in gendered terms of seafarers living with the sea and the elements. They sometimes cast the sea itself as male or female. More often, the maritime environment challenged and confirmed the manhood of seafarers. Men could be awestruck by natural phenomena, and moved to poetry and spiritual musing; at other times, they came to fear and loathe the sea. However, authors who witnessed this, or felt it themselves, were conscious of shipmates who reacted differently, and who were suspicious of emotional attachments and responses. All this testimony points to an unease among maritime writers about how men should react to nature, and the appropriate place of aesthetic appreciation and emotion in the lives of stereotypically tough seafarers.

Literary scholars have noted that Herman Melville and other mid-century writers had already established the sublime impression that the deep sea could make on seafarers, to the point where men on lookout might lapse into contemplation, rather than keeping watch as instructed.[3] Indeed, by the time of the autobiography boom in the early twentieth century, it was hard to find anything new to say about the enormity of the elements, manifest in the great storms that forever threatened to overwhelm ships through generations of sea stories. Nonetheless, our authors tried to recapture and express the connection that they felt with the sea, sometimes as a privileged relationship that they could take ownership of, and often as a way of defending themselves against the petty rules and impositions forced on them by the close confines and rules of the ship.

Liam O'Flaherty, who grew up in a fishing village in the west of Ireland, claimed the Atlantic Ocean taught him the male side of nature from an early age. If life on shore was 'the gentle, female half of beauty, so was the giant, ruthless sea the masculine, more beautiful because it was more strong.' O'Flaherty regarded the sea as a 'theatre' in which his people 'performed dramas of heroic courage and endurance.' It cured the sick, both physically through its fresh airs and mentally through its sounds and rhythms.[4] Later, O'Flaherty was disillusioned by the contrast between his heroic fishermen and the sailors he encountered working on deep-sea ships; it was not inevitable, he discovered, that the sea's masculinity would carry through into the men who encountered it.

William Jones also gave the sea a male character, although he envisaged more specific anthropomorphic forces at work keeping seafarers in their place. Many authors called the dark, white-crested waves of the deep ocean 'greybeards,' but Jones went further, giving the 'Greybeards of Cape Horn' a pronounced identity as gatekeepers of that route. Jones first refers to them, with hindsight, as a foil to his pride at becoming a sail apprentice and acquiring his first 'brassbound' uniform: all this 'made greater the fall which the greybeards of Cape Horn were even then preparing for me.' The greybeards were tricksters, feigning leniency to draw ships into their waters. After its first easy passage past the Horn, Jones's ship *British Isles* was driven backwards again by gales and huge seas; he thought the greybeards were 'laughing uproariously at us, in derision, because with our puny strength we have dared to challenge their supremacy and invade their solitudes.' Later, luck seemed to have turned, but in reality the greybeards 'were only chuckling at us.' Sheer perseverance, though, could ultimately defeat the greybeards, who 'were compelled to acknowledge that the *British Isles* had won the right to pass through their portals.' Even after letting the ship through, however, they still 'claimed a victim' with the death of a crew member who had previously sustained head injuries.[5]

Others thought the sea was feminine, albeit in more negative womanly stereotypes than those Liam O'Flaherty had listed. At the very start of his memoir, Herbert Lightoller characterised the sea as 'a hard, unrelenting mistress' with no patience for fools: 'she tried to drown me several times, yet I beat her; she nearly broke my neck on more than one occasion, but we still remain the best of friends.' He returned to this idea more than once, claiming that the sea was 'harsh and bitter,' yet 'full of captivating smiles and surprises'; 'but you must laugh in her face, when she hits you hardest, and, above all, never fear her.'[6] That gendered personification of the sea as a female force to be overcome by the male seafarer often went hand-in-hand with the common idea that ships were woman-like creatures, and we will return to that point in the final section of this chapter.

Arthur Mason characterised his relationship with the sea in more directly emotional terms than most authors. He described this as both friendship and love, and made unusual claims about the sea as a living force that could communicate and match moods: 'The sea and I have been friends; we have understood each other's thoughts. The sullen moods, the tranquil, and the boisterous, each in its own tone, have blended together in harmony, so that the Soul of the Sea is forever *en rapport* with the heart of its lover. I love the sea, and shall continue to, as long as I have eyes to see its indigo and emerald coloring, and ears to hear its rumbling echoes on crest and crag.'[7] That merging of thoughts and senses between man and the elements is often hinted at in memoirs, although most authors probably thought expressing such an emotional form of masculinity was at odds with the 'simple sailor' persona they claimed in their prefaces.

If part of their motive for going to sea was to find a better kind of manhood, free from petty limits, some authors claimed to have found this in their relationship with the elements. For Rex Clements, the ever-changing forces of the sea meant that seafarers lived on a heightened level, with such extremes of experience that the lives and worries of people on land seemed trivial: 'whatever the sea-farer does, he does largely.' Clements believed that constant danger bred a different set of ethics, focused on crew cohesion and cooperation. In religious matters, too, Clements thought that doctrinal detail was 'thin' at sea, but that sailors were well aware of the larger questions of faith. Clements seems to be arguing that exposure to the sea created a shipboard community with an appropriately rough masculinity – loud, wild, and untameable – yet one that prioritised techniques of group survival in ways that the 'sheltered folk ashore' had lost touch with.[8] James Bisset reached similar conclusions from the opposite direction: his seafarers also lived lives untrammelled by shore conventions, but that was because they knew they were 'insignificant in immensity,' aware of the 'rotation of the universe' in a way that land-folk had no sense of.[9]

Many authors wrote that they felt most in tune with the elements when they were high up on the ship's masts. This was often a solitary experience. Men went aloft in numbers when hard work was required with the sails and rigging, but alone or in pairs for lookout duties or just to get away from their crewmates for a while. Authors wrote of the spirituality of such individual exposure to the sea and sky, invoking wider tropes of the isolated, stoic man who faced down the elements in Romantic-era stereotypes. The great panorama of the southern seas in fine weather appealed to Walter Runciman's sensibilities: 'What ineffable days and nights they were! The soothing silences filled the mind with a sweet confusion of happiness and pensive regrets.'[10]

Frank Bullen suspected that his readers might accuse him of waxing lyrical when he wrote about the beauty of nights at sea in the West Indies, but insisted that his youthful self genuinely responded in that way, especially when the elements contrasted so sharply with the 'squalid surroundings' on-board ship.[11] Fred Farmer was fascinated by the 'magnificent spectacle of a sky as black as Erebus, supported on a disc of heaving roaring whiteness.' At such a moment, he believed, 'a sailor is wooed and won – or lost – for all time.' Still, Farmer was conscious that this was a little esoteric for most seafarers. His own sense of the occasion was dented by a crewmate who complained that the wind was making it hard to light his pipe.[12]

Some authors wanted to believe that seafarers could take control of their relationship with the sea, and that the crew's skill and experience gave them power over the elements. James Bisset thought that the 'glory of life under sail' was in 'men taming and making use of the power of the wind.'[13] He extended the animal metaphor, arguing that the wind was the servant of the crew, not its master, but that like a beast it might turn on the ship and destroy it. That distinction was important to Bisset – men were always the masters in this relationship, even if he admitted that their servant might rise up and drown them.

Others believed that the power of the elements could reinforce the seafarer's inner strength as an individual. Arthur Mason's moment of revelation came when the ship's mate forced him back up the mast to re-furl a sail that he had not tied properly the first time. Furious about the indignity of this treatment, Mason suddenly gained a sense of scale and perspective. The ship he looked down upon seemed 'like a helpless bug being borne away by the whim of the sea,' but far from being afraid he felt he had gained a power the mate could not take away. This was very much an internal strength: 'the mate might abuse me, but he could never destroy the spirit of the sea that was born in my soul.'[14] Simply going to sea might not free a man from the pettiness of authority, but once there, a further step toward embracing elemental forces might finally secure that manly self-esteem.

Some authors saw science as part of the answer, wanting to understand what they were witnessing in modern terms, and thereby better able to overcome its dangers. Frank Bullen recalled being fascinated by the sea during his first voyage, staring over the side of the ship and watching for sea creatures. This habit persisted throughout his career. To Bullen, this interest was essential if he was 'not to die mentally,' which he feared some crewmates had already done. He was amazed to find that the sailors could tell him nothing factual about 'the wonders of the ocean,' although they kindly made up fabulous yarns in answer to his questions. The ship had no books that could enlighten him, only the essential navigation texts in the captain's cabin. Bullen believed he was the only person on board intrigued by the great mass of seaweed in the Sargasso Sea; everyone else cursed the ship's slow progress through it.[15]

As ever with Bullen, we have to wonder how much of his writing could really be an accurate memory of his boyhood worldview, and how much stemmed from the years of reading and writing that followed. He wanted, retrospectively, to portray the proper sailor as a self-taught man with an enquiring mind, interested in both the science and the aesthetic pleasure of the marine environment, and to categorise himself in those terms, even if most seafarers, including his officers, lacked such attributes.

Charles Dixon, who went to sea in 1890 and had a longer career as a sailing-ship captain than most of our authors, might be the sort of officer Bullen had in mind. Dixon was proud of his scientific knowledge on several fronts, from oceanography and celestial navigation to less expected fields, such as when he rigged up a condenser to give his crew fresh water after the mate let the ship's tanks run dry. This let him assert his modernity in the face of superstition and ignorance – he thought a great deal of nonsense had been written about the Sargasso Sea, for example. Science also reinforced Dixon's authority as a professional man of reason and an effective sea-captain. All the same, Dixon believed in metaphysical connections beyond man and the sea, unmeasurable by his sextant and tide tables. When paying tribute to a Cunard commodore who helped him out of a difficult situation, Dixon thought that such seafarers 'draw robustness, courage and a vast chivalry from the cleansing depths.'[16]

Such memoirs point to the complexities in our authors' attitudes toward the sea as a force in their own lives, and in moulding the men around them. Sometimes too, authors invoked weird incidents that would, with hindsight, gain greater meaning in an evolving mythology about life at sea. Herbert Lightoller, the most senior officer to survive the *Titanic* disaster, wrote of his first encounter with an iceberg, which took place when he was a sailing-ship apprentice. Lightoller described in great detail the baffling effect of a large berg at night, big enough to disrupt the wind yet essentially invisible until it was very close – and the dawning realisation that the ship must have been sailing alongside a great wall of ice long before the crew realised what was happening.[17] This episode comes close to the beginning of Lightoller's memoir, many chapters before his discussion of *Titanic.* It haunts the reader, as it evidently haunted him.

SUPERSTITION AND FAITH

The idea of the sea as a supernatural presence, and as a theatre for uncanny forces, was part of a wider system of belief, religion, and superstition described by maritime authors. In part, they were responding to public stereotypes about seafarers, knowing that their readers would expect stories about shooting albatrosses and whistling for winds. Some authors put superstition on a spectrum, at best a quaint hangover from an ignorant past, and at worst a persistent brake on rational progress. Folklore scholars have recognised that men working in dangerous jobs have historically used superstition and ritual to exert some control over their lives, taking comfort and agency from believing that they have a say in their actions.[18] Superstition allowed seafarers to insist on certain behaviours among themselves, reinforcing crew cohesion in the name of respecting sailors' traditions. It gave them something, or someone, to blame if those rules were broken and the ship ran into trouble, and simultaneously served as a menace and a means to prevail against the odds.

Superstition was also a target for evangelical Christians seeking to reform the seafarer through a more formal belief system, and there were religious seafarers too, some of whom found their faith strengthened by their experiences at sea. Religion was an aspect of authority and order on many ships, more or less explicitly stated. Captains were 'Masters under God' in a common phrase of the time, and while that was usually a reference to their disciplinary powers, some took it literally, leading religious services on Sundays and invoking biblical morals. John Bain is the most prominent example among our authors, but William Jones recalled a ship's mate who lectured younger sailors about their sinfulness.[19] At the very least captains conducted shipboard funerals using Christian rites.

Organised religion had an awkward relationship with masculinity in the late nineteenth century. Clergy were men, but it was common to question their manliness. Congregations often depended on women for their lay activities. Sunday schools could give the impression that faith was a matter for children or the illiterate. Church-led temperance and morality campaigns seemed like attacks on men's traditional leisure pursuits. Melting-pot seaport cities often had sectarian divisions, and scholars of such places argue that men saw religion as a question of allegiance and politics, rather than belief.[20] On the face of it, seafarers should have been good candidates for the 'muscular Christianity' movement in the middle of the nineteenth century, but the clergy who dealt with seafarers were often characterised as condescending, and ignorant of the realities of lives at sea. Given all that baggage, it may be no surprise that few of our authors discuss their religious beliefs in any detail.

Pryce Mitchell's comments about his faith focus on youth and mortality. He claimed to have been religious before he went to sea in 1877. In the run-up to his first voyage, he pondered seafarers he knew who had been lost, and appreciated the gift of a Bible from his father. Witnessing his first maritime collision, which killed the crew of a small schooner, provoked another bout of religious reading.[21] References to religion fade as his memoir proceeds, though, as if it was a relic of childhood beliefs, and a landsman's morbid preoccupation with death that Mitchell would move beyond as he became a seafarer.

Many authors report seafarers living with an amalgam of beliefs, as befitted men at the cusp of great changes in industry and society. For Rex Clements, who first went to sea in 1903, superstition was a part of sailoring being overtaken by modernity. It was unsurprising, he thought, that 'all the old-time sailing-ship men' had superstitious tendencies. Clements reflected that a long sailing-ship voyage was so far removed from rational, civilised experience that it was bound to provoke 'weird imaginings,' and that 'seafarers of a less enlightened age' could be forgiven for their delusions.[22]

Fred Farmer put similar experiences in a religious frame. Being on lookout at night as the ship was carried by the Trade Winds was transformative: 'the most hardened sinner in the fo'c'sle will feel the nearness of that One whose Mighty Hand moulds and re-moulds and shapes our destinies.' Farmer thought that seafarers had souls that could recover while at sea from the 'contamination' they suffered in seaports, even if they were likely to 'plunge deeper' again at their next landfall.[23] Bill Adams reported an ongoing confusion in his own mind, sometimes turning to biblical texts for explanations, sometimes feeling the religion of shore folk could not possibly apply to what he witnessed at sea. He saw men take their hats off to natural phenomena, like when 'all the ocean was a sheer flame of phosphorus.' But this was 'reverence,' he thought, rather than religion.[24]

James Barker's characterisation of his old captain Simon Gunn used superstition and faith to put a nuanced distance between seafaring generations. Gunn's mastery of dead-reckoning navigation, and lack of theoretical knowledge, sat alongside the intense superstition learned in his early years at sea in the 1850s, when, Barker wrote, 'he had absorbed all the beliefs of the period.'

The death of any seabird was a portent of disaster, as was the crescent moon lying on its back. The Roman sea-god Neptune 'was an actual living entity.' At the same time, though, Gunn read his Bible three times a day, claiming the book 'was written by God, man's best shipmate.' Gunn's amalgam of superstition, religion, and rule-of-thumb seamanship impressed Barker, but mostly as a relic of the past: 'he was a character in keeping with an almost forgotten era.'[25]

Some of the religion encountered on ships struck educated authors as being full of blasphemy and heresy, yet in keeping with the eccentric individualism of the seafarer. Walter Runciman recalled the seafarers on his first voyage in the 1860s having an unshakable faith in a divine power, but with no way of defining or articulating what that might be. They seemed afraid of 'offending some subtle force that they believed mysteriously ruled human affairs,' while they also 'steadfastly believed in an indefinable Someone to whom they could pray for aid when they got into trouble.' This vagueness about their beliefs was an indicator to Runciman of their lack of learning; their minds, he thought, were 'scantily developed' and they had no interest in books, although they all had some awareness of Bible stories.[26]

In particular, Runciman's crews showed great interest in the story of Jonah, a favourite subject of waterfront preaching and forecastle discussions alike. He listened as they debated every detail and argued about the kind of sea-creature that must have been involved. Crucially, the sailors then extended this into a 'Jonah creed,' through which they monitored poor weather and misfortunes in an attempt to identify whether one of their number might be responsible. Runciman's crews knew when a sailor had failed to pay debts or committed some offence on shore, which supposedly brought bad luck. Usually, they would then punish the man in 'a semi-goodnatured fashion,' although he had heard of a few cases where men were ostracised.[27]

Such behaviours suggest that seafarers were adding a layer of religious and superstitious validation to an uncertain moral code that they might struggle to implement otherwise. If seamen objected to misconduct by their fellows, they could evidently respond better by invoking a traditional creed. At times, though, stresses became extreme. Frank Bullen claimed that his crew accused him of being a Jonah when he was very young, to the point that he believed they would throw him overboard. The bosun and the ship's Black sailors realised in time that the crew's normal banter was heading in a sinister direction, and rescued Bullen.[28] Sometimes, then, hangovers from seafaring's mythology could re-emerge as drivers of ship-board tensions, or as justifications for acts that would have been unthinkable away from the disconcerting emotional turmoil of tense situations at sea.

Superstitious cruelty to animals is a case in point. This permeates memoirs, as seafarers punished a variety of creatures for perceived threats to the ship and its progress, but again, there is a strange mix of belief, habit, and pragmatism. John Wilson recalled catching birds he thought to be 'Cape pigeons,' which followed ships in large numbers as they rounded Cape Horn. Hooked on a line and brought on board, a bird would be decorated with red cloth and released, whereupon it would be pecked to death by its fellows. Wilson offers no reason or justification for this beyond it being 'sport' and 'amusement.'[29] Half a century later, Rex Clements reported similar cruelty to birds he called 'molly-hawks,' but also noticed his second mate kicking a sailor who deliberately drowned a seabird.[30]

Memoirs have a surprising variety of behaviours toward albatrosses. Walter Dexter saw a generational gap by the time he went to sea in the 1880s, with old shellbacks still believing that the birds were the souls of drowned shipmates, although he thought that most of this came from Coleridge's poem. He and his ship's officers caught birds in large numbers, and the captain traded barrels full of their skins and feathers when the ship reached Australia.[31] Dexter's testimony captures the transition from an older superstitious man to a modern man of business.

Sharks emerge as the seafarer's target in many memoirs. The shark-catching ritual, often performed at the first sight of such a creature during the voyage, was claimed to be punishment for the animal's man-eating habits. Henry Hughes thought sailors lost their reason at the sight of a shark, falling immediately into a terrified fury that could only be assuaged by catching, torturing, and killing the creature. They believed sharks killed sailors sadistically, biting off limbs in a 'progressive amputation' that they found horrifying, and responded accordingly.[32] Leslie Morton thought, with hindsight, that shark-catching showed a degree of cruelty that he regretted; as John Wilson put it, once the shark had been dragged onto the deck, 'the work of torment would commence.'[33] The shark would be mutilated, insulted, and cut open to find out if it was guilty of man-eating. Its tail was hung from the jib of the ship as a warning to other sharks, and to remind the crew of their common enemy. Frank Symondson noted that shark catching was entirely ceremonial – sailors would not eat the fish because they believed it was akin to eating their own lost comrades.[34]

Shark-catching is a major part of one of the more unusual maritime memoirs, that of John Keane. Although he worked at sea for a decade from the age of twelve, Keane saw himself as a sportsman and adventurer as much as a sailor. Writing in the 1880s, before the main wave of maritime autobiography, Keane seems to have doubted whether a memoir about seafaring would be successful on its own. He noted in his preface that 'a certain sporting element' was central to his writing, and duly included four chapters entirely about catching sharks, along with lengthy discussion of fishing and exotic game hunting on shore.[35] Well aware of the shark's place in seafarer superstitions, Keane nonetheless distanced himself by adopting the persona of the gentlemanly hunter.

Captains used shark superstitions to their own advantage. Albert Bestic reported that he never saw a captain refuse permission for the crew to catch the first shark encountered on a voyage. Ships had harpoons, hooks, and other equipment at hand for the purpose.[36] Confronted with nervy sailors, James Barker encouraged their beliefs if it kept them busy and offered them hope in a difficult situation. He ordered a line baited with salt pork to catch a shark when his vessel was becalmed in the Pacific. The crew were enthusiastic, dragging the shark around the deck before hacking it to pieces and nailing its tail to the jib-boom, 'believing that so deserving a deed would gain them favor in the eyes of the Wind Gods.'[37]

If they universally hated sharks, seafarers were more conflicted about other animals, and often sentimental about cats, dogs, and birds.[38] Henry Hughes reported men swimming to save animals that had fallen overboard; suicidal behaviour, he thought, that showed the soft-heartedness of the seafarer.[39] Fred Farmer wrote that ships' cats were crucial to forecastle morale, in part because they allowed men to claim ownership and control of something. Seafarers became jealous if they saw an officer feeding 'their' cat, and the loss of a cat overboard plunged the crew into gloom and foreboding.[40] When Clifford Fenton was an apprentice, he recalled his crew in a burst of superstition when the steward drowned a cat; this was probably part of the rivalry among sailors, stewards, and cooks encountered on many ships.[41]

As that suggests, authors recognised that superstition could be a way of playing out tensions among sailors, or between them and officers. Arguments about authority or status found an outlet in stories about animals, singing, whistling, or any of a plethora of superstitions, and also avoided direct criticism of an officer's decisions. Arthur Mason, working as a ship's mate at the turn of the century, had to pacify his captain's panic when men on the wharf claimed they had seen rats abandoning his ship, a common portent. Mason also had to keep this news away from the crew, at least until the vessel was at sea and they could no longer desert. On one level, Mason plays the story for comic effect, describing his efforts to keep the ship afloat and on course despite the antics and eccentricities of all those around him. He had a more serious point, however. Both the captain and an Irish sailor called Mike made much of these superstitions as part of an ongoing antagonism between them, until the ship was actually in danger, when they reverted to their usual competence, 'as a real sailor will do every time.'[42] Although Mason had no doubt that everyone believed in the superstitions, he thought they were sufficiently modern men to avoid endangering the ship over them.

Charles Dixon, writing in the 1930s after a long career as a sea captain, was not so sure. Although he thought his crews compared well with men on shore, he claimed they had a streak of innocence that left them vulnerable to fear and superstition. He believed Finnish seamen, for example, were a bad influence, spreading the 'legendary nonsense of their race' to 'simple-minded sailors.' Although 'all right in fairy tales,' thought Dixon, 'it caused all sorts of trouble in a ship.'[43] The stereotype that Finns had an unlucky effect on the weather was common, but Dixon goes further than most authors in suggesting that it was not harmless, and in arguing that other seafarers were easily led astray in the emotional stresses of the voyage.

Uncanny tales and folk beliefs helped our authors locate the sailing-ship mariner in an older, more elemental kind of masculinity, from which they could distance themselves without ever dismissing entirely. Their argument seemed to be that it was part of the complex package of life and work in sail, appropriate in its day, but mostly a quaint relic by the time they were writing their memoirs. Still, they knew that weird yarns were part of the expectations of their audiences, and could never cast off that element while remaining true to their simple sailor's persona.

SHIPS AS LIVING BEINGS

Many writers used a range of anthropomorphic or zoomorphic analogies to ascribe living behaviours to ships, and some seafarers seem to have believed their ships really were living creatures. The idea that sailing ships were alive gained new force as men drew contrasts with steamers. Writing of his first voyage on a steamship, Herbert Lightoller recalled that he 'sadly missed the feel of something living under my feet.'[44] For others, the living ship was a descriptive and narrative device that enabled an author to explain either the ways that ships worked, or the feelings that seafarers had for them. Walter Dexter saw a direct physical link between the ship and the seafarer. The looming presence of the great sails and the movement of the vessel inspired him to adapt his body to work in tandem; he swayed with the roll and pitch, built his muscles to do justice to the demands of ropes and sails, and was proud to fall under the vessel's spell.[45] As always, there are implications for our understanding of seafaring masculinity. Authors wrote of seafarers who loved their ships, and some claimed to have done so themselves – there was evidently nothing unmanly about expressing love for a sailing ship, at least in retrospect.

Albert Bestic offered an extended discussion of how a sailing ship was a wild animal imprisoned in port, until it returned to the sea and became 'once more a living child of Nature.' At sea, his *Denbigh Castle* sat above the crew's squabbles and grumblings, and even the commercial purpose of the voyage; for the vessel, it was instead a 'lonely pilgrimage.'[46] John Bain recalled an unusual meteorological event off Newfoundland, when a sudden gale froze the ship's sails almost instantly; by next morning the decks were also covered in thick ice, and it spent ten days surrounded by an ice field. This was a huge physical challenge for the crew, many of whom lost fingers to frostbite when trying to free the frozen rigging and tackle. What struck Bain most, though, was the effect on the ship, which took on 'a strange, ghostly appearance. Instead of being a thing of life, she looks like a stiffened corpse. Her elasticity is gone.' Eventually, the weather freshened and the ship began to thaw: 'it is grand to see every hour giving fresh life and vigour to the paralysed and stiffened limbs, until she bounds once more, free and unfettered, on her onward course.'[47]

Arthur Rostron wrote an extended elegy for his old ship *Cedric the Saxon*, not least because he thought that few would remember the sensory experience of being on a sailing ship making fast runs in heavy seas. As well as being an 'inspiring sight,' 'the spars are groaning and moaning – or should I call it singing?' In the midst of all this, the crew watched and listened, 'keyed up to the highest pitch' for the slightest change that would require them to act.[48] Many authors described the process of 'wearing' a ship (a difficult turning manoeuvre), but Fred Farmer was unusual in portraying this as an aural experience. He heard it as a 'weird unearthly note, changing from a deep moan as the ship rolls to leeward to a shrill piercing scream when she returns to windward.'[49] Sailors could also tell by listening whether their ships were struggling. Walter Runciman referred to 'the weird incoherent song of a belaboured ship when its vital parts are pained, which no one but a sailor understands.'[50]

The idea that ships, as well as their crews, could have emotional responses to their circumstances comes across in many memoirs. Frank Symondson told of the way his 'frightened' ship struggled through Atlantic gales with a 'dead cargo' of grain that made its movements sluggish and slow.[51] Bill Adams, steering his ship in the Pacific, thought that the ship had lost the sternness of the rougher parts of the voyage, and was expressing 'an eagerness, yet also a sort of peace.' Later, he believed his ship was afraid, when heading for rocks near Cape Horn: 'you could sense the old girl's sudden fear.' This was all inextricably connected to Adams's own emotional state, at least with the benefit of hindsight and maturity: 'I loved my ship. Maybe I could not then have said it. Today I know I did.'[52]

As these accounts suggest, by far the most common way of representing a ship was as a woman. In that sense, many authors did not see themselves as being without a female presence during their voyages, because they regarded the ship itself as an entity that was womanly in character and behaviour. Authors searched for elaborate parallels and metaphors to connect their ships with what they regarded as inherently feminine attributes. This reinforced their sometimes battered sense of manliness, because they were at sea in the company of, even in partnership with, a female being who needed their protection, care, and command.

Fred Farmer devised a mixture of gendered metaphors to portray the sorry condition of his ship when it was unable to make any progress in difficult weather. The vessel was like 'some once well-clothed beauty, now dressed in the rags of poverty, alone in the deserted streets of a city on a wet and dreary winter's night.' Carrying little sail, 'the pitiful nakedness of the ship seems almost human.' Although written in the 1920s, Farmer's melodramatic vision seems entirely Victorian, equating his struggling ship with long-standing stereotypes of fallen women and street waifs. Pondering the fate of a relatively new ship he had once sailed on, he wondered whether 'she is still the spotlessly clean maiden as when I knew her in my youth, or whether she has since become a dirty, slovenly hag in her old age.'[53]

Farmer pitched an entire argument around the idea that a sailor's love for his ship was the true reason for putting up with the hardships and dangers of working in sail. A seaman's first sailing ship was very much his 'first love.' The call of the sea, Farmer believed, was a myth: it was the call of the ship that brought him back for another voyage. This explicitly emotional interpretation is unusual in seafarer memoirs, and Farmer recognised that the seaman himself would 'scoff at the suggestion,' while making 'an ingenious effort to conceal his secret love' through back-handed compliments to the ship. With the end of sail, the old shellback had to work on shore, 'dreaming of his Lonely Queen, but no longer hearing her call.'[54]

Rex Clements alluded throughout his memoir to what he saw as womanly characteristics in his ship. He explained the task of changing sails in terms of clothing: 'a ship, unlike the majority of her sex ashore, always wears her best clothes in bad weather.' He thought the changing character of the vessel over the course of a long voyage was best equated to different moods and foibles of womanhood: the ship was 'an exacting mistress,' 'a heartbreaking wench,' and 'a Cleopatra.' Such imagery was common enough, but Clements went a step further and invoked the idea of a genuinely loving relationship between sailors and their ships. This too was profoundly gendered; the men set the course and direction with their 'sea-cunning,' while the 'woman-like' ship 'would respond to every thought and act of one who understood and loved her.'[55]

Many ships had an iconic representation of womanhood on board in the form of the figurehead. Robert Ramsay joked that the carving was his 'new sweetheart' after having to leave behind a girl on shore, and recalled the other sailors seeking the figurehead's views about their romantic problems, as the 'only piece of femininity in sight.'[56] Some testimony reads oddly until we remember that authors are transposing their adult mentalities back onto their boyhood selves. Henry Hughes went to sea as an informal apprentice in the 1890s, sailing in a ship belonging to his grandfather. His mother had been the model for the vessel's figurehead. Hughes only reveals this at the very end of his memoir, when he is leaving the sea, and able to confess that climbing out on the bowsprit to see her face had been a great comfort during voyages. Early in the book, he adopts a much more adult-male persona, concocting the idea that the recently-refitted ship reminded him of 'a smartly-dressed middle-aged woman who had been to a beauty specialist to have her face lifted in an endeavour to keep abreast of her younger rivals.'[57] That statement points to the time-warping impact of autobiographical recollection, perhaps nowhere more evident than in changing attitudes to mothers, wives, women, and ships as authors themselves passed through phases of the male life cycle.

Tellingly, authors who spent long careers as captains of large passenger liners had a particular audience in mind when pondering the gendered characteristics of their old sailing ships. The tone is a kind of after-dinner-speech sexism. Edgar Britten couched his explanation for the tradition of regarding ships as female as an answer to his wife's repeated questions about the subject. Britten used 'capricious' twice in less than a page, and focused on the alleged unpredictability of ships, with 'their whims and their fancies, their virtues and their weaknesses.' A seaman never knew if he would be kissed or kicked, claimed Britten, and 'the capricious wench was capable of doing both' in quick succession. He also favoured clothing metaphors: the vessel was never 'dowdy,' but 'always trim and neat.' Sails were the 'pretty finery' in which a ship would 'romp along full of pep and vim' when the sun was shining.[58] Albert Bestic included a similar summary late in his memoir: 'A sailing ship, like a woman, while possessing beauty and courage, can show weaknesses which but increase the love of those who man her. She can bestow favours and she can be exacting. She will at times respond to commands with obvious delight, or sullenly acquiesce, according to her mood.'[59]

The idea that ships are always referred to as 'she' was an established habit long before our authors went to sea, as was a broader range of animal, and especially equine, metaphors. Still, seafarer memoirs rarely just repeated those tropes, and instead offered readers extended discussions of why ships might be female, or horse-like, or a still broader assortment of living things. All these ideas carried a deal of gendered weight, sometimes for comic effect, usually much more serious. A man's role, authors argued, was to control these creatures, but also to cherish and protect them, and some of the most persistent discussion of seafarer gender roles relates to the sailor's relationship with his ship. In addition, not only officers claimed such ties; all seafarers could see themselves as men alongside their womanly ship, and perhaps this gave them a sense of command and agency that they otherwise lacked, for all that it reinforced their paternalist assumptions.

*

Maritime memoir-writers had some genuinely unusual experiences to recount in terms of their engagement with nature and the elements. Although many people made ocean journeys every year in the late nineteenth century, these were increasingly on large steamships. Britain's seaborne passenger traffic was dominated by the liner routes on the North Atlantic, and through the Mediterranean and the Suez Canal to the East. Some faced rough passages, discomfort, and even disasters, but most passengers had a relatively mild time of it. This was literally a world away from the environments faced by the deep-sea sail routes in high southern latitudes. Whether around Cape Horn to and from the Pacific coasts of the Americas, or across the broad expanse of the southern Indian Ocean to Australia and New Zealand, cargo-hauling sailing ships worked in waters that few of their readers could ever have seen. A seafarer familiar with such waters had a remarkable story to tell.

It is striking, then, that so many authors did not content themselves with mere descriptions of the wonders they saw. Despite the difficulties of writing about emotion, authors worked hard to convey their responses, and those of the men around them. Some stressed the spiritualism of the seafarer, as a counter to his rough reputation; others tried to explain his superstitious excesses as reactions to the enormity of the forces ranged against him and his ships. And ultimately, any sailor could feel more of a man if he cast his ship as a womanly being, to be protected, nurtured, and sometimes bullied though the dangers of the voyage. Bill Adams spoke for many in claiming that constant care and attention made the ship his, rather than the shipowner's: 'when had ever *he* steered her through a southerly buster in the night's roaring blackness?'[60]

Indeed, most authors did not seem to regard the traditional technologies of the sailing ship as technologies at all, reserving that language for the innovations of steam. This let them frame life and work in sail as an older mindset and worldview, invoking folk beliefs, uncanny events, living vessels, and a seamless merging of crew, craft, and ocean. Acknowledging that there was much they could not control did not belittle them as men, so long as they felt they had command of themselves. By the time they wrote their memoirs, most thought this was a lost kind of seafaring manhood, but they persisted in believing it a better one.

7

Facing the Deep

The elemental extremes discussed in the last chapter had far-reaching impacts on the bodies and minds of seafarers, and if some were inspirational, others were brutal. While authors usually claimed that seafaring turned sailors into better men, they all remembered shipmates who had lost their manly health and vigour to injury, overwork, and illness. They witnessed deaths at sea, many of which challenged Victorian ideas of propriety and dignity. Authors also made clear that even when sailing-ship mariners avoided the worst dangers, they endured long voyages of uncertain duration, with poor, and ever-deteriorating, food and living conditions.

Most of our writers argued that seafarers faced those trials with great courage, and their memoirs perpetuate an already long-established stereotype that spanned naval and mercantile shipping, hailing what they called 'Jack's pluck.'[1] Still, courage could be a difficult issue for memoir-writers. Men were expected to play down bravery and fear alike, and authors had to balance the competing demands of modesty and dramatic storytelling. It was also hard for them to apportion blame for poor conditions at sea. Even authors who held shipowners or captains responsible for bad food and unsafe ships usually saw seafaring primarily as a struggle against the forces of nature.

Portraying seafarers as heroes certainly helped validate our authors' lives and careers by association. It might also have addressed some insecurity on their part. If Victorian audiences had embraced books about self-help and commercial success, they had also been uneasy about suggestions of greed and avarice.[2] Stories of seafaring courage enabled our authors to depict ordinary, mercantile men who were also heroic. Maritime memoirs are full of warlike, combative, and confrontational language, although these ships and men were fighting the elements, and not actually engaged in warfare. Such rhetoric was a powerful invocation of a hegemonic manly outlook.[3] Running through all this testimony is the perennial concern about sailors' bodies, and whether their fabled strength and resilience was still a match for the conditions faced in the later days of sail. Some authors wrote of fragile mental states too, pondering their own vulnerabilities, and those of the men around them.

WORK, DISCOMFORT, AND DOMESTICITY

Writing about seafarers' responses to hardship invoked controversial perceptions well beyond the sailing-ship sector. Many depictions of stoicism and courage were doubtless meant to be complimentary, but they fed into wider narratives about working people bravely overcoming material deprivation to build and maintain their moral character. These tropes were far more comfortable to the mainstream reading public than any suggestion that workers might improve their lot through class war and revolution.[4] They were also, of course, convenient for captains and shipowners, who resisted spending more on food, clothing, accommodation, labour-saving equipment, and safety procedures.

Shipowners made much of the legal tradition of 'assumed risk' in trying to limit their responsibilities for health and welfare. After all, sailors could hardly argue that they were unaware of the dangers when they joined the industry.[5] As in factories on shore, difficult working conditions at sea were often internalised by seafarers themselves, who saw contempt for danger and suffering as part of their identity as men and seamen. Historians have noted the irony of hard men in many industries who neglected safety procedures, however rudimentary, only to find themselves suffering injuries and illnesses that made them dependent on others, and struggling to maintain a sense of their own masculinity. Such men were, in a sense, trading their bodies for confirmation of their male identities, a bargain that ultimately failed.[6] The nature of seafaring employment also tended to conceal its longer-term impact on the well-being of seafarers. Men who were too weak to work were not signed on in the first place; those who became ill during a voyage would be left on shore at the next port. It was not like living in a mining community, say, where the sick and disabled continued to live alongside the working men. Seafarer authors could easily forget the human consequences of their industry's poor conditions.

This background is important because many authors argued that suffering had been character-building for new sailors: if weak boys were to grow into strong men, they needed to endure a hardening process that bred manly indifference to domestic comfort. Such sentiments can be found in most memoirs to some extent, although notably among authors who had long careers, and who had a clear survivor's bias in believing they had been well-served by the process. Looking back on his early days at sea in the 1900s, Rex Clements couched hardship as a call and response: 'Was the life hard? – one slept the sounder for it. The food poor? – salt pork tastes better to a man in Fifty South than a banquet to an epicure. The pay paltry? – there is other wealth, thank God, than that of gold.' This masochistic anti-modernism reveals a widespread worldview that was brought into sharp focus by new techniques and technologies, and their attendant social and cultural impacts. Clements contrasted the 'simple joy of living' that he claimed to experience on a sailing ship with the crude efficiency of steamers, achieved by cramming the maximum 'work and worry' into the day.[7]

Without any apparent irony, authors who became steamship liner captains eulogised the supposed spartan character of the sailing-ship mariner, a man who worked for a higher purpose and scorned luxuries and comforts. Edgar Britten thought that the 'terrible hardships experienced in windjammer days' had moulded the 'strongest and the fittest' seafarers, who had 'a due respect for discipline and authority.'[8] Arthur Rostron believed 'it was a healthy life and fitted us for the exposures and trials that were to come.'[9] James Bisset thought the sea was a profound elemental force that 'conquers the mind of sailors when they are far from land and enables them to endure discomforts that they would never tolerate on shore.'[10]

Despite the ubiquity of such commentary, there are notable differences over time. Our earlier authors were still describing an industry with minimal safety regulation, and some wrote in part to expose the scandal of 'coffin ships.' Frank Bullen first went to sea in 1871, on an old vessel that was far past its best. The rigging was rotten, the sails in rags, the ship had to be constantly pumped out, and there was little material in store to repair or replace anything that broke. Bullen remembered the fears of the crew, and their embittered sense that the ship had been sent to sea with no care as to whether it returned.[11] William Lord and Frank Symondson reported similar experiences. Lord suffered through a voyage in the 1860s on a ship that would not have been allowed to sail under the seaworthiness regulations in force by the time he was writing in the 1890s.[12] Symondson's first voyage in 1872 had several false starts before the vessel was finally considered sound enough to attempt its journey to Australia.[13]

By the time our later authors went to sea early in the twentieth century, some changes are evident. The parsimony of owners continued to underpin much discussion of hardship at sea, but most writers were no longer so concerned about the seaworthiness of the vessels themselves, which had improved in a generation. Now, the need for extreme economy was manifest in the number of sailors employed and in the amount of work expected of them. Food and living conditions remained problematic. Especially at the end of long winter voyages, crews could be so debilitated that even the strongest ships were put at risk. These pressures exacerbated the old 'cracking-on' culture that we have already seen in some captains, who took pride in making fast passages in difficult seas, and who had inherited generations of assumptions to that effect.

Unusually, we have two accounts of the same 1905 voyage of the vessel *British Isles* round Cape Horn to cast light on the ways authors represented these questions. William Jones was an apprentice on the ship; James Barker was its captain.[14] Jones's running theme, the under-manning of later sailing ships, comes through in his diligent narrative of injuries, accidents, illness, and fatalities as the voyage progressed. He demonstrated how an already small crew could be reduced over months at sea, and the impact this had on those remaining. Barker, on the other hand, had nothing to say about crew levels. His themes throughout are the importance of moral and physical strength, hard work and obeying orders, with the captain's belief in his own authority matched by the deference of the crew. In a brief summary toward the end of his book, Barker recorded the same number of deaths as Jones, but devoted less space to non-fatal illnesses and injuries, and logged these as being due to the 'assaults of the elements.' In Barker's telling, events occurred and were resolved in quick succession, usually by his own interventions, with none of the lingering fear and stress captured by Jones. Barker's book reveals the mindset of a driven ship's captain; Jones captures the impact of a long and unlucky voyage on a crew of seafarers, but is ultimately at its best in revealing the effect of those traumas on himself as an impressionable teenage trainee.

Without criticising Barker, Jones makes his views clear. Jones thought officers 'of the old school' believed that 'men before the mast in sailing-ships could be driven to the limit of human endurance.' One example that still outraged Jones half a century later was Barker's response to a fire in the hold. Barker ordered all hands on deck for several days to dig out tons of smouldering coal, hoist it up on deck, and douse it with water. Jones testified that 'there was a perfectly good donkey-engine, with a boiler and winch, in the engine-house, within four feet of the forward end of the main hatch, where the fire was.' Barker could have ordered its use to winch the coal up out of the hold, but did not, because that would have needed fuel. Barker gambled on fine weather persisting long enough for his exhausted, choking, and filthy sailors to finish the job before they were needed to handle the sails and rigging in the next storm. Only later in the journey, with his crew reduced by half through illness and accident, did Barker use the donkey engine to help turn the ship when it was coming dangerously close to ice. In Jones's evidence, the risk had to be existential before Barker would supplement human power that he had already paid for, with steam power that incurred additional expense. The problem with labour-saving devices was that they only saved labour if they were actually used – the alternative definition of 'labour-saving' was to make fewer seafarers work harder.

If the underlying reasons differed from ship to ship, and over time, sailing ships were rarely comfortable places for their crews, especially in the cold, stormy seas they predominantly had to traverse by the early twentieth century. Two sensations – cold and wet – characterise almost every description we have of sailing-ship voyages. In the 1870s, Frank Symondson reported that waves regularly swamped the apprentices' half-deck, sea-chests simply floated around, and it was impossible to maintain dry living quarters.[15] Two generations later, Alan Villiers remembered the miserable living spaces of commercial vessels, where crew quarters in the bow were exposed to the seas and often flooded: 'there was no warmth in the ship, no comfort, no dryness.'[16]

Food also emerges as an ongoing controversy, although again, authors drew different lessons. Most repeated a familiar trope about the acceptance of poor food being a measure of seafarers' stoicism and manly detachment from domestic trivia. There may also have been an element of obedience, and a cultural attitude, widely inculcated in childhood, that working people should count themselves fortunate to eat whatever they were given.[17] Like the food, authors' accounts vary little. Fresh produce was exhausted early in the voyage because sailing ships had no refrigeration, and the crew moved onto a limited diet of dried and salted goods.

Memoir-writers often report sailors using humour as a defence against the food problem. One of James Bisset's older shipmates wound him up with tales of 'wind-puddings' – deep breaths of sea air – which were supposed to counteract hunger. There were also gruesome legends, told with great enthusiasm during yarning sessions, about the kind of meat actually contained in the new-fangled cans of mutton taken on board in Australia.[18] Walter Dexter claimed sailors had 'food dreams,' and talked constantly of what they would eat in their next port.[19] For some authors, food signified the petty humiliations of the British class system and its growing bureaucratic apparatus. Arthur Mason objected to the oppressive distribution of provisions on his first deep-water British ship in the 1890s: 'She was a real lime-juicer. Everything we had to eat was weighed out, and our water was measured.'[20]

Some authors went further, though, arguing that the food provided on British sailing ships was emasculating because it was hardly fit for animals, let alone men.[21] These were long-established ideas, stretching back into the Georgian navy at least, when food carried many layers of symbolic meaning about the rights and privileges of seamen.[22] Having to eat poor food, and indeed feeling bound by manly performance to enjoy or at least tolerate it, just added to the un-manning of the sailor. Sailors suffered many knock-on effects from a diet heavy in salted meat and fat, and lacking fruit and vegetables. At sea in the 1850s, John Wilson concluded that 'the food we had to eat at sea was death to a man's digestive organs, and conduced to scurvy.'[23] Crews suffered boils and other skin conditions, especially at high latitudes and in bad weather, when the already tired seafarers had low resistance to disease and infection.

Madden Jardine reported that after five weeks of trying to round Cape Horn in 1881, hardly any of his shipmates were working at full strength, most were in chronic pain, and life on board had become 'a bleak, hideous nightmare.'[24]

By the time the last of our authors went to sea in the early twentieth century, owners had little incentive to reform conditions in sailing ships. British sailors were abandoning sail for steam, but foreign seamen appeared plentiful and uncomplaining. Owners and captains knew that improvements would only squeeze their margins further, and the suffering of seafarers was part of the race to the bottom in a declining sector. More philosophically, older men believed that rough experiences built the characters of the young, as, they claimed, it had built their own. It seemed safer to put the next generation through similar trials lest something be lost in any process of reform. This climate encouraged all involved to rationalise bad conditions as the maintenance of tradition, in a nostalgia for hardships that supposedly never did them any harm. It also allowed dangerous practices to carry over into the tramp end of the steamship sector, hidden behind the public's fascination with the old days of sail, and their assumption that such hardships were in the past.

COURAGE

The best-known trope about manly maritime courage in the nineteenth century was the doctrine of 'women and children first.' While mostly relevant to the passenger liner sector, it created a set of expectations that no seafaring writer could ignore. Every schoolboy also knew that captains were supposed to be the very last person rescued, even if they were not expected to actually go down with the sinking ship as was apparently the tradition in the fighting navy. Both ideas are rooted in reinventions of chivalry, selflessness, and responsibility as key manly attributes within the Victorian class system. Awkwardly, they were devised in the mid-nineteenth century following sinkings where officers and seafarers abandoned their passengers. In addition, the reality was one of 'ladies' rather than 'women' first, and the aim was to maintain order among the seafarers and lower-class passengers who might, it was widely believed, lack discipline in a crisis.[25]

Our authors recalled tensions between their experiences and such received traditions. William Lord described his crew having to abandon their water-logged ship in the 1860s via a small dingy, which required several trips before everyone was safe. The crew was in disarray, and only gradually was the captain able to persuade them to cut some cargo loose in an effort to steady the ship. When they had to leave, the captain's wife went first – 'it goes without saying' – but only after an argument because she would rather have stayed with her husband. The strongest seamen then took priority for themselves. Lord, still a boy sailor, left at the end with the captain, but would have gladly relinquished what he called 'the position of honour' for an earlier departure. Lord's account of this episode is far from heroic.[26]

The tragedy is that memoirs are a poor source for the worst disasters in the age of sail, because commercial sailing ships that were lost tended to sink without trace or survivors: men whose ships went down in deep water were very unlikely to live and become memoir-writers. Most of the dangerous situations our authors experienced were therefore threats to individuals rather than risks to the ship. Nonetheless, many authors put collective courage at the heart of their characterisations of seafarers. Looking back from the 1920s, Fred Farmer couched seafaring heroism in classical terms: 'no calling ever produced so many or greater heroes than did the sailing ship,' he claimed, and even the idea of working aloft seemed to come from 'an already forgotten period of unsung heroes and Stoics.'[27] Farmer's shellbacks belonged to a pre-mechanised, valiant society where men and ships had to battle the elements using centuries-old techniques and technologies.

For Walter Runciman too, the most extreme weather revealed not only the courage of the crew but their communal strength as seafarers. The violence of the wind and waves could be such that officers ceased trying to shout orders, and just relied on every man to do what he could for the ship. Runciman's picture is the same as Farmer's – 'desperately brave fellows' rooted in a mythic vision of seafaring manhood.[28] Arthur Rostron was disturbed to see 'fear in the eyes of men' during a storm in the southern Pacific, but the thing that stuck most firmly in his memory was the mate's shouted efforts to pull the crew together: 'if we've got to die, let's die like men.'[29] What the seafarers thought of this appeal to their courage and manliness is unknowable, of course, but it fitted Rostron's worldview as an apprentice and, decades later, as a senior captain crafting his memoirs.

Such epic models made it hard for authors to write of their own bravery, while still conforming to manly norms of self-deprecation and modesty.

Indeed, when authors reported their own courage, they usually did so indirectly, writing of setting an example, or showing leadership, which was more appropriate than boasting about their valour. James Barker, for example, set up lifelines in a gale for the two mates and the men at the wheel, but not for himself: 'I had, by reason of practice and tradition, to move about without that feeling of security which a lifeline imparts.' His job, he believed, was to be a prominent presence, 'infusing courage into those two sturdy old time sailormen at the wheel.' As a result, Barker was swept across the deck several times, breaking two of his ribs. He revealed nothing to the seamen, however. Only when the ship seemed safe did he go below to get his ribs strapped up by the steward, under cover of consulting the charts. Barker believed that seamen would 'trust in good luck and the "Old Man,"' but only if he played his role appropriately.[30]

Other authors hid courage behind understatement, and thought that the ignorance of youth might be at the root of a lot of seafaring bravado. When William Crutchley's crew found themselves being blown onto a lee shore, with several minutes to contemplate the likelihood of shipwreck, his fellow apprentices seemed indifferent rather than courageous: 'needless to say, we were all a little curious as to what the next few minutes might bring about, though honestly speaking I do not think young people care very much what faces them.' Indeed, Crutchley thought the only person on board who was actually being brave was the captain's wife, because she was behaving beyond his normal gendered expectations.[31] Sailors themselves liked to play down any sense that they were being courageous. A man called Collins caught the young Frank Worsley when he lost his grip aloft, but refused thanks and swore him to secrecy. Worsley concluded that 'an honest old seaman' would not want to be associated with a fuss around having saved a life at some risk to himself.[32]

Some authors noticed that officers tried to anticipate terrifying situations, shoring up the courage of their men, and recognising that even experienced seamen could be frightened into making errors. When a ship was moving ahead of a high sea, for example, officers rigged canvas behind the helmsman to prevent him seeing the waves, which would appear to be looming over the stern of the ship. A number of authors witnessed this. Leslie Morton believed that 'the sight of such seas can make a man lose his head momentarily,' sufficient to pull the ship off course and risk being swamped.[33] In fact, the wave was not about to crash down, because the ship was being pushed upwards by rising water, and the wave would not overwhelm the ship if it kept its line. The optical illusion, however, was formidable.

John Wilson recalled being in that situation, and looking back to see 'the huge wave towering right above us with a great curl on its crest.'[34] Walter Runciman remembered a sailor who panicked, leaping into the rigging for safety; fortunately, the second man at the wheel held on and saved the ship.[35] It is revealing, though, that the authors who discussed this issue thought that officers had to intervene, and that the ordinary courage of seafarers was insufficient for the occasion. Such testimony points to an odd mix of appreciation of bravery and a paternalist sense that seafarers lacked the education or intelligence to recognise when a natural phenomenon was not what it seemed.

Seafarers did not only require courage in harsh weather and dangerous seas. Climbing the masts was well known as a risky activity, but of course it was particularly disturbing for those with vertigo. Officers knew this, and only allowed new seafarers aloft in favourable conditions until they proved capable. Nonetheless, working at height was an essential part of the job, and an inescapable rite of passage. Bill Adams wrote that he had struggled to defeat vertigo throughout his apprenticeship. He knew his fellows were contemptuous of that kind of fear, so he did not confide in anyone. He would climb the masts – run up them, even – with a sailor called Tom Swift, so as never to give Swift any hint of the problem: 'I had to live up to his confidence.' Rounding Cape Horn, Adams claimed that he and Swift did the work of four men handling the uppermost sails, then stayed aloft 'to watch the fiery skies and roaring seas, and our old enemy Cape Stiff.' On his next voyage, wanting the approval of the new second mate Clegg, Adams climbed to the very top of each mast, where there was a ball that had to be painted gold. He did this while trying to hide his shaking, remembering the exact places from which crewmates had fallen. Adams claimed it was all worth it just to have Clegg call him a 'damned handy sailor.'[36] Like many of our authors, Adams was uncomfortable discussing individual courage except in the validating fraternity of the crew.

The opposite traits to courage and stoicism were also to be found at sea, and many authors condemned what they saw as cowardice and malingering. It is telling that they used such language, full of military connotations that had become much more current during the Great War. Writing in the 1930s, Clifford Fenton looked back at the old sailing-ship route from Australia across the Pacific to Chile, describing it as the voyage most likely to expose 'the chicken-hearted seaman' who would stay in his bunk and refuse work.[37] Nationality and class permeate these accounts. As we have seen, most authors thought British seamen were superior to foreigners in any crisis. Bertram Hayes told of the only time he ever saw a crew refuse duty, and emphasised that they were foreign 'squareheads' who should never have been on a British vessel.[38] In most memoirs, however, such generalisations sat alongside positive accounts of individual foreign men whose courage was not in question.

That sense of fraternal alongside individual courage, sometimes marshalled by officers who knew from experience when nerves might be most stretched, is a common thread in seafaring memoir. It was entwined with feelings for the ship, sentimental attachments to home, and often to a more generic sense of the reputation of seafaring men. It was also something that sailors owned, and part of the gulf of incomprehension that they perceived between their experiences and the ideas of people on shore. The irony was that this suited their employers too, because it signalled an acceptance of the unchanging, inevitable hazard of working at sea.

BROKEN BODIES AND MINDS

Some authors were lucky in their time at sea, not only avoiding injury themselves, but rarely witnessing ship-board calamities. Charles Protheroe, one of our early writers, reflected that he had never seen a fatal fall in twenty years at sea, despite how often sailors were 'hanging on by the eye-brows' aloft.[39] Most memoirs, though, have accounts of deaths, injuries, and near-misses. Fred Farmer reported falling from a yard, but he caught some rigging on the way down and saved himself. He was relieved that no one saw him fall, because it spared him embarrassing banter from his shipmates. Only later did he reflect on the danger, and the wider implications: 'how many men have fallen from aloft and disappeared in a mysterious manner, to pass unseen and unheard into Eternity?'[40] Rex Clements too had a close escape. A flapping sail knocked him into space but he was able to grab the footrope as he fell past it; he badly strained his arms and shoulders doing this, but could swing down safely to the deck. As well as the physical pain, he was haunted by reliving the fall in his mind: 'Lucifer himself never fell so far as, all night long, I kept doing in sudden fits and starts.'[41]

Some authors wanted to convey to their readers the kind of trauma that seafarers could suffer as a result of their experiences, and even just from events they had witnessed. Alan Villiers wrote of a second mate who, years before, had been a boy sailor steering his ship in a storm when he saw his entire watch swept overboard by a wave. The boy could not leave the wheel or turn the ship, because that would have caused the vessel to founder. No one could hear his shouts for help over the gale. He was stuck at the wheel for hours, having to face alone the enormity of what he had seen, until the off-duty watch realised something was wrong and came to his aid. Villiers learned all this in the aftermath of a new disaster, which killed a sailor and left the second mate incapacitated with guilt; confined to his cabin for the rest of the voyage, he took years more on shore to recover. Villiers has nothing but praise for all involved. The captain patiently nursed his shattered officer, and with food running low, shepherded the rest of the crew home safely too. There is none of the posturing about strength of character encountered in some memoirs.[42]

Others reported a mixed set of responses to the mental illnesses suffered by crewmates. Albert Bestic wrote of 'Hans the Swede,' who broke down during a voyage when supplies were running low. He suddenly tried to turn the ship, insisting that they should steer north 'to catch fish for food.' The crew took away his knife as a precaution, but concluded that he was harmless, especially because he seemed to retain enough awareness to turn out with his watch. He stopped working, though, and just gazed at the horizon, which Bestic concluded was generally demoralising.[43] Bill Adams wrote of several occasions when sailors lost their best friends at sea. His crew showed great sensitivity to a Nordic sailor called Kylon whose friend had died on board, and who became increasingly eccentric, wandering the decks talking to God and the dead sailor. Although he was put in chains briefly when the men became afraid of him, the captain decided he posed no danger, and everyone became used to him. He did no work, and ate less and less as the voyage went on, but was treated kindly.[44]

Much more troubling was Adams's account of a fellow apprentice called Wood, not least because Adams had to confront his own role in the marginalisation of his shipmate. Wood came from a wealthy background, and had been a first-class passenger on liners, giving him a laughable misconception of life at sea. Adams had his own insecurities about class and privilege, having been a scholarship boy at an elite school, and felt inferior to those, like Wood, with real wealth and connections. Adams also learned that he and Wood both suffered from vertigo. Wood did not hide this, and it reinforced the view on board that he was unfit to be a seafarer. After weeks of what must have been constant trauma, Wood refused to go aloft and do his work. Adams went instead, keen to show that he was a very different prospect. Wood began staring into space, and old sailors would tell him yarns but get no response. Finally, on the voyage home, Wood went aloft, but came back down laughing and clapping his hands: 'Wood was mad – made mad by horror of the rolling spars. It wasn't nice to see.' When the ship reached Liverpool, Wood was taken away by his father. Adams's conclusion was that 't'was better in the half deck with the madman gone.'[45] Adams defined Wood's problems as self-inflicted: he announced his fears rather than working silently and stoically to overcome them, and he did not value the comradeship of the crew. That appears to have ensured an unsympathetic response from his shipmates, leading to a further downward spiral.

It was harder to deal with more senior men who were struggling with their mental health. James Bisset reported his ship's carpenter becoming moody and depressed, frightening the apprentices with tales of shipwrecks. He became obsessed with 'the bells of the sea,' which he believed were portents of doom. During one voyage when the ship was struggling in the doldrums, he claimed for days that he could hear bells, to the point where the crew locked him in his workshop and derided him as mad.[46] Crews tolerated eccentricity, but not unnerving behaviour, even, perhaps especially, in valued and essential shipmates.

There was something pathetic about such strong men suddenly brought low. Herbert Lightoller remembered 'Olsen the Swede' losing his night vision, and thought 'it was pitiful to see him feeling his way round the decks.' Lightoller cultivated a nonchalant performance himself, borrowing a smallpox victim's coat because he claimed to fear the cold more than the disease.[47] Others thought that sailors were supportive of sick crewmates, especially if the men kept working. Stoicism was appreciated, although this was sometimes self-interested. Henry Hughes wrote approvingly of a man called Jeff, who continued working even when in great pain and largely immobilised by illness. What the men seem to have appreciated most, though, was that Jeff moved out of the forecastle to stop disturbing their sleep with his restlessness.[48]

The prospect that disease or injury would lead to permanent disability clearly preyed on seafarers' minds. Madden Jardine recalled a sailor named Hesketh whose finger was mangled in an accident and seemed to be taking a long time to heal. Hesketh became obsessed with the possibility of gangrene, and had Jardine inspect the wound periodically. Jardine was able to reassure him every time, and 'restore his balance' until the doubts began preying on him again.[49] Jardine believed that it was mostly fear of letting his crewmates down that was worrying Hesketh, but sailors also dreaded amputation and disability because it struck at the core of their self-image – quite literally for those who signed on as Able-Bodied Seamen. Sailors were, after all, known as 'hands': if they could no longer hold ropes, sails, the wheel, or myriad other parts of the ship, they could not be seafarers.

Sometimes injuries offer insight to a broader scale of value-judgements and priorities. Soon after joining the shipping company that would be his employer for the rest of his career, Henry Moffat badly injured his arm. The doctor initially favoured amputation, but was persuaded otherwise by Moffat and his officers, who testified that he had 'a good character for sobriety.' The doctor then took the time to operate and set the bones in Moffat's arm, enabling his seafaring career to continue. Although Moffat's body was the immediate focus, his character and reputation determined his value to the shipping company, in a mixture of old and new measures of seafaring masculinity. Years later, Moffat's body began to fail him again when he suffered declining hearing, but by that time he was a long-serving captain and an even more useful asset, and his employers gave him an important administrative job on shore superintending fleet logistics.[50]

As always, seafaring memoirs have a survivors' bias, and nowhere more so than in discussion of men's responses to illness and injury. Still, more authors than we might expect recalled harrowing periods when they wondered if they would overcome their own debilitation, and many recounted in detail the trials of the men around them. Being left behind in a foreign hospital was a grave prospect, partly because no one had confidence in the treatment on offer, but also because it seemed an emasculating humiliation in the eyes of shipmates.[51] The amount of space authors gave to these events may reflect an awareness, with hindsight, of how lucky they had been to reach an age when they could tell their tales.

LOST AT SEA

Deaths at sea were hard to locate in our period's wider assumptions about mortality, grief, and mourning. Few fit with conventions of a 'good death' as promoted by religious evangelicals in the nineteenth century. They were often too sudden for any preparation of the soul, and even when men died after lengthy illnesses, religious guidance to aid repentance had usually been unavailable. Seafarers had their own rituals and cultures, and responses to the loss of crewmates could seem alien to popular sensibilities. Passengers were sometimes shocked by what they regarded as sailors' blasé attitudes toward deaths and funerals. By the time most of our authors were at sea at the turn of the century, however, the extremes of Victorian preoccupation with death were waning. Certainly when authors were writing in the 1920s and 1930s, the national experience of mass fatalities in the Great War had altered perceptions of how individuals and families should manage grief.[52]

Seafarers may have been in advance of shore customs. They were long familiar with the realities that so disturbed the broader population after 1914. Deaths at sea were always remote from family, who might only learn of them belatedly and with little detail. They were followed by simplified funeral services and burials with no memorial that could be visited by the grieving. When ships, and therefore their crews, were posted missing, families faced a long wait before accepting the worst, a reality that would also afflict many on the home front in wartime. That said, most seafarers who died on board had at least some form of funeral surrounded by their shipmates, irrespective of their status, means, nationality, or faith.[53] This was in some contrast to the pauper burials feared by the urban poor.

Rex Clements thought that the monumental forces of the open ocean overshadowed all else: 'death itself would be a small thing in such surroundings.'[54] Ships and men vanished with a suddenness and finality unknown on land. Clements seems to have regarded this with a kind of liberating fatalism. Still, losing men overboard had a profound impact on the remaining crew. Men who fell from far out on a high yard could well be killed when they hit the surface of the sea. Heavy clothing and sea boots could drag them under immediately. Even if a man remained conscious and afloat after hitting the water, he could only expect to stay that way in calm, warm seas. In addition, sailing ships were usually moving faster than a man could swim, and even if commands were issued to slow or turn the ship and launch a boat, that took minutes at best, by which time ship and man were far apart. In rough seas, sudden course changes could endanger a ship, and small boats were unsafe. Rescue efforts were widely believed to put many lives in danger for a slim chance of saving one.

Authors remembered feeling powerless as a result. Frank Symondson reported a man called Johnson falling from aloft. The scene on deck was one of 'indescribable confusion,' he wrote, as men ran to all parts of the ship and climbed the masts desperate to catch sight of Johnson in the water. The irony, he reflected, was that Johnson could probably see the ship all the time, but had no chance of reaching it in heavy seas. When Symondson's watch next had to climb the masts, everyone was very subdued, pondering the loss.[55] Charles Stevens told of a man who fell from the end of a yard into the sea. The crew threw him a lifebuoy, but they could not turn the ship – running in ballast in heavy seas, changing course quickly might have capsized the vessel. Stevens thought that 'it was a hard sight to see him on the top of each wave struggling for life and we making no effort to pick him up.'[56]

Some captains were sensitive to the emotional impact of a loss overboard on their crews, and to the potential for trouble from angry or grieving sailors. Bill Adams described his crew searching for two hours when a sailor called Furst fell into the sea, before concluding that he must have drowned. The captain gathered the crew in front of the afterdeck and asked, 'Anything more you want me to do, lads?' When the crew told him there was nothing, the captain resumed normal working by ordering the vessel onward.[57] Charles Dixon did the same when he was captain, asking the crew if he should continue the search, and having them sign the log to confirm that it was hopeless.[58] Conscious that emotions would be running high, captains were keen to avoid any grievance around the seriousness of the search, and manoeuvred the men into feeling they were taking the decision.

Most of those lost overboard had no funeral, adding to the sense that such deaths were unnatural and disturbing. Perhaps to compensate, seafarers who died on board, or whose drowned bodies could be pulled from the sea, were buried with whatever ceremony the crew could manage in the conditions. Authors were much affected by ship-board funerals, even decades after the event, writing poignant accounts that stand in contrast to the matter-of-fact tone they often maintained elsewhere in their books. Funerals were something of a leveller, with all the crew and officers expected to play their parts. There were rituals to perform, most notably by the sailmaker, who was responsible for sewing the body into a canvas shroud.

Preparing for a funeral could alter the normal use of space on board the ship, opening areas normally closed to ordinary crew members. When a sailor known only as Harry died in the night, James Barker had him carried to the main cabin, where there was a large enough table for the sailmaker to sew the body into canvas. Other members of the crew were told they could see Harry before he was sewn up.[59] Those seafarers would only have been in that part of the ship in rare circumstances, underlining the seriousness of the situation and how disruptive death could be to ship-board conventions. Normal use of space was restored as soon as possible, with the seamen sent forward again when they had performed their necessary roles.

Deaths at sea demanded work from seafarers that would normally be done by women on shore. 'Laying out,' preparing bodies for burial and making them presentable for mourners, were tasks performed by local women in most communities.[60] At sea, preparing the dead was appropriate work for men, and indeed it added to the status of the sailmaker. There is some testimony, however, of deaths so shocking that normal responsibilities broke down. Clifford Fenton wrote of a man whose body was so badly shattered in a fall onto the deck that the sailmaker refused to touch him. An old sailor had to be bribed with whisky to sew the remains into a tarpaulin for burial.[61] While most authors maintained that standards were upheld and decent rituals performed following ship-board deaths, it is clear that some conventions were fragile, and that the authority of the officers was not certain in such circumstances.

Authors wrote of the loss of seafarers in many different ways. John Keane was one of the few authors to openly ponder his own likely emotions if he found himself washed overboard. He did not write of courage or fear, but rather wondered whether he would be consumed by rage and fury, or lapse into calm resignation. Keane also contemplated slower deaths from disease, in particular the painful decline of men suffering from scurvy that he witnessed in the 1860s. Although Keane argued that sailors were kind-hearted men, disturbing deaths like these brought out a selfish, callous side to them, and the surviving crew would waste no ceremony in burying the dead sailor.[62] Walter Dexter agreed that crews coped better with accidental deaths. Having to watch a sailor die of disease preyed on their minds, for all that they had a 'rough sympathy.'[63] Frank Bullen also recalled the 'horrible' task of looking after a sailor dying from a disfiguring infection. His crewmates picked on him as the youngest sailor on board to perform this feared and unwelcome role.[64] Some crews seem to have regarded this as nursing, and therefore a job for women or boys, although there are many examples to the contrary.

William Lord drew an unusual distinction between losses overboard and deaths from illness and accident. He recalled early in his career being haunted by the sight of sailors drifting away from the ship after being washed off the deck in a storm. The powerlessness of all concerned to save the men was 'heart-breaking' and 'preyed on my mind with little cessation for long afterwards.' Oddly, though, Lord does not seem to have defined these as deaths – writing of a time years later, when he was captain of a steamer, he reported the death of a fireman as 'the first death that had ever happened at sea on board of any ship that I had sailed in.' Perhaps losses overboard were just that in his thinking; with no body to bury, the surviving crew suffered from the loss, but without having to confront the corporal reality. A death on board, with the continuing presence of the dead man and the rituals surrounding his body, struck Lord in a different way. He admitted that leading the funeral service was almost too much for him, and after he returned to the privacy of his cabin, his 'feelings utterly prostrated me for some time.'[65] This is in contrast to the accounts that we have from most authors, who painted dramatic pictures of deaths and funerals, but usually without admitting to serious emotional impacts on themselves.

Disturbingly, the deaths of seafarers also featured in superstitions, and the idea that a sacrifice to the sea gods might be needed periodically if a ship was to be favoured with good passages. Authors reported captains who encouraged this thinking, pragmatically accepting any help they could get in difficult sailing conditions. Indeed James Barker admitted to this himself, allowing the crew to draw their conclusions from the various deaths that occurred during the 1905 voyage of *British Isles*. Immediately after the funeral of the sailor called Harry, the wind came up from the right direction to drive the ship on its proper course: 'here was a slant at last.' Later, when Jansen the Dane was lost overboard, Barker reported discussion in the forecastle that the man had been a Jonah. Although the officers had no doubt that Jansen was a fine sailor and a great loss, Barker had to acknowledge that the crew 'responded as though inspired with new life.'[66]

Most authors who remembered deaths at sea thought they cast a temporary gloom over the survivors, but usually nothing more. Stoic acceptance of death was part of their own self-image, quickly absorbed by young sailors from the behaviour of the fatalistic old shellbacks who had seen many such losses before. By the time they were writing their memoirs, the rise of steam had made seafaring safer, and deaths could be explained away as another artifact of the age of sail, even if in fact the improvement was only relative: shipping remained, and still remains, a remarkably dangerous occupation.

*

William Crutchley concluded his memoir with a commonplace statement about the manliness of seafaring, but then added an unusual qualifier: 'it is a man's life in a properly found and officered ship.'[67] After forty years working in prestigious steam liners, Crutchley evidently thought there was a bargain to be kept, and that safe, professional ships with comfortable quarters and good food provided a proper workplace in which men could be men. The testimony in the first third of his book, when he recalled his days in sailing ships, suggests that he knew this had not always been the case. Rather than hailing the rough masculinity of old-style sailors in the face of adversity, Crutchley's implication was that poorly provisioned, leaky sailing ships run by eccentric captains did not offer proper conditions for working men, and were perhaps more likely to create animals or brutes.

Crutchley was no radical speaking up for workers' rights, so it is revealing that he couched the relationship between seafaring labour and capital in these terms. Robert Ramsay also complained that a long-standing contract had been stretched and broken in the later days of sail. He felt his own moral compass had been knocked off course when he witnessed the parsimony of shipowners, and came to sympathise with any sailor who felt driven to pilfering or malingering.[68]

However, most of our authors rejected the idea that men were reduced to beasts by working on sailing ships, and indeed favoured the contrary view that they became better men. By the time they were writing, though, the realities were safely in the past, and the men and beasts alike inhabited the growing mythology of the age of sail. Charles Dixon stoked the legends, concluding that public enthusiasm for each new record set by the great Atlantic steamship liners was misplaced, because they were essentially technological achievements. Far more impressive in his view were the passages of the old clipper ships, made possible when 'officers and men pitted strength, courage and an endless endurance against the fury of sea and wind.'[69] The sheer number of seafarer memoirs published from the 1920s assured the promotion of those legends, even if a few told a more sceptical tale.

8

Traditions, Rituals, and Cultures

We have already seen memoir-writers depicting a vibrant and multifaceted culture rooted in seafaring work and tradition, whether it was rivalry between watches, cruelty to marine animals, or superstitions about weather. This chapter takes a closer look at how authors represented some day-by-day fundamentals of sailor culture, focusing on language, talk, song, and personal possessions. The ability to participate in, pass on, and ultimately create occupation-based traditions has long been regarded as a positive masculine characteristic, reinforcing the tendency of so much historical writing, as well as memoir, to locate men in workplaces and women in homes. Seafaring is probably an extreme case, given the isolation of the ship during its voyage, but also the turnover of crews, and hence a constant renewal and reinforcement of rituals, stories, and behaviours.[1] Sea voyages exposed men to a mental world in which ancient seafaring practice and the events of the current passage were continually recycled. Seafaring culture moulded shipmates from individuals who joined the voyage as strangers, transmitting from one crew to the next the attributes of the 'proper sailor,' not least of which was a manly balance between self-interest and collective strength.

Officers had an awkward relationship with seafarer culture. Looking back on their early days at sea, those authors who had moved up to higher ranks remembered admiring the expressive power of sailor talk and song, as well as what they thought was a surprising depth of feeling and character revealed in quiet conversations. Over time, though, they had come to realise that these could also be subversive arts, conveyors of subtle insults, and even of mutinous resistance during tense voyages. Our later authors especially believed they were recording a lost way of life, and offered their experiences to readers as if they were enthusiastic amateur anthropologists. Others were conscious of the distance that had always existed between them and the men of the forecastle, and admitted that they struggled to recapture, let alone understand, all they had seen and heard.

LANGUAGE

Maritime authors over centuries have made intensive use of sailor talk, knowing that they needed to 'fulfil a stereotype if they were to be believed as seamen.'[2] Our memoir-writers maintained the genre convention that sailors talked differently from people on shore. Most highlighted technical and obscene language, both of which have long been coded as male, as indicators of how sailors conceptualised their bewildering surroundings, and also how divorced they could be from social norms and domestic restraint. There are substantial variations in the extent to which authors wanted to convey their shipmates' words. Some included very little dialogue, while others wrote lengthy speeches and conversations, and of course we have no way of assessing how any of this might relate to words actually spoken.[3] Still, most authors clearly thought that sailor talk was important to the picture of the sailing-ship mariner that they wanted to convey to their readers.

Mastery of technical language was an indicator of both crew cohesion and seafaring skill, and therefore a tool for transmitting both to the next generation of boy sailors. Some authors thought nautical terminology was a great leveller, and a glue that held shipmates together. James Bisset called it 'the Esperanto of the sea,' comprehensible even by illiterate sailors, and by the many whose English was weak.[4] Memoir-writers brought their readers into this maritime world by naming the parts of the ship. Some authors eased the audience in gradually, starting with full names in their early descriptions and then moving to the abbreviations that officers used to give orders. William Jones, for example, recounted the proper names in the early chapters of his book, but before long his forecastle had become a fo'c'sle and his topgallant sail a t'gans'l;

he also provided a detailed sail plan and a glossary.[5] Other authors assumed existing knowledge, expected readers to do their own research, or thought readers would just be impressed by the bewildering argot. William Lord, for example, wrote that 'it may be interesting to describe the process of reefing' – and then did so with little explanation of the many technical terms he used.[6]

The other stereotyped characteristic of seafarer language was prolific swearing and obscenity. Walter Dexter thought this was a key reason for sailors being excluded from shore society, albeit with subtle changes over time. Once, swearing had signalled real wickedness and godlessness, now perhaps just a lack of education and vocabulary. Looking back from the 1930s, Dexter likened sailors to British Tommies in the trenches of the Great War, or Australian 'diggers,' hard-swearing men who did not think they were causing any offence among their peers, but who immediately changed their speech in the presence of women or social betters.[7]

One common tale was that it was a good sign when sailors were swearing, because it signalled normal working practice on the ship. If they ever stopped, it pointed to some looming disaster.[8] John Wilson reported the 'tremendous' obscenities being yelled by his captain in a moment of peril as 'sweet music to me,' acting as a 'paean of victory and a song of assurance, which drove away my fears completely.'[9] A seafarer could use language of a kind unacceptable on land to shout down a storm, reinforcing more general ideas about the other-worldly demands of their working environment. Swearing and obscenity were also a point of controversy surrounding sea shanties. Most commentators agreed that lyrics were lewd and unprintable, and published shanty collections tend to have sanitised words. Seafarers themselves apparently had clean versions of popular songs that could be sung on passenger ships when there were respectable people within earshot.[10]

The irony, of course, was that while memoir-writers insisted that sailors swore, they could never tell their readers what those words actually were. Melbourne Garahan claimed that part of the authenticity of his book was getting closer to sailor language than most authors, but conceded that the reality would always be unprintable. In particular, he was amazed by the 'extraordinary' blasphemy of everyday sailor-talk, and reported men having profanity-laden arguments with God, as if every adverse wind were a 'personal affront' to be remonstrated over.[11] Frank Bullen made an almost identical point about the 'continual blasphemy of sailor-talk,' of which he never became tolerant, although in other ways he admitted to speaking as crudely as anyone during his years in the forecastle.[12] However, publishing convention in the early twentieth century located seafaring memoirs as mainstream works that had to be cleansed for the general reader. Most blanked out even minor swearing, especially when it might offend the religious, so that 'God damn' became 'G— d——,' and harsher language did not appear at all.

Other authors tried to explain swearing as part of broader moral codes among seafarers. William Crutchley recalled that most men tolerated very rough language, but that 'son of a bitch,' with its insult to mothers, would always lead to a fight, even when an officer used it against a seaman.[13] This was a long-standing convention. Although he went to sea four decades after Crutchley, Hans de Mierre also reported being greatly offended by that slur. As a senior apprentice he told his ship's new second mate to stop using it: 'we don't talk to each other like that in these ships,' he told the officer, who remarkably backed down.[14] There was also a nationalist undertone to de Mierre's complaint, because 'son of a bitch' was especially associated with American sailors and officers, and de Mierre was claiming higher standards of civility for British vessels.

Most norms around swearing involved age and class. Clifford Fenton recalled being told off by an old Dutch seaman who thought it a shame that 'a young boy like you' should be swearing. He also reported a clear sense that it was inappropriate in apprentice officers, for all that real officers ranted and swore throughout memoirs.[15] Pryce Mitchell wrote that he had not been allowed to swear during his early voyages, because the older sailors, not the officers, forbade it among the ship's boys. The same men reportedly refrained from telling 'blue yarns' when the boys were in earshot.[16] In part, the crew were reserving some behaviours for themselves as grown-up men, but they also regarded setting an example to boys as proper manly behaviour.

What seafarers called one another also reinforced their hierarchies and distinctions, and similar language runs through most memoirs. It is no surprise, but striking nonetheless, that virtually all these terms relate to some phase or kind of maleness. When giving orders, officers called sailors 'men,' and apprentices 'boys' or 'lads.' The traditional last order given by the mate on arrival in the home port, for example, was 'that'll do the men, carry on the boys.'[17] This released the before-the-mast crew at the end of their contracted work, but reminded the apprentices that they were bound to the shipowner for the duration of their indentures, not the length of the voyage. Occasionally we hear of someone who took offence, reading into persistent use of 'boy' a diminution of his role on the ship. John Mason recalled (unsympathetically) the complaints made by a disgruntled apprentice called Clarke: summing up his time at sea, Clarke's words were apparently 'it was "boy this" and "boy that."'[18]

Everyone on board seems to have called apprentices 'my boy,' 'my lad,' or 'my son,' emphasising the youngster's status, but also a mixture of ownership and paternalism. Indeed, 'm'son' was James Barker's favoured address for boys and men alike when he was trying to be encouraging, according to both his own testimony and that of William Jones, who was one of his apprentices.[19] Barker was already a captain in his mid-twenties, so perhaps adopted that verbal tic as part of appearing older and more paternal than he was. Among themselves, apprentices continued their schoolboy habits, calling each other by nicknames, or by upper-middle-class affectations like 'old chap' and 'old man.'[20] Sailors used 'mate' among themselves, and 'sir' when addressing officers; older sailors and senior apprentices might sometimes have a licence to call officers 'mister,' like the captain did.

All occupations have linguistic traditions and habits, but few matched the widespread public imaginary surrounding seafaring language, thanks in the main to sea fiction. When our authors came to write their books, they knew that readers were already familiar with what they perceived to be sailor talk, however much disagreement there might have been about what that really meant. This is inevitably a huge topic, and one that has been worked extensively by literature scholars as well as historians, mostly using the language crafted by maritime novelists.[21] What follows has a more targeted focus on how our authors reported sailor culture in relation to the image, and self-image, of sailors as men.

TALKING AND YARNING

The idea that seafarers had a rich and active oral tradition is hardly surprising, but it does sit in tension with some of the realities of work at sea. As well as not being permitted to talk while on watch, men slept for much of the time during off-duty watches, and did not appreciate chatty shipmates in the forecastle. In the evening dog watches, though, discipline slackened and crews could talk openly among themselves. On Sundays too, there was often free time for conversation. When weather and seas were calm, especially at night, seamen had to be on deck but were not always working, and it was possible for men to talk quietly away from the officers. The fact that talking was a privilege rather than a right may have given seafarers an incentive to claim some agency over it.

Broadly, authors divided seafarers' talk into everyday conversations (which could also become debates and arguments) and yarns, which were a more theatrical performance, usually delivered by one sailor for an extended period. Some authors described a third category, 'growling,' in which sailors muttered complaints, almost to themselves, that served as an outlet for frustration and grievance. Growling would begin early in the voyage and never really cease, but usually without escalating into confrontation. Walter Runciman recalled leaving a northeast England port on his first voyage and heading south; in the few days it took the ship to reach the English Channel, 'the crew had got to know each other, and began to sing their songs, tell their yarns, and practise their growling, as became their calling.'[22] All this talk was central to crew cohesion and relationships, for good and ill.

Some authors argued that the most revealing sailor talk was in quiet moments. Men could sometimes chatter unobtrusively, often smoking as well, at lookout posts where they were a long way from the officer on the afterdeck. An extended conversation might run over many watches. Exchanges would be more intimate, recalling family, or telling stories from times on shore that might be nuanced in comparison with ribald yarns performed in the dog watches. Issues that caused tension in difficult sailing conditions could be discussed more peaceably during a tropical night. Fred Farmer thought that in such circumstances 'some of the scales of mud' might drop from a seafarer's soul.[23] He believed men could, in the quieter moments, step away from the constant performance of being a seafarer, strengthening their camaraderie and fraternity within a narrower compass.

Formal yarns were often elevated to a higher level by memoir-writers, who felt, by the time they were writing, that these represented a lost maritime culture. Indeed, historians and literary scholars have long been conscious of the yarn's potential as a narrative device, and it is no accident that novelists adopted it in their own work. Joseph Conrad, whose use of the yarn has been widely studied, appropriated it as a medium through which educated men of the officer classes – his character Marlow being the most prominent – narrated weighty stories to small groups of their peers, and hence to Conrad's readers.[24] That growing sense of the yarn as a literary form may have distanced our later authors from its reality. Memoir-writers were looking back at the yarns they had heard in their youth through the filter of those eloquent novelists' constructions.

Still, our earlier authors probably captured yarning culture quite well, and certainly thought they were explaining an unknown culture to their readers. They depicted a form of oral transmission that celebrated great feats of seamanship and fitted them into a continuing living history. In addition, seafarers' yarns were often insider jokes, told with endless technical detail. Frank Symondson, for example, recalled American sailors who joined his ship at a port of call and regaled the crew with legends of hard-driving Yankee captains. Demand for speed, they claimed, had led to the invention of ever-more exotic (and, the listeners knew, imaginary) types of sail to be carried on ever-taller masts. Above the conventional skysail, one ship was supposed to have had a 'moonsail, cloud cleaner, stargazer, sky scraper and an angel's footstool.' It was an important part of shipboard etiquette to respect any yarn: 'nobody questioned the veracity of any of this.'[25] Such yarns cemented the seafaring identity of the listeners. Only they had the technical knowledge and experience to know when their legs were being pulled, and the ability to appreciate the seamanship that went into a yarn gave them membership in an exclusive club.

This authority also meant that yarns, as with the set-piece recitations of other oral societies, drew status from the reputations of the men telling them as much as, and often more than, their intrinsic content.[26] Yarning old shellbacks reinforced their own authenticity and the acceptance of their stories. Walter Dexter appreciated sailors' yarns, but took a more sceptical view than most authors. He thought you could always learn something from old sailors, but that yarns were really only about 'women, wine, and the last ship.'[27] In other words, they enabled the teller to replay his experiences in a favourable light, whether they related to his exploits on shore, or to an amalgam of previous voyages during which the eccentricity of captains, the brutality of mates, and the foibles of cooks and other shipmates could be dissected.

John Bain devoted some space to defining and characterising the yarning phenomenon. Yarns could be short or long, he thought. The short kind usually related to something from the most recent voyage, while long yarns told of older events from years ago, and their telling might stretch over a month, in daily instalments of two or three hours. Improvisation, digression, and embellishment prevailed in these: 'the story which the sailor intends relating usually forms but a small part of the yarn he spins.' According to Bain, shipwrecks and disasters were the most common subject matter for yarns, although extreme changes of fortune in other contexts were also popular. During his first deep-water voyage, he heard three men tell of being cast away on desert islands, while two others specialised in tales of the Australian gold rushes, and the brief periods of wealth and prosperity that they enjoyed before being fleeced by men on shore – that idea of the land as a place of danger was often the moral of a sailor's yarn.[28]

People on shore also seem to have assumed that seafarers' tales might be far-fetched, especially because the most dramatic events happened away at sea and left no obvious trace by the time the crew returned home. Arthur Rostron complained that his friends and family did not believe his stories. On one voyage, the captain and steward failed to acquire enough supplies, and the ship ran out of bread and flour only three weeks after leaving Australia. The crew were reduced to starvation rations for months, but the captain put into a French port and bought extra food for the last week of the voyage: Rostron reached England so well-fed that no one accepted his tales of privations.[29] It was also a point of pride on some ships to repair any damage to the vessel by the time it reached port, and the last stage of a voyage was spent painting and polishing. Leslie Morton reported his ship thoroughly tidied so that it could be berthed 'without losing any face of dignity.'[30] This made it hard for outsiders to believe tales of swamped decks and ruined rigging, and also explains why sailors compensated with the rule that their yarns went unchallenged by their shipmates.

A few authors feared that yarning was a subversive weapon in the hands of the wrong kind of sailor. Earlier writers especially had a foible about 'sea-lawyers,' men they blamed for undermining the authority of officers and the good discipline of crews. William Lord thought that such men used the 'most wonderful yarns,' about how they had made their previous captains and owners pay, to egg their crewmates into radicalism and mutiny.[31]

This seems rarely to have been the case, however. Indeed, it is more likely that sailors' yarns were a conservative driver of a stoic seafaring culture. Men recounted hardships in terms of their own ability to overcome them, against a backdrop of timeless constants. The very fact that they had lived to tell – and constantly retell – their tales was the whole point. The British merchant marine had dominated the world's shipping industry for longer than any of them had been alive, and the food, accommodation, and weather had never been any different. Pryce Mitchell recalled 'Old Sam' keeping up his shipmates' morale by making mocking comparisons with his past tribulations: 'what are you, men or jellyfish?'[32] Clifford Fenton thought the sea-lawyers on his ship were thespians rather than revolutionaries. They entertained the dog-watch crowd by pretending to be real lawyers, holding a mock court to indict an archetypal bully captain.[33]

Indeed, the other-worldliness of yarns enabled them to persist when more down-to-earth topics of conversation could not. Albert Bestic reported his fellow apprentices running out of things to say during a lengthy voyage. They did not have the years of experience needed to concoct real yarns, so spent the first part of the voyage swapping stories about their homes and school experiences. After months at sea, these tales became so familiar that they started telling each other's stories, and then stopped talking altogether beyond the necessary.[34] This inability to maintain the seafarers' oral culture was demoralising to Bestic and his fellows, and was an uneasy premonition of the decline of the yarn in the age of steam.

For Walter Runciman, the intense oral culture on board his early ships in the 1860s was the hardest thing to describe: 'It would tax one's descriptive powers to reproduce those exhilarating forecastle narratives and discussions, delivered in the rolling northern vernacular, and flourishing of big phrases, and the flavour of wonderful words scattered about in aimless profusion. I have lived in the atmosphere of it and felt its glow, but I can never pretend to reproduce it as it was. Nor is there anything in nautical literature that impresses me with its accuracy.'[35] Still, many of our authors persisted. While some memoirs have more dialogue than others, they collectively have tens of thousands of words ostensibly spoken by otherwise unknown sailors. For all the uncertainties in how we should interpret them, memoirs give us an unusual and vivid sense of the rhetorical world of the later sailing-ship mariner.

SONGS AND MUSIC

Our authors often wrote of the musical cultures on board their ships, and by the end of the nineteenth century were contributing to a wider interest in sea-songs. Shanty collectors became a specialist part of the much broader folk-song revival, and it was in this era that a published canon of sea-song was established.[36] While most memoirs did not go into great detail about sea-songs, they add up to an important body of evidence about music on sailing ships. Authors certainly wanted to convey this culture to their readers, and in some cases to argue that the decline of the shanty in the age of steam was part of a wider neglect of the proper sailor.

Broadly, sea-songs fell into two categories. Shanties (sometimes spelled chanties) were work songs, with a call-and-response structure that helped the crew pull or push in unison when handling ropes, sails, and capstans. The second category, sometimes known as forebitters, were off-duty songs with melodies and lyrics that had a greater crossover with popular songs sung on shore.[37] That distinction had already become the standard way to classify sea-songs by the late nineteenth century. John Bain, for example, writing of his early voyages in the 1860s, thought off-duty singing was an extension of yarning: 'The singing of songs goes along with the spinning of yarns on board ship. Gathered round the focs'le-head, one shipmate after another expresses his emotions in song.' Bain then discussed shantying, citing lyrics for the long-pull songs 'Haul the Bowline' and 'Hanging Johnnie,' followed by 'Round the Horn' and 'Santa Anna,' which were sung when turning the ship's capstans. Across all forms, Bain's emphasis was on the power of fraternal, manly singing – 'the full chorus of male voices' – that could unite a crew, whether in work or in off-duty comradeship.[38]

Unlike forebitters, shanties were sung in the presence of officers, and several authors reported them being used subversively, criticising the behaviour or ability of the mates, or more generally as a way of working off resentments. Albert Bestic reported his first encounter with shantying as a give-and-take between the crew and the ship's mate. The shantyman began 'Blow the Man Down' conventionally, with lyrics about encounters with women on shore, and the men hauled the rope accordingly. After a while, Bestic thought the sail was 'almost as tight as a board,' and that there was little to be gained by further effort. The shantyman then gave up his story and began a verse with

'I thought I heard the chief mate say,' suggesting that he was expecting an order to stop hauling: the mate 'took the hint' and moved the crew on to other tasks.[39] Such testimony suggests that shantymen were not only inventive for the amusement of the crew, but also as a means of indicating their views about the working of the ship, which would not have been tolerated in plain speech. The fact that Bestic reported this happening at the start of a long voyage also points to the crew probing the authority of a new officer, to ascertain how far they might go in making their voices heard.

Sometimes authors reported ironic use of shanties, which presumably raised the morale of the crew at the expense of officers' dignity, but without any real malice. After leaving London for the long voyage to Australia, Frank Symondson's ship barely made it into the English Channel before turning back for additional ballast and cargo adjustments; the men struck up a homeward-bound shanty of the kind normally sung when leaving distant foreign ports.[40] More seriously, Rex Clements reported a shanty used to signal discontent by briefly doing no work: he claimed that if the shantyman sang 'I've got a sister nine foot high,' the crew would shout 'way down in Cuba' and jump on the spot three times instead of hauling. Invariably, Clements wrote, the mate would order a stop to this after the first line, but the message had presumably been received.[41] The shanty 'Leave Her Johnny, Leave Her' was widely used when tying up in port to mark the end of the voyage, but if men started to sing it at any other point, it signalled serious dissatisfaction to the point of mutiny. John Mason recalled a crew singing it in protest against a drunk captain.[42]

Some authors pointed to shanty culture as an expression of seafarers' sense of independence, and drew a particular contrast with the working practices of the Royal Navy, which had large, well-drilled crews and no work songs.[43] Whatever the wider lessons authors derived from shantying, the common thread was the manly strength of group singing. If off-duty forebitter singing could have its melodic and even feminine moments, there was no question in our authors' minds that the roaring, howling din of the working shanty was a masculine musical form. It accompanied prodigious physical labour and cemented the collective identity of the seafarers in relation to people on shore, in their superiority to other kinds of sailors, and against their own officers if necessary.

Authors also used shantying in debates about Britishness at sea. W.B. Whall, a former captain and shanty collector, thought the rising proportion of foreign seafarers working on British ships marked the end of shanty tradition. He believed the 'ancient, wild hooraw choruses' of the British seafarer would never be matched by multinational crews.[44] Others argued that British sailors were just part of an international culture of shantying. Frank Bullen located its origins and continuing vitality in the ports around the Gulf of Mexico, and several authors singled out African and African-American seafarers as the most powerful shantymen.[45] Racial stereotypes and prejudices infused this debate, and it became entangled with the wider folk-music revival movement's preoccupation with defining heritage within national boundaries.[46]

Memoirs have some extreme examples of seafaring musical culture, appropriately enough from the edges of Britain's maritime world. On the west coast of South America, large fleets of British sailing ships congregated to load cargoes of guano and nitrates. This was a challenging place for sailing-ship mariners, inhospitably dry and hot, and exposed to the constant swell of the Pacific. Ships stayed for months while crews loaded noxious cargoes, creating a transient floating community of seafarers, apprentices, and officers who suddenly found themselves surrounded by hundreds of their counterparts after deep-water solitude. They shared a sense, often a grievance, of having to do hard, unpleasant, and un-sailorly work in a place where there were few attractions on shore.[47]

Even more so than usual, therefore, going back to sea was a welcome event for crews on the guano ships, and leaving the major harbours of the region became an important ceremonial expression of sailor culture. Rex Clements recorded a time when seventy large sailing ships were moored in the harbour at Iquique, with daily departures and arrivals maintaining roughly that number for an extended period.[48] Every night the ships due to leave the next morning would be cheered round the port. This ritual had several elements, most involving some adaptation or subversion of normal sailorly activities.

First, the departing ship hoisted its youngest crew-member aloft on a cargo sling accompanied by relevant shanties, waving the Red Ensign and passing round a bottle of spirits. Then, the sailors lashed up a timber frame with lights attached to represent the shape of the Southern Cross, the dominant constellation in the skies on the route around Cape Horn. This was hoisted to the top of the mast with favourite hauling shanties. Violent ringing of the ship's bell – a sharp contrast to the measured strikes of normal watch-changes – heralded the cheering. The man with the loudest voice on the ship called for cheers in the name of the next ship in line, which were returned by that ship's crew. The process was repeated until all the ships in the harbour had been hailed. This could take two or three hours, until the Southern Cross was lowered, and everything stowed for departure, with a final farewell shanty.

Cheering round the port reflected three important elements in sailor culture. For sailors to know and name every vessel in the harbour showed a remarkable interest in ships and in other crews, for all the fierce individualism that seamen demonstrated in other ways. The sailor's grapevine compared ships and officers, while men quickly identified new ships and refreshed their memories of familiar ones. Second, shantying and cheering were the two loudest and most boisterous forms of sailor communication. They required group cohesion, and strong peer pressure to participate in full. Cheering was a way for regimented male groups to express themselves, common in military and maritime contexts, and also in schools.

Finally, the ceremony established a community of purpose and experience for those sailing far into southern latitudes. The symbolism of the Southern Cross is important, because many seafarers never saw it. Most of the world's major shipping routes, and especially the steamship tracks, were in the northern hemisphere, and it was possible to have a varied career at sea without ever crossing the Equator. The constellation reinforced the self-image of the Cape Horn sailors not only in relation to stay-at-home landsmen, but to other – and in their minds, lesser – kinds of seafarers.

The shantying and cheering at Iquique was an unusual case, and Clements recounted it in great detail as an anthropological spectacle. There was no equivalent in European ports, or on passenger ships, or anywhere that non-seafarers might witness it. Yet if sailors took pride in the closed world of seafaring, and did not willingly share their culture with outsiders, most of the detail of sailors' songs and stories was nevertheless rooted on shore and in the time they spent in port. As will be discussed in the next chapter, what seemed to be the total institution of the sailing ship could never escape the land, however much seafarers liked to make a show of their wandering independence.

WORLDLY GOODS AND HABITS

Seafarers lived in a complicated material culture, surrounded by equipment, tools, machines, and fittings that intrigued and bewildered new sailors. They also wore clothing unique to their occupation. Many of our authors went further, identifying personal possessions, and attachments to objects or habits, as important elements in seafarers' lives that they wanted to convey to their readers. The fact that seafarers had belongings at all sometimes surprised authors, given how often sailors were characterised as footloose men who arrived on board ill-equipped, and who deserted with only the clothes they stood in. But several authors point to a material culture of seafaring, a habit of collecting meagre but meaningful items that men protected and secured as far as possible. Inventories of sailors who died at sea reveal a wide range of possessions, ranging from clothes and tools to more domestic items.[49]

Almost every sailor carried a knife. While this was primarily a tool for everyday work, it took on additional significance in times of danger. A knife could be the means of saving lives, or even the ship, when rigging had to be cut away, or sailors had to extricate themselves from tangled ropes or sails. It was also a weapon when the threat was human rather than elemental. Several authors reported their fascination with knives as boy sailors, much to the exasperation of their elders. Melbourne Garahan recalled that the most prized part of his initial seafaring kit was 'a huge jack-knife' that his parents confiscated until it was time to join his ship.[50]

For all that, British seafarers liked to associate knife-fighting with foreigners. Walter Dexter called it 'a low-down thing,' and reported that he had made a point of beating knife-wielding sailors to demonstrate what he regarded as the superiority of gentlemanly fist-fighting.[51] Although most accounts alleged that knives were a particular proclivity of unmanly southern Europeans, they sometimes appear in tales about the berserk rages that northerners were supposedly prone to. Hans de Mierre's recollection of a fatal knife-fight on the quayside in Australia stands for many. All those involved were Finns or Swedes, and de Mierre stresses the point that the craft and technical skills of such seamen were second to none: they could 'make anything' with their knives from a bit of timber. De Mierre was therefore surprised to find such noble men using knives as weapons.[52] Most ship's mates emphasised their disdain of knives by carrying belaying-pins – wooden rods used for securing ropes, which essentially served as truncheons – believing that these placed them morally above any knife-carrying seaman.

Other aspects of seafarer culture mixed manly expectations with the life-cycle rites of passage that young mariners associated with becoming accepted into proper manhood. Tobacco carried a great deal of symbolic weight in terms of gender, age, and class. It was forbidden to respectable children, yet almost universally accepted in men. The decision whether or not to become a smoker offered young seamen a chance to assert a new individuality, one way or another. Some boys signed pledges to avoid tobacco in this period, akin to the better-known anti-alcohol tactics of the temperance movement. Smoking became a muddled indicator of respectability and manliness, with competing pressures on boys to take sides.[53]

Bill Adams remembered being encouraged to smoke by the senior apprentice on his first ship, who emphasised tobacco's restorative qualities in difficult working conditions: 'a pipe'll damn near save a chap's life sometimes.'[54] Although it was a social activity during the dog watches, smoking was usually couched in memoirs as a more individual practice. Its morale-boosting qualities were invoked in the more isolated phases of the seafarer's day, when ship-board routines and discipline could force men to live almost in parallel with others rather than together. Fred Farmer thought tobacco was a solace to sailors, 'as with most men who live solitary lives.'[55]

At the same time, smoking provoked a puritan streak in some writers, especially when they connected it to perceived moral failings on the part of their crews. Madden Jardine reported an unusual aspect of his crew's need for tobacco in Rio de Janeiro. Having refused to work unloading cargo, the crew held a debate in the forecastle about whether to give in to the captain and start work again, or face being sent to jail on shore. One of the crew voted for jail, although he warned the others of the greatest hardship of incarceration, the lack of tobacco. In a pointed yarn, he recalled his time in jail in Calcutta, when his sanity was saved by a visit from crewmates who smuggled him some tobacco. Another man agreed that were it not for the tobacco ban, foreign jails would be full of British seamen because they were otherwise an amenable alternative to being on most ships.[56]

The use of tobacco in different forms was a signal of seafaring manhood often performed for the benefit of those on shore, albeit with varying consequences that were entangled in class and social expectations. When Hans de Mierre returned home from a voyage as an apprentice and casually produced a Hamburg cigar, his businessman father proudly shouted 'good boy!'[57] The message was slightly different for lower ranks, however. William Crutchley worked his passage home from Australia before the mast after he deserted his apprenticeship, and learned to chew tobacco, 'so that I might be able to demonstrate undeniably to my people at home the fact that I was an AB.' He duly reported his mother's horror when she met him at the quayside.[58]

Some authors remembered tobacco as a prevalent ship-board currency, which made life awkward for non-smokers.[59] Apprentices who were determined to abstain found that they still needed to engage with the tobacco economy. James Bisset was caught in a boyish dilemma midway through his apprenticeship, having watched a sailor spend a year making a ship in a bottle. Bisset wanted to buy it to take home to his mother, but the sailor asked for payment in tobacco, which was more use to him than cash. Bisset, a determined non-smoker, had to overcome his embarrassment and approach the captain for some tobacco credited against his eventual wages. This uncomfortable conversation just emphasised that Bisset was still a boy. He had to assure the captain that he would not smoke the tobacco himself, and also persuade him that this was a good use of the allowance that he was supposed to be conserving against any profligacy.[60]

Bisset's interest in sailor craftwork was part of a broader cultural assumption that seafarers were experts at carving, sewing, and small-scale artificing in general. This was a masculine coding of technical skill, but also of ingenuity, and in making good use of unpromising raw materials. It sat on a continuum, with men like bosuns and carpenters expected to be able to save their ships by rigging clever fixes in emergencies, while all sailors should turn out rope-work, rag-rugs, or ships in bottles. Most authors represented this as an affirmation of tradition, and a wholly positive, even sanitised, image of the sailor. Very occasionally, though, we hear of sailor craftsmanship doubling as an ironic comment on working and living conditions. John Wilson recalled sailors carving small boxes not from wood, but from chunks of salt beef so old as to have acquired similar properties.[61]

There also seems to have been a division between what was acceptable activity on and off duty. Rex Clements reported that his captain was happy to teach apprentices intricate knots and splices, but that they had to practice in their off-duty hours; to make fancy rope work on duty would have been 'effeminacy.'[62] Presumably this was to stop apprentices wasting time on elaborate work when simple versions would do for everyday use, but it is revealing that the rule focused on whether these were properly manly activities during deck watches. Although former captains have little to say about their own craft activities in memoirs, we know from surviving examples that they made items for their children, just as ordinary seafarers did, and remained part of the material culture that connected their ship and shore lives.[63] Still, their silence probably indicates some unease about whether such work was entirely in keeping with the management and command of the ship at sea.

Sailors kept their possessions in another iconic piece of seafarer material culture, the sea-chest. The chest and its contents were personal and individual, a small but valued element of private space in crowded, communal living quarters. Former apprentices recalled a moral code whereby they never locked their chests, trusting each other not to open anyone else's. Leslie Morton wrote of an apprentice named Stutter who attracted suspicion by locking his chest; he turned out to have been stealing other boys' tinned fruit and luxuries, and was duly beaten for his crimes in a story that could come straight from a public school memoir.[64]

However, the sea-chest also served more collective, ritual purposes. Albert Bestic and Charles Protheroe both wrote of the Sunday tradition of the 'sailors' pleasure,' in which off-duty seafarers turned out their sea-chests to dry and repair clothes, compare unusual items, and then re-pack everything in good order. When Bestic's apprentices did this, it could take hours, punctuated with storytelling inspired by the old photographs and letters they found in the process.[65] Early in his apprenticeship, Frank Worsley was surprised to find that a sailor nicknamed 'Cockroach' had a great pride in his possessions, and was happy to show Worsley the numerous trinkets he kept tidily in his sea-chest. These ranged from sharks' teeth and a pipe made from an albatross bone, to three prized photographs – of his mother, a woman he called his 'regular tart,' and a sailor chum long since drowned. Worsley was fascinated, not least because 'Cockroach' seemed otherwise to be one of the more disreputable members of the crew.[66]

Frank Symondson paid more attention than most to sailors' material culture, perhaps because he appreciated the contrast between such concerns and his own disappointment about the conditions he faced during his first and only voyage. Symondson emphasised the sentimentality of sailors who clung to keepsakes: 'Jack has more of sterling good in his chest than lands-people credit him with – relics of past voyages; bygone years' little gifts from home, perhaps given when he was a boy, and to which he clings fondly, though he may not have seen that home for many long years.' Married seamen had even more emotionally valuable items, Symondson thought, although almost every sailor kept something that would bring to mind 'his Poll.'[67]

Symondson also describes the tradition of selling a dead man's effects to raise money for his dependents, a ritual that linked the living with the dead, and sailors with those left behind on shore. After a man called James Johnson was lost overboard, the sale of his effects was a theatrical and cathartic affair. Johnson had come on board in Hong Kong for the voyage back to England, and seems to have had a range of clothing: 'trousers, boots, Crimean shirts, dungarees, ducks, go-ashore togs.' The mate took a jocular turn as auctioneer amid laughter at the condition of some of the clothes. He marketed an old tarry pair of dungarees as an 'elegant sailor-like pair of trousers,' and sold them to the cook for four shillings. Someone paid £2 for a nearly new pilot coat. Only Johnson's Chinese sea-chest itself went unsold, perhaps, thought Symondson, because of some superstition.[68]

The use of a dead man's belongings to show respect for him and his family appears in many memoirs, and authors believed it demonstrated honour and nobility among shipmates. Men would pay inflated prices so that the dead sailor's family might receive some compensation.[69] Occasionally, though, we see another side. Frank Bullen recalled an instance when a crew member drowned in the dock before the ship had even sailed. Unusually, the rest of the sailors rushed to divide up his clothing, so that they would be better prepared for the voyage.[70] They had not yet come to know the lost man, or each other, so perhaps the ritual surrounding the sale of relics only became relevant during the voyage, as the crew coalesced into a unit and individuals identified with their shipmates. In port before setting sail, men's relationships were still impersonal and mercenary, and a man's possessions lacked the meaning they would acquire during the voyage.

Our authors chose to cast a good deal of light on the material culture of seafaring men, perhaps not least because they thought readers might be pleasantly surprised by such suggestions of domestic habits, and of attachments to their people on shore. Henry Hughes sailed with a crew that had previously worked on ancient, filthy collier ships, and he thought they made the most of the chance to create a comfortable space on their new vessel. As well as keeping their forecastle clean, they furnished each bunk with photographs of their families and with trinkets and mementos.[71] As always, though, we have to recognise that such representations are really commemorations of a lost sector, rooted in the long, uncertain voyages, and traditional seafaring skills and craft of the sailing ship. By the time most of our authors were writing, the new steamship crews had worked on timetabled voyages for decades, saw their families every few weeks, and were not at sea long enough to make sculptures from shark bones.

*

Seafarer culture was complex in itself, but translating it for the benefit of the reading public's expectations was one of the harder tasks facing memoir-writers. Its opacity was one of the strongest indicators of its authenticity, and readers were probably suspicious of sea stories that did not bombard them with bewildering language, boisterous singing, and a range of stereotypes about pipe-smoking and ships-in-bottles. At the same time, our later authors knew that their accounts looked back on a seafaring world that had already been broadly represented in sea fiction, and in earlier memoirs. While some could still offer unusual material, like Rex Clements's testimony from the guano coast, there is a real sense that later authors were struggling to contribute anything new.

Some of our memoir-writers were also conscious that simply publishing their memories placed them outside important aspects of sailor culture. Several authors noted that sailors were reluctant to tell their tales to outsiders, not least because they did not know how to translate their jargon and rough language for the benefit of respectable people. Walter Runciman, for example, blamed seafarers' clannishness in part for the low profile of the shipping industry: however garrulous they were among their peers, nothing could persuade sailors to talk that way with landsmen.[72] Our authors decided to speak for their former shipmates, but in so doing they contradicted their own efforts to maintain the persona of the 'simple sailor,' unaffected by the wider literary imaginary of seafaring.

9

Looking Landward

While time at sea takes up most space in maritime memoirs, authors knew that the shore was crucial to seafarers' self-image, and also to representations of the seaman in popular culture. The waterfront districts of major seaports were a battleground for conflicting visions of seafaring manhood, as some sailors quietly went home to their families and others became embroiled, more or less voluntarily, in the vice and depravity associated with bar-and-brothel sailortowns. Many seafarers looked forward to what they called 'a good run ashore,' and did not always see a contradiction between respectability at home and brazen behaviour abroad. Transient seamen complicated the already debatable meaning of 'home' as an indicator of class, gender, family, and respectability. There were life-cycle changes too, as attitudes to being on shore evolved with age, rank, and responsibility. Much has been written about the sailortown phenomenon in recent years, and this chapter does not attempt to summarise it.[1] Rather, it asks what our authors wanted to convey about their sense of being seafaring men on shore, and how they wanted to contribute to that established public perception.

Most obviously, going ashore was to arrive in a world of women. Journalists, politicians, and social reformers periodically recycled the riotous, scandalous spectacle of 'Jack and his Jill,' crowded into waterfront streets. At the same time, they praised the wives, mothers, and sisters who provided a stable family environment for some, and the middle-class women who were prominent in missions and charities. There are few opportunities to hear the voices of these women, or indeed of the ordinary seafarers. Maritime memoirs can help to some extent, but with many limitations, not least because our authors were recalling time spent in port as boys and youths, filtered through the attitudes of their respectably-married later selves. Apprentices and officers had different experiences on shore from those of the crew before the mast, and most memoirs are thin on descriptions of bars, brothels, and boarding-houses. Authors could be judgemental about seafarers' behaviour in port without knowing much about it, and were prudish about revealing what detail they did have. Only a few memoirs mention women to any significant extent, as is a common feature of autobiography by men across social classes.[2] Many authors were so focused on work and seafaring that they barely discussed lives on shore. Such silence, an unconscious part of the worldview of our authors but frustrating to historians, inevitably reduces the pool of evidence we have about some key issues.

Those claiming to reform the lives of seafarers usually targeted aspects of their identity as men, whether it was excessive drinking, frequenting brothels, fighting, or, on the upside, breadwinning and domestic respectability. Sailortown reformers often campaigned on the emasculating effects of diseases caused by drink and vice, arguing that men who could not control themselves on shore risked losing their manly health.[3] In turn, many of the objections seafarers raised against religious missions, Sailors' Homes, and temperance initiatives were expressed as a desire for manly independence, and a reluctance to submit to institutional conformity while in port. And if the men before the mast were not expected to show much restraint, apprentices and officers knew that time on shore exposed them to situations that might compromise their reputations and damage their careers, as much as anything they did at sea.

THE PERILS OF FREEDOM

If working at sea was an expression of being free from the petty restraints of life on shore, seafarers soon learned that a commercial sailing ship had many restrictions of its own. These in turn could only be escaped by returning to the land. Over time, repeating that cycle became a way of life. The most domestically-oriented sailors visited their families, then signed on for the next voyage. Others came on shore in a nautical bubble of bars, brothels, and boarding houses, created to separate men from their wages, and to ensure that they went back to sea as quickly as possible. And all sailors arriving anywhere except their home port always had to navigate that latter kind of urban waterfront.

Sailing-ship mariners had little continuity of employment. They were paid off when their ship returned to its home port, and owners had no obligation to hire them again for the next voyage. As ever, having most of our testimony from men who always intended to be officers makes it hard to understand the worldviews of ordinary seafarers approaching such gaps in employment. Concerns about money, always rather abstract at sea, became more pressing. On shore between his early voyages, Frank Bullen feared running out of money (and therefore food and accommodation) before securing his next berth; he rushed from ship to ship, caring little which job he took. Bullen's testimony probably captures the insecurity that preyed on many ordinary seafarers between voyages. He did not consider himself free, but rather as suffering 'from the misery of being masterless.'[4] Only when he began to train as an officer, and had at least the prospect of more secure employment, did Bullen feel he could move away from a hand-to-mouth cycle.

Other seafarers appeared to embrace their transience. Large numbers deserted from their ships when they reached foreign ports in the late nineteenth century, provoking legislation and international controversy.[5] Some were labour migrants or adventurers, and a working sea voyage was their way of reaching a country with better job opportunities or an open frontier. Fred Farmer admitted that he fell into this pattern himself early in his time at sea. Working as an Ordinary Seaman in the 1890s, he was more motivated by adventure and new experiences than by building a career; when he deserted in Buenos Ayres, he had no concerns 'so long as I was seeing something.'[6] Such behaviour made it easy for shipowners and their allies to depict feckless, unreliable workers who abandoned their contracts and shipmates in the delusional pursuit of better prospects on shore. The dilemma for memoir-writers was whether to admire such men, who seemed to be perpetuating the kind of adventurous lives that many of our authors aspired to at the beginning of their careers, even if they subsequently recognised the broader damage caused by desertion.

Matters became more complicated when men were coerced or misled by the notorious crimps. These were boarding-house keepers who persuaded sailors to abscond, only to send them quickly to sea again on another ship for a profitable commission. This was a culture of violence and extortion, but arguably sailors and crimps alike suffered poverty and exclusion from respectable shore society. Evidence about crimping comes overwhelmingly from its opponents, and parts of the service offered by crimps were valuable to seafarers, especially in relation to finding accommodation and future jobs.[7] There was also much hypocrisy, because ship's captains did not hesitate to hire sailors from crimps.

Some authors expressed outrage about the treatment of sailors on shore. John Masefield remembered crews arriving in Liverpool after long voyages. At sea, he thought, these men 'had known only manhood and shipmates: now they were ashore among scum and sneak-thieves.' Worse, having endured such hardships for the profits of shipowners, no one on shore seemed to care.[8] Charles Dixon, writing after a long career as a captain, thought that falling into the hands of crimps took away a seaman's liberty, not just on that occasion, but in the long term: 'a sailor seldom battled his way back to the old rugged freedom.'[9]

Even the kinder commentators criticised seafarers for being apathetic and fatalistic, simple souls who could not be trusted to look after their own interests. Walter Dexter recalled sailors at sea threatening great retribution against crimps, only to go along with them again at the next port.[10] Exhausted by long and difficult voyages, some men seemed not to mind which ships they sailed in, and believed that they had little power to make their lives better or worse. While admiring the physical strength of their shipmates at sea, memoir-writers equally doubted their moral and mental resilience in the face of temptations on shore.

From whatever perspective, therefore, debates over the character of the merchant seafarer, and whether or not he was a responsible working man, often focused on a supposed spiral of on-shore behaviours that led to desertion. Most authors thought drink was the first step. Almost all accounts of ships arriving in port have them being met by boarding-house runners who plied sailors with liquor, often assumed to be laced with sedatives. If they made it to a waterfront bar, the dangers multiplied; bartenders and the women who frequented those bars were all reckoned to be agents of the crimps. Most authors claimed to have been abstemious themselves. William Lord admitted going ashore in Spain with his crewmates, but only to buy fruit in the market.[11] Arthur Rostron expressed sympathy with those who sought comfort and escape in port, but hurried to insist that he was not among them: 'beer was not to my taste, and as for the other "attractions" of life in port, they had no lure for me.'[12] While Henry Moffat told some picaresque tales of sailors carousing on shore, he was a 'total abstainer' himself.[13]

We have, therefore, rather little first-hand testimony about the entanglements of crimps, seafarers, and the sailortown complex of freedom and exploitation. What we do have is often self-justifying, as authors tried to explain away poor conduct. William Crutchley, for example, deserted from his apprenticeship in the 1860s after a violent falling out with his captain in Australia. He got a job as an Ordinary Seaman on another ship, and his experience points to the cynicism of all involved. Crutchley's new captain was short of crew, was willing to overlook Crutchley's desertion, and even lent him the money to pay his fine.[14] This amoral behaviour by captains was part of the reason desertion persisted; captains knew that owners cared far more about the progress of their own ships than abstracts like the causes of desertion.

Pryce Mitchell offers an unusual perspective, claiming not only to have been the victim of crimping, but to have worked for a crimp. Having deserted from his ship in Melbourne in the late 1870s, Mitchell worked for a boarding-house keeper called Mother Doyle in exchange for her protection from the authorities. After a while, in his telling, he confronted her about the mistreatment of sailors, resulting in him being 'shanghaied' back to sea. While careful to call crimping 'an unspeakably rotten business all through,' he saw this as excusable adventure-seeking behaviour for a young man exploring the world. Mitchell even claimed parental endorsement; his father forgave his activities on the grounds that he had learned self-reliance at such a young age, and Mitchell was able to resume his career.[15] That sense of entitlement, of a world in which manly self-discovery justified the suffering of others and the loosening of moral codes, underpins much behaviour on shore, although Mitchell's account is unusually transparent.

Mitchell's tale also raises the gendered representations of crimps. Much of the fascination and fear provoked by Mother Doyle came from the fact that she was a woman wielding power and influence in a man's world. Male crimps were also discussed on a spectrum of masculinity. Authors characterised 'runners,' who did the dirty, violent work, as primitive sorts, little better than beasts of burden drawn from a waterfront slum-dwelling underclass. While acknowledging their physical toughness, authors had no doubt about their unmanly character, full of deceit and corruption, with no sense of fair play or justice. Rather than get honest, manly jobs themselves, they preyed on sailors.[16]

Perhaps oddly, though, authors could understand why seafarers fell under the spell of the wealthier crimps – whatever else they might have been, these were imposing, charismatic men. Leading crimps had a reputation for flamboyant clothing, designed to impress seamen who liked to make a visual impact themselves when on shore, but also as an ironic indicator of prosperity and respectability. John Mason claimed that his crew rescued a notorious San Francisco crimp named Franklin from drowning in the harbour, and were struck by his clothing, jewellery, and $200 watch; even at death's door, Franklin persuaded the steward to desert, threatened the mate, and was clearly a power on the waterfront.[17]

Other accounts cast crimps as cool men of business. Charles Dixon recalled his meeting with the Rio de Janeiro boarding-master Steve Breen in the 1890s, when Dixon was working as an Able Seaman on his father's ship. This encounter caused Dixon some soul-searching, wondering how his father ('the most honourable of men') could not only work with someone like Breen, but be friendly with him. Breen was suave, well-dressed, and dangerous, but more like a lawyer or banker than a sailortown thug. Dixon had to accept that captains in foreign ports were pragmatic, and that the demons of forecastle gossip might turn out to be soft-spoken, modern men in sharp suits.[18]

If few of our authors admitted to familiarity with sailortown boarding-houses and bars, they were more forthcoming about institutions that hoped to reform and rescue the seafarer from waterfront dangers. The second half of the nineteenth century saw a global movement of religious mission organisations, alongside the usually secular Sailors' Homes, intended to provide morally safer alternatives to boarding houses.[19] They had a mixed record of engagement with seafarers. To Walter Dexter, such places were 'smug and respectable,' full of what the seafarer regarded as rules and hypocrisy; the freedom of the boarding-house, whatever its drawbacks, seemed preferable in a seaman's self-image.[20]

Mission pastors were a particular focus of attention. John Bain thought that flowery preachers offended seafarers by appropriating nautical metaphors; in the cult of practical seamanship, everyone could tell immediately that the minister had never been to sea.[21] Other authors, though, believed that seafarers could accept some pastors as manly role models. Recalling time on shore in the first decade of the twentieth century, Rex Clements thought such preachers were 'the finest type of sky-pilot – real "men" as well as parsons,' and were willing to do visiting seafarers 'a good turn.'[22] Clements's testimony points to deeper assumptions about the place of religion in seafaring masculinity: it was not something to make a fuss about, and it was manifest in upright and manly behaviours rather than piety.

John Mason invoked another masculine trope, claiming that padres working for the Missions to Seamen in the 1890s literally fought crimps in the Pacific ports of the Americas. Men like Kearney in San Francisco or Hardy in Valparaiso were, Mason claimed, well-known as 'fighting parsons,' able to match seafarer standards of manly conduct, despite being in a profession that was easy to dismiss as effeminate. Even Mason believed, however, that it was apprentices who benefited from the efforts of mission staff, and that many ordinary seafarers kept their distance and preferred the alternative waterfront institutions of the bar and boarding house.[23]

Rex Clements's point about preachers doing sailors a good turn reflects a widespread view: mission activity was more successful with adult sailors when it toned down doctrinal teaching and offered social and economic support. By the early twentieth century, missions also had an increasing sense of national cultural purpose, as the major seafaring countries established institutions abroad to offer itinerant seamen a means of connecting with their homelands.[24] Partly an effort to improve the reputation of their nation's seafarers in other countries, mission activity could expose competing ideas of masculinity. Seamen sometimes resisted pastors' attempts to send wages back home, for example. Even when seafarers acknowledged that they should be aspiring to a breadwinning role, they also wanted to be good shipmates who would freely spend money for the benefit of all those around them.[25] Missionaries promoting one kind of manliness while failing to recognise the other threatened to emasculate and infantilise seafarers, and drive them away from their services.

For all that mission padres exercised a restraining influence on apprentices during their time on shore, boys still assumed they could let off steam when they were away from the ship. Some authors thought apprentices should be forgiven what they called 'skylarking.' This could involve fights with locals, petty thefts, and anti-social behaviour, and often involved a degree of nationalistic superiority and entitlement. Herbert Lightoller thought that 'other nations don't appreciate the Britisher's love of a skylark, particularly when played by a set of boys.' For all that he celebrated bad behaviour by apprentices on shore, though, Lightoller claimed this was a very different thing from the real dangers of the waterfront. Writing of the 'dives' he encountered in American ports, he thought that visiting one really was 'a dive, morally, intellectually and physically.'[26] It is no accident that 'skylarking' seems more akin to a public school, boys-will-be-boys culture than the perils of sailortown.

Some of our authors struggled to strike a balance, both in their behaviour at the time and in their subsequent testimony. Leslie Morton's memories of a drinking session in New York when he was an apprentice were conflicted. Although with hindsight he felt he had to disavow such behaviour, he was frank about its impact on his self-image and his sense of belonging in a properly masculine environment: 'it all seems very petty and sordid now, but how manly it felt to be in the company of such he-men on that occasion.'[27] Morton knew that this behaviour was especially transgressive because it happened on shore; listening to a forecastle yarning session by similar he-men on his ship would have been less daring. That thrill and pride in just being associated with such men suggests that many of our authors may not have been hiding nefarious behaviours on shore when they crafted their memoirs. Perhaps it really was enough for them as apprentices to stay on the sidelines, enjoying the spectacle while keeping the distance that would preserve their reputations and career paths. As the next section shows, this was certainly the case for many authors when they discussed their associations with women.

WOMEN'S COUNTRY

Although sailing-ship mariners lived and worked in a male society at sea, they went on shore into a world of women. Maritime mythology had long-standing assumptions about what that meant, with clichés about sailors who had wives in every port, and women who had husbands on many ships. Such ideas were jocular or scandalous depending on who was telling the tale.[28] Merchant seafarers therefore offer another example for debates around the sexual morality of Europeans abroad, which to date have often been conducted around histories of the fighting navy and of army regiments. Research in those areas has revealed strategies of surveillance, medical intervention, and bureaucratic processes to control, or at least channel, sexual behaviour by men, while usually directing the most intrusive efforts at regulating women.[29]

In fact, while many commentators were outraged by the activities of merchant seafarers and women in sailortown districts, the British state chose not to apply the most punitive regulatory regimes at its disposal. The notorious Contagious Diseases Acts, implemented in naval ports, army towns, and a number of colonies in the third quarter of the nineteenth century, were not extended wholesale to Britain's commercial seaports, despite campaigning. Politicians and officials made a distinction between state-employed Royal Navy sailors and commercial seamen, apparently concluding that regulating the behaviour of the latter was either an overreach of the state's role, or a logistical impossibility.[30]

That limit to state surveillance, however, did not mean that our authors felt any licence on shore, and former apprentices certainly remembered being scrutinised in foreign ports. Missions deployed matronly women to remind apprentices of their mothers, and of their respectability as officers-to-be, openly pandering to stereotypes about hearty boys who were doubtless obsessed with food after a long voyage, and who could thereby be steered away from anything less wholesome. Albert Bestic remembered that 'the ladies of the Mission to Seamen' in Fremantle, Australia, had a hamper waiting for his ship's apprentices when they arrived in port around 1910. The boys thought this was 'jolly decent,' but did not ponder the gentle nudging behind the gift.[31] James Bisset got the point more clearly: the ladies at Melbourne Seamen's Mission in 1900 'were motherly and kind and gave us a reminder of home' in the form of tea and cakes, and singsongs round the piano.[32]

Writing decades after the event, most authors resisted telling whatever tales there were to tell about encounters with women. Perhaps some of this was due to the coyness of the publishing business during the memoir boom of the 1920s and 1930s, but even when it became possible to publish racier stories, most authors insisted that their connections with women had been naive and innocent. This fits with other studies, which have found that many people from all social classes in the late nineteenth and early twentieth centuries were ignorant about sex, often intimidated by members of the opposite sex, and keen to behave in what they considered proper ways toward them.[33] Often derided as a culture of denial, secrecy, and suppression (which it certainly was), it might sometimes be viewed as a respect for privacy, and the maintenance of a boundary between public and private lives.[34] That was certainly the way most of our authors wanted to represent it to their readers.

There are many examples. Hans de Mierre and William Jones wrote similar accounts of their time on shore in Australia early in the twentieth century, meeting the daughters of respectable families at what read like Edwardian church picnics, or country-house visits. For de Mierre, everything was 'very sedate,' and he claimed to value a sophisticated, middle-class propriety that expected innocence in young men as well as women. He emphasised this by criticising his captain – 'very much the simple sailor' – who embarrassed everyone with some clumsy innuendo.[35] Jones and his fellow apprentices also appreciated Australia for 'the opportunity of meeting women and girls of a nice kind, on shore, speaking our own language.' His recollections are as much about food and showing off his uniform as they are about the girls he was promenading with. Race and nationality, as well as class, helped apprentices feel comfortable in Australia. Jones's first foreign port of call had been Pisagua, Chile, and he wrote in derogatory terms that Indian pedlars and prostitutes were the only women to be seen. There were none of the 'beautiful *señoritas*' he and his fellow apprentices claimed to have dreamed about.[36]

Authors often wrote about women with self-deprecating humour. Melbourne Garahan had his 'first love affair' with a nurse through the Seamen's Mission in Newcastle, Australia, but doubted if she noticed his 'dog-like admiration and devotion.'[37] James Barker claimed to have been struck dumb in the presence of women when he was a young sailor, fulfilling another common stereotype about awkward boys. He also recalled his old captain Simon Gunn's suggestion that Barker should marry one, or even both, of his daughters, as an indication of Gunn's quaint eccentricity, although doubtless Gunn had been amusing himself at the expense of his strait-laced junior officer.[38] Walter Dexter thought he had learned a lot about sex from the yarning of sailors, but claimed he and his fellow apprentices were content to just walk past and talk to the women who solicited outside the dockside brothels: that was enough to 'play with fire' and have something to boast about. They would also sneak into bars, and dream of running away with the barmaids, but always went back to their ships.[39]

At the same time, authors thought the crew before the mast saw shore encounters with women differently, believing that in their eyes a seaport was a huge brothel, existing to serve the base instincts of arriving seafarers. In a few cases, authors stated this as an obvious truth needing little elaboration; in others, it was part of their struggle to understand the motivations of the men they were observing. It is no accident, however, that open discussion of sexual attitudes is rare in the memoirs of those who adopted the plain-speaking-sailor persona, and that we find most discussion in the writing of authors who saw themselves as literary men. Even there, reticence is common.

Liam O'Flaherty, for example, thought Rio de Janeiro was a place of astonishing beauty, but also an object of his desires: 'it seemed to lie before me, waiting for ravishment.' All the talk in the forecastle, he wrote, was about women, and he had one of his crewmates claim that, 'It's all one big whorehouse. I wish I were ashore.' But O'Flaherty next wrote that he was 'exceedingly mortified' when a newsboy approached him on the street in Rio and offered to direct him to a brothel: locals clearly believed that sailors on shore were not only easily recognisable, but had only one thing on their minds. The irony, however, was that O'Flaherty actually was looking for the red-light area. He claims in his memoir that he had no intention of visiting prostitutes, and just wanted to see for himself what the fabled brothel district of a city like Rio looked like.[40]

Leslie Morton's experience of Callao as an apprentice was confusing and conflicting. He was taken to a brothel by the second mate, 'Mr McWattie,' but only to ensure that McWattie got back to the ship safety when he was drunk. There seems to have been a code that apprentices under officers' protection were not served drink or solicited by women. Morton was even told to wait outside the brothel because it was no place for children. Thinking that he had grown up a lot during his first voyage, this brought Morton back to earth, and he felt that his 'manhood was sorely impaired.'[41] Typically, though, Morton's account of McWattie's visit to the brothel focused on drink, rather than the uncomfortable topic of sex. The lesson Morton drew at the end of the story was about McWattie's ability to turn out for duty a couple of hours after apparently drinking himself unconscious. For Morton, that was clearly a more appropriate indicator of McWattie's masculinity for discussion in his memoir.

James Bisset, whom we last encountered with the 'motherly' ladies at Melbourne Seamen's Mission when he was an apprentice, told a different story later in his memoir, but within careful limits. Bisset completed his apprenticeship in Callao, and signed on as an Able Seaman for the voyage back to England, where he would take his exam for second mate. Before the ship sailed, though, that change in status meant he could go ashore 'as an A.B. free to do as I liked, and I was determined to sample the "flesh-pots."' In fact, Bisset made clear that while most of the crew went off with women, he and a respectable shipmate merely drank and ate too much. They became embroiled in a bar fight by bad luck, he claimed, and had to be bailed out by their captain.[42] For all his bravado, then, Bisset's story of fleshpots was anything but. The vices of sailortown were conducted out of sight, by the rougher men of the crew, while Bisset only admitted to some youthful exuberance around drink and fighting.

If most authors had little to say about seafarers and women, they wrote even less about the women themselves. On the rare occasion when we do meet women with names and personalities, they often just represent the author's bewilderment about being on shore, and a sense that his attitudes were becoming coarse and mercenary. When Bill Adams went home to stay with his aunt after his first voyage as an apprentice, he struggled to fit in. Awkward among non-seafarers, he had little sense of whether it was night or day, and would get soaked in the rain without noticing. Adams met a girl called Annie, and spent much of his leave with her. Tellingly, he invented a fictional male friend to avoid his aunt's disapproval. As soon as he started back to his ship, though, Adams claimed that he forgot Annie, because 'I was a sailor.' He traded Annie's photograph for food with another apprentice, and later in the voyage gave her bracelet to a girl working in an Oregon brothel as payment for her services.[43]

Adams used the idea of Annie to assert his manliness in relation to the other apprentices, without, he conceded, giving her any thought for weeks on end. Adams's attitudes to women also reinforced other elements in his developing sailor persona. The three women whose photographs he and fellow apprentices swapped around were nicknamed 'Fore, Main and Mizzen' after the ship's masts. More generally, he approved of seafarers who could walk away from women without hesitation. His ship's new first mate confessed that he had joined on a whim, just because the vessel looked beautiful at the quay, and despite being due for a holiday with a 'grand woman,' who 'gave me hell for chucking her for a ship.' To Adams, this indicated a man with the right priorities, and it 'tied me to him for good and all.'[44]

Albert Bestic also wrote of apprentices swapping photographs and stories of the women they left behind, and while he took a less cynical stance than Adams, this still had more to do with status in the half-deck than with romantic commitment. Bestic had to save 'a much thumbed photograph of my sweetheart, Daisy Green,' when it was almost washed away from his flooded quarters. Most of his mentions of Daisy then involve competition with other boys. He thought his adventures at sea might encourage Daisy to pick him over a rival at home, who would be made to feel 'small.' When a letter from Daisy caught up with him in Fremantle, Bestic thought he gained standing among the apprentices, none of whom received letters from women on that occasion.[45]

If groups of apprentices ribbed each other about girls on shore, they could become judgemental if they felt real priorities were at risk. Clifford Fenton wrote of a fellow apprentice, Dunkin, who deserted in New Jersey while denying it had anything to do with a girl called Anna. Fenton and the other boys told Dunkin cautionary tales, as if from their vast knowledge: 'lots of fellows have run away in the Colonies because of some girl,' lectured Fenton, but women were never worth throwing away a career for. It transpired that Anna's family liked Dunkin and thought he would be better off working in America rather than training unpaid on a sailing ship; Fenton sniffed that 'they did not, evidently, appreciate the apprenticeship system.' Fenton thought he was living out a vocation, and was mystified by Dunkin's rejection of that for the sake of a girl and a paying job. Dunkin's indignant denials suggest that he shared enough of that creed to be self-conscious about his actions. For all that, Dunkin went, and his fellow apprentices covered up for him with the captain.[46] Charles Dixon, when he was a captain, had a similar condescending view of his apprentices' entanglements, believing that two young men had been led astray in New Caledonia by 'pretty and seductive little minxes.' He had the apprentices brought back to the ship for their own good, and thought they looked 'a bit silly.'[47]

Shipmates' attitudes toward women offered another opportunity for judgemental authors, often in an amalgam of other stereotypes. Black seafarers were commonly subject to the racist tropes of promiscuity and immorality, although the supposed evidence offered was always second-hand or conjectural.[48] John Mason, for example, introduced his ship's steward as a West Indian who was 'fairly good looking for a negro,' but did not give his name. Mason's first sight of the steward was when three women saw him onto the ship at the start of the voyage. Although the steward said they were his wife and sisters, Mason found this 'very amusing.' Then, in Australia, the steward was fired for allegedly having two women in his cabin.[49] The overall impression in this and other memoirs is of women as contamination, whether in the minds of men who should have been thinking about their jobs, in seafarers' bodies on shore, and even in the ship itself. But racial and social prejudices also made it easy to blame some seafarers for welcoming that contagion aboard.

Some authors accepted the idea that seafarers were transient in their relationships as in everything else, but claimed that this did not mean they lacked respect for women. Arthur Mason returned to the point several times in his memoir, setting out a philosophy that was extremely convenient for the men involved, but nonetheless revealing of how Mason sought to explain some seafarer stereotypes to his readers. It was true, he thought, that sailors sought comfort with women in foreign ports, but that everyone, including their wives at home, accepted this as an inevitable part of being a man adrift in the world. What really mattered, Mason argued, was that sailors never lost their love of home and the women who cared for them there: the 'average sailor of the old school' was happy 'to be bossed by someone who is feminine and has their interests at heart.' Mason contrasted this with the immorality of the wealthy man on shore, who kept a young mistress and frequented brothels, while maintaining the façade of a respectable home life with his wife and daughters. A contented sailor, thought Mason, was in love with a woman on shore who served as his ideal, and his compass; he claimed that conventional ideas of fidelity or promiscuity could not grasp the realities of life for sailors and women, but that this led them to a higher morality, not a lower one.[50]

Older seafarers returning home to wives and families often had a difficult role to play, caused by the unpredictable voyage patterns of the age of sail. A few authors went into detail about their periodic returns to family life and the resulting relationship adjustments with the women in their lives. William Lord noted that he spent only eight months at home during fifteen years of marriage, and reported a revealing change in his status over that period. On his first visit home following the birth of a son, Lord admitted to being emotional, but couched this in terms of being 'an affectionate father,' and of showing support for his wife: 'I do not feel at all unmanly in candidly confessing that never before that moment had I felt more strongly inclined to drop a few tears – for company.' Later in his memoir, though, he had the confidence to joke that he was no longer the master at home, but only the chief mate, and that his wife had 'undivided responsibility' for managing a house full of children.[51]

Robert Ramsay was one of the very few authors who discussed his marriage regularly through his memoir. Ramsay claimed to have avoided sailortown temptations by concentrating on his 'love of the home folks, and the family circle,' and a sense that he would one day marry his own girl: there was 'nothing like the love of a good woman to keep a man straight.' He and a Glasgow girl called Aggie endured a long courtship because her parents thought him unsuitable. Finally able to marry Aggie when he became an officer, Ramsay confessed to years of drink problems that were a trial to his wife. Ironically, Ramsay's experiences overturned the usual stereotypes about the clean sea and the corrupting shore. It was the monotony of life as a junior steamship officer that exacerbated his drinking, and he eventually became sober after working as a stevedore and cargo manager in American ports. The rarity of Ramsay's testimony comes not only from his acceptance of his own character flaws and weaknesses, but his apparently sincere concern for the impact these had on Aggie. The tone and content of Ramsay's reflections on his own married life are unique among the memoirs discussed here.[52]

The idea that a good woman at home was the seafarer's best defence against the deprivations of the job was evidently common among sailors, at least in the advice they liked to give to others. Madden Jardine recounted several conversations urging him (a fifteen-year-old apprentice in the 1880s) to marry as soon as he could and avoid the fate of the rootless sailor; on other occasions he overheard men valuing their own marriages or regretting that they were single. Jardine usually links this to broader indicators of manly responsibility. In one scene, he has a man called Thomas equate marriage with financial respectability; Thomas only got married after saving his wages for eight years, and was able to move into his own home immediately after the ceremony. Later in the voyage, another seafarer spun a morality yarn for Jardine, about how he had drunk away all his opportunities since losing the woman he had planned to marry decades before; he concluded that an early marriage would save Jardine from a lifetime of regrets. Elsewhere in the book Jardine made attitudes to women serve as insights into the characters of several seafarers. One of Jardine's heroes, a man called St Ives, frequently pondered what his saintly mother would think of his actions; in contrast, both of his villains, Keely and Cockney, talked dismissively of the disposable women they encountered on the waterfront.[53]

For many of our authors, therefore, women acted as reference points for their sense of a moral self, and for the depravity of some seafarers. Only very rarely do those women come across as rounded individuals, accorded anything like the level of discussion and detail that authors gave to their shipmates, or even their ships. The presence of that world of women, somewhere out there over the horizon, was crucial to understanding the lives of sailing-ship men on long, isolating voyages. But even in their discussions of time on shore, most of our authors never went beyond its symbolic importance.

LEAVING THE SEA

Almost all our memoir-writers had left the sea by the time they wrote their books. We have some testimony about the circumstances in which their careers ended, although perhaps not as much as might be expected. There was reticence, even embarrassment, about admitting that they no longer worked at sea. This is an ironic counterpoint to another established part of seafaring culture: large numbers of seamen swore in the later stages of every voyage that they would never go to sea again, before signing up for their next ship after a short stay on shore.

There are many examples. As they fought through a South Atlantic storm, Rex Clements's group of apprentices not only talked each other into leaving the sea, but promised to denounce the life so that no one they knew would ever work on a ship. In the event, Clements admitted that the most sincere intentions 'only lasted as long as the weather.'[54] To Henry Hughes, even the best sailors showed this fickleness. He told of a man who had been at sea for fifty-five years, yet groused incessantly about it, hating the sea until he reached port, at which point he could not wait to sail again.[55] Melbourne Garahan and Charles Dixon offer more detail than most. Garahan's crewmates were going to use their accumulated wages to buy shops, restaurants, or even an orchard; one would visit his mother for the first time in years. Dixon reported men who planned to join the Post Office, and to work in a warehouse. As both authors expected, given their broader scepticism about seafarer mentalities, none of these intentions survived a few days on shore.[56]

Nevertheless, after all these abortive plans to leave the sea, there eventually came a point when men stayed on shore for good. Frank Bullen was open about the financial incentives pulling him landward, although these were linked to resentment about the limits he felt had been placed on his seafaring career. Having worked himself up from the humblest origins to serving as a mate in the early 1880s, he could go no further. At the age of twenty-five, Bullen decided to abandon 'a profession that then offered me nothing better than mate of a tramp at £6 per month, and accepted a berth in a public office ashore at £2 a week.' Bullen had a wife and child and no way to furnish a house for them.[57] What particularly rankled with Bullen was that he had worked in vain to break the pattern by becoming an officer. Coming to view seafaring as a career rather than a job made it all the harder to lose it.

Hans de Mierre, although much wealthier than Bullen at the outset, made a similar decision in the end. After fifteen years at sea, and having made the transition to a junior officer on large steamships, de Mierre was faced with many more years in the same job before he had any chance of command. He realised that men of his class and skills were paid far better on shore, and wanted to provide for his wife. Those conflicting ideas of manliness bothered him, but the breadwinning homebuilder who could hold his own among the conventional middle classes eventually trumped the seafarer. Not without some farewell histrionics, though: de Mierre thought he was going to 'join the midgets, the pygmies who wielded pens among dog-eared ledgers behind all those lighted windows.'[58]

Illness drove some of our authors on shore, as indeed it ended the careers of many seafarers. Nineteenth-century seafaring in that sense was like soldiering: while recruits doubtless expected to die heroically in battle, or in a Cape Horn shipwreck, they were actually more likely to succumb to cholera or typhoid. Those invalided out of seafaring reacted in many different ways. When

John Patterson left the sea crippled by rheumatic fever, he had already begun the transition to being a poet and writer, and seemed unperturbed by the end of the nautical chapter in his life. Seafaring had been an act of adventurous rebellion for him, and he had already collected enough experiences to provide him with the literary material he sought.[59] Bill Adams, in sharp contrast, discovered in California that he had a lung condition that made continuing at sea life-threatening, and struggled to make sense of the sudden ending of his career. He too became a writer, but remained obsessed with the sea and his time as a seafarer. He stayed at sea in his mind, Adams thought, until he was finally able to write about the experience decades later.[60]

Arthur Mason's decision to leave the sea was part of his transition from boy to man. Many factors came together for him; a general sense that his 'youth was gone' was brought home by the death of a seafarer he called Liverpool Jack, who had been his first mentor and who periodically came and went from his life for years. Mason also knew from experience that seafaring work had little culture of saving or security, and that the odds of funding his dream of a small farm beside his mother's in Ireland were slim. But it was the indifference of the sea to all this that focused his mind: 'the sea, however much she may still the thirst for change, is no husbander of men's strength against the future, and has no care for their material provision.'[61]

For Mason, then, the very timelessness that attracted a man wanting to get lost from the realities of shore-life and responsibilities – the primal continuities that formed his sense of seafaring manliness – were also those that risked making him unfit to re-join that world. The sea encouraged a state of mind that made it hard to develop beyond a certain point, and a man might find that he could only grow any further by growing out of it. Maybe here are the roots of that common perception that seafarers lived stunted, contradictory lives, combining some of the most extreme manifestations of masculinity with a strange childishness. If they stayed in sail, they became men out of time, stuck on the edges of the modern world without being part of it.

John Wilson, one of our earliest authors, claimed a number of incentives to end his three-year seafaring career in 1860. Forced ashore to recuperate from illness, he found that 'old associations and habits' had a strong pull on him. He returned to the Durham coalfield to lodge with old friends. The home comforts he experienced there were a strong factor, compared to the 'dingy, confined forecastle' of his time at sea. Finally, he was nursed by his childhood sweetheart, who soon afterwards became his wife.[62] We know that seafarers often left the sea when they wanted to marry and settle, and statistically even coal mining was safer than working on a sailing ship in the nineteenth century. While it is unusual for us to have the personal testimony of a man in Wilson's circumstances, it is reasonable to assume that he spoke for many others.

Frank Symondson's memoir concluded with the end of both his first voyage as an apprentice and his seafaring career, but is abrupt, unreflective, and even farcical. He was so keen to leave the ship that he found himself on the West India Dock Road in the middle of the night, before realising that he faced a long walk into central London. Sheepishly returning to the vessel, he left again a few hours later without any ceremony and took the train to the owners' offices to have his apprenticeship cancelled.[63] Perhaps he felt that his dissatisfaction with seafaring had already been clear throughout his memoir, and saw no need to state his views in conclusion. In another sense, though, Symondson's actions were common enough. Many authors reported that they and other seafarers would walk away from ships with a remarkable lack of sentiment, almost like a shore worker leaving his factory at the end of the day. Only in retrospect did they come to see deeper meanings to these actions.

✳

Most authors did not leave the sea at the end of their time in sailing-ships, but rather moved into the steamship sector to continue maritime careers. Tellingly, though, they used the same language, in what must have been a widespread and poignant saying: men who switched to steamships said they were 'leaving the sea to go into steam.'[64] Indeed, this sense of a fundamental change in direction, to what felt like a different way of life, comes across in the structure and content of many memoirs, even when it is not stated so explicitly.

James Barker's memoir, for example, is entirely about his time in sail, with only the briefest mentions of steam at the very beginning and end. His introduction combines sadness with the hard-headed business reality that he wanted to convey as a ship's master: 'Most horny-fisted "Old Timers," men haunted by lingering memories of more venturesome days, must experience a certain feeling of sadness with the realisation that the era of the sailing ship has passed forever. However, they will all agree that, owing to the course of events of recent years, it was inevitable.' At the end of his book, Barker simply noted that his move to steam was 'a radical change,' before concluding with a final tale of how he saw his old sailing ship once more in Hamburg, provoking memories of 'startling clarity.'[65] He had nothing to say of his two decades in steamships. Barker was, as we have seen, a man of great confidence and self-belief, but even he struggled to regard his steamship service on a par with his years in sail, and certainly not as something the reading public might be interested in. The next chapter will consider in more detail this afterlife of the sailing ship mariner, and his symbolic place in the age of steam.

Afterlives: Sailing-Ship Men in the Age of Steam

If the 1920s and 1930s were the peak decades of the sailing-ship memoir, they were also a period of soul-searching about industrial, urban modernity and the threat it seemed to pose to traditional life. Responses ranged from a reactionary rejection of all things new, through comforting nostalgia, to more sophisticated awareness of tradition and heritage in a changing world.[1] While dominated by rural manifestations of Britishness, like stately homes or village folk music, that wider cultural movement provided the backdrop for the memorialisation of the age of sail and those who worked through its later stages.

Just as sail and steam coexisted for decades in the shipping industry, so the sailing-ship memoirs of the inter-war years sat alongside new genres of writing about life at sea. Some catering, engineering, and technical seafarers published memoirs and fiction about their time in steamships.[2] Writers, critics, and commentators revisited Britain's place as a seafaring nation, in large part driven by anxiety about the lessons of the Great War. Some complained that the general public was forgetting about shipping again, as it usually has in peacetime, except perhaps for the opulent world of Atlantic liners and their movie-star passengers, captured in newsreel images against the Manhattan skyline.[3] Still, sail remained the focus of much maritime publishing. As well as the memoirs used in this book, there was a surge in voyage accounts by journalists and adventurers, who signed on Nordic sailing ships to capture what they saw as the very last of commercial sail.[4]

When so many of our authors devoted most, or even all, of their books to their time in sail, that was itself a statement. Even those who reported being happy to move into steam could not avoid the impression that the later phase was of less interest to them, and probably to their readers. Equally, regretting the demise of the old-time seafarer implied that the new steamship crews were poor successors, and cemented the idea that the only seafaring worth writing about was in the past. Seafaring autobiography was a personal expression of recollecting and ordering the author's past, but also a public act of remembrance that contributed to the collective memory of the industry and its place in the national psyche. Our authors' desire to honour life in sail pushed the current shipping industry back into the shadows, and even demeaned it, however unintentionally.

Memoirs became part of the wider movement throughout the twentieth century that equated maritime heritage with the public spectacle of 'tall ships.' It gave less profile to the reality that those ships had been, in the words of one maritime museum pioneer, 'the most dangerous form of transport ever devised.'[5] The very fact that much nostalgia seems harmless, and even affirming, makes it particularly problematic when encountered in violent or dangerous historical circumstances, and when many of the 'traditions' being celebrated turn out to have been invented quite recently, to promote narratives of imperial and national supremacy.[6] For Britain especially, the maritime history of the twentieth century has been a peculiar mix of that celebratory nostalgia and a case study in national decline. This concluding chapter pulls together some of these threads, assessing what seafaring memoirs can tell us about the broader role, and fate, of the seafaring man in twentieth-century Britain's continuing ambivalence about the sea.

⁕

Our memoir-writers held a range of attitudes toward steamships and the crews who worked in them. Fred Farmer, who sailed as an Ordinary Seaman in the 1890s and wrote his memoir in the 1920s, was probably the most outspoken. To Farmer, steamship men were just 'paint washers.' He reported that his crewmate Old Tom told of a steam voyage as if he 'had lost all self-respect and sunk deeply into some form of utter degradation.' In particular, Farmer thought that the steamship sector was unmanly. It was giving away important seafaring values by pandering to female passengers. Liner operators, he believed, saw women's views as key to their marketing, and wanted their officers to prioritise the social niceties. Old-style mates had put the ship first; as such, thought Farmer, they were respected by male passengers, but 'rarely popular with the ladies.' Everywhere Farmer looked, some aspect of modern shipping was contaminating and emasculating his seafaring men.[7]

Most authors were more ambivalent than Farmer, not least because they had made their own move into steam as officers, and whatever their feelings, could not deny a large part of their careers. They confessed to anti-steam sentiments in their younger selves, while accepting that their views had changed with the times, and with age and maturity. Also writing in the 1920s, Walter Runciman's attitude to the sail-to-steam transition was rooted in his successive careers as seafarer, shipowner, and politician. On one level, he was pragmatic. The first time he was offered a steamship command it nearly doubled his pay after years of hard work in sailing ships, and while he claimed to have 'strong prejudices' against steamers, his battle between 'judgment and sentiment' was soon resolved.[8]

Runciman also tried to locate his own feelings in a wider context. Many people had justified doubts about early steamships, he thought, but those had been steadily overcome by level-headed Victorian men, whether seafarers, builders, or owners: overall, it had been a 'wonderful' phase in the mercantile history of the world. His only doubt by the time he published his memoir in 1924 was whether the ruined world left by the war could afford steamers, or whether humanity might need to revert to old technologies and a slower pace of life.[9] Runciman captured the ambivalence of much writing about sail and steam, and the realisation that there was more than one kind of maritime Britishness. For all that sail seemed to invoke patriotic traditions going back centuries, steam's promoters could also claim to represent common national, and indeed manly, tropes – invention, technology, entrepreneurship, and empire.

Many authors evoked peer pressure about staying in sailing ships. Leslie Morton recalled his group of apprentices meeting the second mate of a steamer in port in 1912. The boys knew that this man represented their future selves, but they all assured him that they would stay in sail all the way to being captains. Morton could 'still remember the rather sardonic grin he gave us.' Morton's first exposure to the extreme end of the steamship phenomenon came three years later when he worked on the Cunard liner *Lusitania*. He was confused by the vast ship, which was 'very much not to my taste; innumerable people, noise, passengers.' His accommodation was like a 'workhouse dormitory,' three decks down: the contrast to his normal berth in the deckhouse of a small sailing ship was striking. For all that, Morton was impressed by the way the ship cut through the water at eighteen or twenty knots, a visual thrill when viewed from the porthole near his bunk. He was also fond of playing the 'real' sailor for the passengers, demonstrating how to splice wire ropes, and other skills derived from his training in sail which, completed a few months before, seemed quaint now.[10]

Authors who became public figures as senior liner captains could differ widely in their attitudes to sail and steam. By the time they wrote their memoirs, they were company men, subject to the bureaucracy of steamship firms, and managing huge floating workplaces in roles far removed from the autonomous, freebooting captains they worked for in their early voyages. At the same time, though, they claimed a continuing identity as seafarers and shipmasters. They believed in command, authority, and responsibility, amplified by the scale and complexity of the giant ships, and would not have accepted any equivalence with factory managers on shore.

Arthur Rostron, for example, claimed never to have considered working in steam during his apprenticeship in the late 1880s: 'Steam was no sort of job for a real sailor! It was for the worn-out, the decrepit, the soft-hearted.' Rostron even returned to his old sailing ship when he found his promotion path blocked in steam, claiming that he loved the work and 'wanted to be a hundred per cent sailorman.' Still, he went on to captain Cunard liners, and accepted that the industry needed a different kind of man by the 1920s: the steam-trained seafarer 'may not be an all-round sailor, but he can be a thoroughly efficient seaman.'[11]

Bertram Hayes took a more radical stance. Hayes, who served a sail apprenticeship and eventually became commodore of the White Star Line, thought anti-steam sentiments were driven by envy, and that training in sail was obsolete even as he completed his apprenticeship in the 1880s. 'Most of us,' he claimed, saw sailing ships 'as merely a means to an end. Nobody wished to remain in them any longer than he could help.' Indeed, Hayes was unusually blunt about this, when many authors hedged their bets. Hayes could see no reason why 'being half-starved in a sailing ship in one's young days' produced better steamship officers in the long run, and had 'no fear for the well-being of the Merchant Service now that sailing ships are a thing of the past.' Sail training was part of a broader conservatism in the industry that Hayes pushed against, just as he advocated less reliance on age and seniority, and earlier promotions for promising young officers.[12] Officers like him, to be sure, but the self-serving edge to his comments did not necessarily make them wrong.

Steamships did indeed change the lives of seafarers, and often for the better. Death and injury rates fell overall, because fewer men were exposed to the dangers of working at height and on wave-swept decks. Still, the stokehold crews suffered new diseases caused by hard work amid extreme heat and fumes. There were also new stigmas, with firemen and trimmers regarded as unskilled brute labourers. Depictions of steamship work became a graphic thread of modernist writing, and conditions in the stokeholds seemed to be an extreme example of the (literally) hidden depths of capitalism, as men laboured in heat and dust far from the view of the first-class passengers. Others faced worse still, as a new stateless, nomadic underclass whose tramp ships could vanish without any apparent consequence, as portrayed in writing like B. Traven's *The Death Ship* (1926), or in Eugene O'Neill's plays of the 1910s and 1920s.[13]

Changing ideas of Britishness, Englishness, class, and authority emerged from maritime memoirs in the 1920s and beyond, as authors read their own current perceptions back into the past. Indeed, seafaring was just one of many issues that seemed to speak to a collective national anxiety in this era.[14] Fear of a crisis of masculinity was often part of anti-modern and anti-industrial ideology, especially between the wars. Some maritime authors believed a great degeneration and decadence had taken place, and they held up their old shellbacks as exemplars of the kind of manhood that had been lost. Arthur Mason returned to this point more than once in his memoir, arguing that sailing-ship work had lessons far beyond the shipping sector: 'as the years drift by I can see that a Cape Horn training for our sailors to-day, nay, even for our business and society men, would make better men of the men, and men of the sissies, and perhaps help to perpetuate the strength of the human race.'[15]

Walter Runciman, too, railed against 'Machiavellian reformers' in 1920s politics and society more generally, contrasting them against his heroic seafarers. In an extended footnote to his account of an early voyage, he questioned what street agitators knew of 'real hardships' or the 'mill of hard work' that his remembered sailors had been through: 'some of them are effeminate, and others are insolent bullies; few of them have any real value in human affairs.'[16] John Mason made similar points, reflecting that merchant seafarers had saved

Britain from starvation during the Great War, while 'other classes of men on shore tried to hold the country to ransom.'[17] John Sutherland thought it fitting that old merchant sailing ships were used as 'Q' ships in the war, intended to entice German naval vessels close enough to be attacked. This heroic anachronism seemed to sum up the character of the seafarer, but also, somehow, the age of sail itself; to cap the symbolism, as we have seen, Sutherland even had Joseph Conrad as his guest on one mission.[18]

Such authors saw the seafarers of their youth as an idealised counter to the new industrial masses and their potential for revolution. Praise for manly stoicism, however, was also an argument that working men should bear their burden and know their place. Walter Dexter criticised the steamship workers of the 1930s for not accepting how well off they really were, compared with the hardships endured by his own generation: 'the old blustering, bullying, ill-fed, ill-paid life bred a race of seamen.' He thought old shellbacks had once been men apart when they went on shore, a proud attribute sacrificed by a new generation who seemingly wanted to be like other working men.[19]

Narratives of British decline continued to colour memories of maritime life and work for decades. Proper sailors had risked their lives for love of their ships, argued Fred Farmer in the 1920s, but 'that was in the days of England's greatness, before the milk-and-water days of the "dole" began to sap the character of the race and build up a nation of "work-shys."'[20] Leslie Morton, writing in the 1960s of events just before the Great War, recalled his excitement at being homeward-bound for England. While that was a common enough sentiment among young seamen, Morton gave it another layer, adding that 'in those days the name England meant England, not a shadow of England as it means today.'[21]

Always, though, we have to ask which lost England our authors were mourning. The sailing ship symbolised many versions, often mythological, and conveniently distant. Almost all writers who concluded with tributes to doughty old shellbacks had also written about deserting, malingering sailors; the superhuman captains might have more space in memoirs than the tyrannical drunks, but the latter are there nonetheless. The sail sector combined what some authors saw as the English genius for individualistic, thriving, small-firm shipping entrepreneurs with its shambles of amateur, gentlemanly muddling-through, often on the same ships, and in the same memoirs.

What, then, can seafaring autobiography tell us about these broader questions of national decline and maritime identity? Much of the long debate about British economic decay has highlighted perceived divisions between commerce and manufacturing, or between aristocratic and bourgeois cultures. The focus has been on elite society and politics, on the public schools, and on institutions of government and finance.[22] Many of our authors certainly offer support for the existence of conservative attitudes, suspicion of innovation, and rigid class structures in British shipping. Nonetheless, that industry was by any measure an international leader in the decades before the Great War. Nostalgia for the sailing ship encouraged some ships' officers to write poignant memoirs, but only after they had enjoyed long and successful careers in steamers. And even if shipowners had shared such views, it did not stop them building the world's largest steam fleets.

While the decline of Britain's maritime industries in the twentieth century certainly coexisted with sailing-ship commemoration and nostalgia, it is very hard to establish any causal link. Scholars agree in broad terms that decline was rooted in a reluctance to invest in advanced approaches from the 1920s onwards – diesel rather than steam engines, new shipbuilding techniques, and innovative types of vessels like tankers.[23] If anything, it was a persistent commitment to the age of steam that held British shipping back in the mid-twentieth century, not an even older affection for sail. In addition, shipping has demonstrated many times that it can operate successfully in the face of public ignorance and indifference, so tall-ship nostalgia in popular culture is hardly a barrier to those leading the industry.

Seafaring memoir-writers offer us some intriguing insights, but also remind us of the dangers of extrapolating those into broader theories about their industry. This is especially true for the many authors who had no such ambition, and for whom the transition from sail was a personal issue tied up in their own sense of identity. Most obviously, it signified their lost youth and the need to face, as grown men, the realities of a world that was changing as fast as they were aging. Few truly resisted the move to steam personally, nor would they have expected or even wanted their industry to remain wedded to the old technologies. It was more a question of ensuring that what they saw as valuable aspects of sailing-ship culture were retained, most obviously in the character of the proper sailor and officer.

Although James Bisset wrote as lyrically as the rest about his adventure-seeking early days at sea, he expressed little nostalgia for his last sail voyage. Nor was he embittered, and the balanced tone of his reflections is unusually clear. Looking back from the 1950s to the end of his apprenticeship in 1903,

Bisset thought he had experienced a key moment. Sailors and officers alike would only have become demoralised by working any longer in sail: 'all their skill and science, so laboriously acquired, was of little avail against the competition of mechanical power.' Small wonder they were often surly and morose; if he stayed, he feared, an inevitable souring would be the result. After six years at sea, and a voyage as second mate, he felt his 'youth had gone,' and that he had 'matured to manhood's responsibilities and the burden of care.' Bisset rounded Cape Horn for the last time on his twenty-first birthday, and while he still thought the Horn was the landmark of the proper sailor, it also represented for Bisset a reckless phase in his own life that would now give way to the order and predictability of the steamship routes. Whether or not Bisset was deliberate in the heavy masculine symbolism tied up in his closing pages, it is obvious to us – his father welcomed him home at the end of that voyage by telling him that he had done well, and that he was a man now.[24]

Bisset's testimony captures the multiple transitions made by those who moved from being sail apprentices to steamship officers at the turn of the nineteenth and twentieth centuries. As children, they had dreamed of going to sea, inspired by a pantheon of heroic British sailors, real and fictitious. As boys, they learned the ropes and lived out their fantasies. As youths, they gained their second mate's certificates, and saw themselves as the last inheritors of an ancient tradition of seafaring manhood. As men, though, most were pragmatic and reasonable, and joined the new world of steam. Years later, they used their memoirs to rationalise that path through the inevitability of modernisation, but also to indulge their nostalgia. They memorialised the men who had stayed in sail, whether the incorrigible old shellbacks before the mast, the thwarted mates who could never get promotion, or the otherworldly, eccentric captains. But they did so from a safe distance. As Frank Bullen put it in 1929, not many men with sail experience 'would leave a comfortable life ashore to renew it, no matter how much they valued the advantage it had given them, or how much they loved the old ships.'[25]

Notes

INTRODUCTION

1 Kirkaldy, *British Shipping*, appendix II.

2 Smith, *Coal, Steam and Ships*; Kubicek, 'The Proliferation and Diffusion of Steamship Technology,' 100–10.

3 Harlaftis, Tenold, and Valdaliso, *The World's Key Industry*; Boyce, *Information, Mediation and Institutional Development*; Keeling, *The Business of Transatlantic Migration*; Feys, *The Battle for the Migrants*; Tabili, *We Ask for British Justice*; Balachandran, *Globalizing Labour?*; Hyslop, 'Steamship Empire,' 49–67.

4 Graham, 'The Ascendancy of the Sailing Ship,' 74–88.

5 Craig, 'Printed Guides for Master Mariners,' 23–35.

6 Davies, 'British Shipping and World Trade,' 39–85; Sturmey, *British Shipping and World Competition*, 13–19.

7 Apollonio, *The Last of the Cape Horners.*

8 Foulke, 'Life in the Dying World of Sail,' 105–36; Gorski, '"Purely a Question of Policy,"' 1–34; Woodman, *More Days, More Dollars*, chapter 2.

9 Gorski, 'Employers' Liability and the Victorian Seaman,' 68.

10 The fundamental text remains Sager, *Seafaring Labour*.

11 Broeze, 'Militancy and Pragmatism,' 165–200; Gorski, *Maritime Labour*.

12 Carter, *Merchant Seamen's Health*; Quinlan, 'Precarious and Hazardous Work,' 281–307; Kennerley, 'Writing the History of Merchant Seafarer Education, Training and Welfare,' 1–21.

13 Burton, 'Sourcing Maritime History Over Four Decades,' 308–29; Fischer, *The Market for Seamen in the Age of Sail*; Costello, *Black Salt*.

14 Burton, "'As I Wuz A-Rolling Down the Highway One Morn,'" 141–56; Beaven, Bell, and James, *Port Towns and Urban Cultures*; Milne, *People, Place and Power on the Nineteenth-Century Waterfront*.

15 Land, *War, Nationalism, and the British Sailor*; O'Hara, 'The Sea is Swinging into View,' 1, 109–34.

16 Glenn, *Jack Tar's Story*; Vickers with Walsh, *Young Men and the Sea*; Gilje, *Liberty on the Waterfront*; Creighton, 'American Mariners and the Rites of Manhood,' 143–64; Creighton, 'Fraternity in the American Forecastle,' 531–57; Schell, *A Bold and Hardy Race of Men*.

17 Fischer and Nordvik, 'From Namsos to Halden,' 41–66; Scholl and Hinkkanen, *Sail and Steam*; Ojala et al., 'Young Lads and Old Tars,' 861–86.

18 The pioneering text was Rediker, *Between the Devil and the Deep Blue Sea*; for a more recent overview, see Parnaby, 'The Many Motivations of Jack Tar,' 199–208.

19 Gray, *Steam Power and Sea Power*; Conley, *From Jack Tar to Union Jack*; McKee, *Sober Men and True*; Colville and Davey, *A New Naval History*.

20 Symondson, *Two Years Abaft the Mast*, vi.

21 Adams, *Fenceless Meadows*, 7.

22 Mäenpää, 'New Maritime Labour?'

23 Anim-Addo, Hasty, and Peters, 'The Mobilities of Ships and Shipped Mobilities,' 337–49; Rico, *Nature's Noblemen*; Hogg, *Men and Manliness on the Frontier*.

24 Behrman, *Victorian Myths of the Sea*.

25 Burton, 'The Myth of Bachelor Jack,' 179–98; Gorski, 'Seafarers, Seafaring and Occupational Identity,' 13–17.

26 Fink, *Sweatshops at Sea*, 35–44.

27 Williams, 'The Quality, Skill and Supply of Maritime Labour,' 273–92.

28 Connell, *The Men and the Boys*; Bederman, *Manliness and Civilization*; Rotundo, *American Manhood*.

29 Baron, 'Masculinity,' 143–60; Parsons and Heholt, *The Victorian Male Body*; Begiato, *Manliness in Britain*; Rosenwein, 'Worrying about Emotions in History,' 821–45.

30 Dawson, *Soldier Heroes*; Heathorn, *For Home, Country, and Race*, 50–5.

31 Harris, *Private Lives, Public Spirit*, 8–13; McClelland, 'Masculinity and the "Representative Artisan" in Britain,' 74–91.

32 Bederman, *Manliness and Civilization*, 10–19.

33 Budd, *The Sculpture Machine*; Baron, 'Masculinity,' 147–9.

34 Brown, 'Cold Steel, Weak Flesh,' 159–61.

35 Beaven, *Leisure, Citizenship and Working-Class Men in Britain*; Taillon, '"What We Want is Good Sober Men,"' 322–6.

36 Allen, 'Men Interminably in Crisis?' 191–207; Francis, 'The Domestication of the Male?' 637–52; Griffin, *Bread Winner*.

37 Tosh, *A Man's Place*, 151–68, 196; Boyd, *Manliness and the Boys' Story Paper*.

38 Cocks and Houlbrook, *Palgrave Advances in the Modern History of Sexuality*; Clark, *Desire*; Lewis, 'Introduction,' 1–16; Maynard, 'Queer Musings on Masculinity and History,' 183–97.

39 Creighton, '"Women" and Men in American Whaling,' 195–218; Burton, '"Whoring, Drinking Sailors,"' 84–101.

40 Grass, *The Commodification of Identity in Victorian Narrative*, 31–8.

41 For example, engineers: Oldenziel, *Making Technology Masculine*, chapter 3.

42 Hackett, 'A Different Form of "Self,"' 208–26; Smith and Watson, *Reading Autobiography*; Popkin, *History, Historians and Autobiography*; Aurell and Davis, 'History and Autobiography,' 503–11.

43 Summerfield, *Histories of the Self*, 135–45; Kelly, *The German Worker*; Maynes, *Taking the Hard Road*; Burnett, Vincent, and Mayall, *The Autobiography of the Working Class*; Vincent, *Bread, Knowledge and Freedom*.

44 Baird, *Women at Sea in the Age of Sail*; Greenhill and Giffard, *Women Under Sail*.

45 Dean, *Umbala*; Williams, *Blow the Man Down!*; Costello, *Black Salt*.

46 Kennerley, 'Aspirant Navigator,' 41.

47 While most of our authors are relatively unknown, a few are the subject of biographies: Clements, *Captain of the Carpathia*; Kennerley, *Bullen's Voyages*; Lance, *Alan Villiers*; Stenson, *Titanic Voyager*.

48 Runciman, *Before the Mast – and After*, 9.

49 Dexter, *Rope-Yarns, Marline-Spikes and Tar*, 258.

50 Burton, 'The Making of a Nineteenth-Century Profession,' 103.

51 Duncan, 'Youngsters of the Seven Seas,' 128.

52 Farmer, *The Log of a Shellback*, v.

53 Klaus, 'On the Road,' 296–310.

54 Barrett, *History From the Bottom Up and the Inside Out*, 39–40; Glenn, *Jack Tar's Story*, 3.

55 *Spectator*, 19 August 1938, 314.
56 Only the first of Bisset's volumes, *Sail Ho!*, is used here.
57 Lowenthal, *The Past is a Foreign Country*, 207; Eakin, *How Our Lives Become Stories*, 100–7.
58 *The Nation and the Athenaeum*, 14 November 1925, supplement, 252.
59 Hurd, *History of the Great War*, 1:2; *Times Literary Supplement*, 10 January 1918, 15; Bone, *Merchantmen at Arms*.
60 Masefield, *New Chum*, 146.
61 See especially Clements, *A Gipsy of the Horn*.
62 Gagnier, *Subjectivities*, chapter 3.
63 Atkinson, *Victorian Biography Reconsidered*, 10–15, chapter 2.
64 Bascom, 'The Forms of Folklore,' 4–5.
65 Stewart, *The Sea Their Graves*, 12–16.
66 Foulke, *The Sea Voyage Narrative*, 13–17.
67 Summerfield, *Histories of the Self*, 169–70; Rakich, 'Savage Fakes.'
68 Cohen, *The Novel and the Sea*; Klein, *Fictions of the Sea*; Bender, *Sea-Brothers*.
69 Bullen, *The Log of a Sea-Waif*, vii–viii.
70 Wilson, *Autobiography of Ald. John Wilson*, 41; Crutchley, *My Life at Sea*, 81, 303; for W. Clark Russell, see Peck, *Maritime Fiction*, 144–8.
71 For a recent interpretation of Conrad's life and work, see Jasanoff, *The Dawn Watch*.
72 Bestic, *Kicking Canvas*, 39; Bisset, *Sail Ho!*, 41; de Mierre, *Clipper Ships to Ocean Greyhounds*, 310.
73 For example, Munro, 'The Canal Boatman,' 293–4.
74 Kennedy, 'By Land and Sea.'
75 Saunders, *Self Impression*, 4–6.
76 Moffat, *From Ship's Boy to Skipper*, 8.
77 Mason, *Ocean Echoes*, 284.
78 Mason, *Before the Mast in Sailing Ships*, 5.
79 *Academy*, 24 August 1912, 233; *Spectator*, 19 August 1938, 314.
80 Barker, *The Log of a Limejuicer*, xiii.
81 Lunn and Day, 'Britain as Island,' 124–36; Robbins, *Nineteenth-Century Britain*, 10–28; Colls, *Identity of England*.

CHAPTER ONE

1 For parallels on land, see Childs, *Labour's Apprentices.*

2 Boyd, *Manliness and the Boys' Story Paper*; Tosh, *Manliness and Masculinities*, 204–8; Peck, *Maritime Fiction*; Bristow, *Empire Boys*; Phillips, *Mapping Men and Empire.*

3 Patterson, *My Vagabondage*, 127.

4 Clements, *A Gipsy of the Horn*, 13.

5 Fenton, *The Sea Apprentice*, 6.

6 Villiers, *The Set of the Sails*, 12.

7 Ibid., 14–16.

8 Vincent, *Literacy and Popular Culture*, 56–8.

9 Runciman, *Before the Mast – and After*, 19–22.

10 Heathorn, *For Home, Country, and Race*, 75–6, 178–84; Conley, *From Jack Tar to Union Jack.*

11 Adams, *Ships and Women*, 16, 21, 36–9.

12 Runciman, *Before the Mast – and After*, 21–4.

13 Ramsay, *Rough and Tumble on Old Clipper Ships*, 3–4.

14 Mitchell, *Deep Water*, 22, 35, 38.

15 Bisset, *Sail Ho!*, 14, 21–9.

16 Randell, *I'm Alone*, 15–23.

17 Moffat, *From Ship's Boy to Skipper*, 13–17, 24.

18 Worsley, *First Voyage in a Square-Rigged Ship*, 42.

19 Garahan, *Ship Ahoy!*, 4.

20 Britten, *A Million Ocean Miles*, 23–6.

21 Bain, *Life of a Scottish Sailor*, 3, 7.

22 McCord, *North East England.*

23 Quotations in this and the following paragraph are from Runciman, *Before the Mast – and After*, 32–5; O'Flaherty, *Two Years*, 75–6.

24 Adams, *Ships and Women*, 23–8.

25 Williams, *Some Reminiscences*, 20.

26 Kennerley, 'Bullen, Frank Thomas'; Kennerley, 'Global Nautical Livelihoods,' 3–24; Bullen, *The Log of a Sea-Waif*, 2.

27 Crutchley, *My Life at Sea*, 8.

28 Jardine, *Leaves From a Sailor's Diary*, 10–11.

29 Jones, *The Cape Horn Breed*, 18, 22–3.

30 Bovill, 'Education of Mercantile Mariners.'

31 Kennerley, 'Ratings for the Mercantile Marine,' 36–8; Evans, *The Training Ships of Liverpool.*

32 Barker, *The Log of a Limejuicer*, 5–6, 13.

33 Garahan, *Ship Ahoy!*, 19, 26.

34 Masefield, *New Chum*, 1–5.

35 Mason, *Before the Mast in Sailing Ships*, 80.

36 Jones, *The Cape Horn Breed*, 35.

37 Kestner, *Masculinities in British Adventure Fiction*, chapter 1; Tosh, *A Man's Place*, chapter 5.

38 Dexter, *Rope-Yarns, Marline-Spikes and Tar*, 17, 22.

39 Barker, *The Log of a Limejuicer*, 7.

40 Bestic, *Kicking Canvas*, 18.

41 Stevens, *A Sailor Boy's Experience*, 30.

42 Bullen, *The Log of a Sea-Waif*, 25.

43 Runciman, *Before the Mast – and After*, 79–84.

44 Bain, *Life of a Scottish Sailor*, 21.

45 Crutchley, *My Life at Sea*, 18.

46 Lightoller, *Titanic and Other Ships*, 2–3.

47 McCulloch, *A Million Miles in Sail*, 32–4.

48 Adams, *Ships and Women*, 58.

49 For evidence in this paragraph and the next, see Wilson, *Autobiography of Ald. John Wilson*, 28–31.

50 *Spectator*, 29 December 1944, 604.

51 *Spectator*, 7 December 1907, supplement, 904; *Academy*, 12 December 1885, 392; *Glasgow Herald*, 21 October 1899, 9.

52 Bratton, 'Of England, Home and Duty,' 76.

CHAPTER TWO

1 Lee, *Masculinity and the English Working Class*, 19–21; Baron and Boris, '"The Body" as a Useful Category for Working-Class History,' 28.

2 Tosh, *Manliness and Masculinities*, 51; Forman, 'Race and Empire,' 109–32.

3 *Times Literary Supplement*, 18 September 1919, 498.

4 Barker, *The Log of a Limejuicer*, 10.

5 Ibid., 34.

6 O'Flaherty, *Two Years*, 77–8.

7 Dexter, *Rope-Yarns, Marline-Spikes and Tar*, 1.

8 Clements, *A Gipsy of the Horn*, 237.

9 Kim, 'Naturalism, Labour and Homoerotic Desire,' 39–62; Fussell, *The Great War and Modern Memory*, 325–33.

10 Symondson, *Two Years Abaft the Mast*, 30.

11 Clements, *A Gipsy of the Horn*, 54; Adams, *Ships and Women*, 211–12.

12 Fenton, *The Sea Apprentice*, 107, 159.

13 Brown and Begiato, 'Visualising the Aged Veteran,' 102–36.

14 Moffat, *From Ship's Boy to Skipper*, 216, 249.

15 Farmer, *The Log of a Shellback*, 142, 157, 214.

16 Jones, *The Cape Horn Breed*, 78–9.

17 Ramsay, *Rough and Tumble on Old Clipper Ships*, ix.

18 Symondson, *Two Years Abaft the Mast*, 61.

19 Fenton, *The Sea Apprentice*, 25.

20 Wilson, *Autobiography of Ald. John Wilson*, 33, 42.

21 Bullen, *The Log of a Sea-Waif*, 183.

22 Runciman, *Before the Mast – and After*, 83, 110.

23 Barker, *The Log of a Limejuicer*, xiii.

24 Press, 'Wages in the Merchant Navy,' 37–52.

25 Stevens, *A Sailor Boy's Experience*, 34.

26 Bullen, *The Men of the Merchant Service*, 163–6.

27 Moffat, *From Ship's Boy to Skipper*, 65.

28 Symondson, *Two Years Abaft the Mast*, 55.

29 Bullen, *The Log of a Sea-Waif*, 142.

30 Bestic, *Kicking Canvas*, 64.

31 Mäenpää, 'Galley News,' 257–9; Bérubé, *My Desire for History*, chapter 16; Baker and Stanley, *Hello Sailor!*

32 For ships' cooks, see Villiers, *Falmouth for Orders*, chapter 10; Bullen, *The Men of the Merchant Service*, chapters 23 and 24.

33 Fisher, 'Working Across the Seas,' 21–45.

34 Tabili, *We Ask for British Justice*; Frost, *Work and Community Among West African Migrant Workers*; Balachandran, *Globalizing Labour?*

35 Bolster, *Black Jacks*, 218.

36 Broeze, 'The Muscles of Empire,' 46.

37 Tabili, *We Ask for British Justice*, 8.

38 Costello, *Black Salt*, 106–11.

39 Bain, *Life of a Scottish Sailor*, 28–9.

40 Hackett, 'A Different Form of "Self,"' 213.
41 Vickers with Walsh, *Young Men and the Sea*, 239–41.
42 Mason, *Before the Mast in Sailing Ships*, 26.
43 Moffat, *From Ship's Boy to Skipper*, 82.
44 Bullen, *The Log of a Sea-Waif*, 9, 13, 15, 33–6.
45 Ramsay, *Rough and Tumble on Old Clipper Ships*, 11, 18.
46 Symondson, *Two Years Abaft the Mast*, 58–60.
47 Bisset, *Sail Ho!*, 36.
48 Symondson, *Two Years Abaft the Mast*, 46.
49 Clements, *A Gipsy of the Horn*, 18–20, 128.
50 Behrman, *Victorian Myths of the Sea*, 58.
51 Jones, *The Cape Horn Breed*, 78.
52 Adams, *Ships and Women*, 67, 180.
53 For example, Keane, *On Blue-Water*, 228–30; Morton, *The Long Wake*, 14.
54 Benson, *The Working Class in Britain*, chapter 1.
55 Thompson, *The Making of the English Working Class*, 913–14.
56 Gorski, 'Employers' Liability and the Victorian Seaman,' 62–75.
57 Bain, *Life of a Scottish Sailor*, 23, 120–4.
58 Lord, *Reminiscences of a Sailor*, 21–2, 37, 41, 77–8.
59 Bestic, *Kicking Canvas*, 14, 35, 37.
60 Adams, *Ships and Women*, 94.
61 McCulloch, *A Million Miles in Sail*, 102–3.
62 Gagnier, *Subjectivities*, 112–17.
63 Mason, *Before the Mast in Sailing Ships*, preface, 16–18.
64 Bisset, *Sail Ho!*, x, 51, 269–73.
65 Moffat, *From Ship's Boy to Skipper*, 64.
66 Jardine, *Leaves From a Sailor's Diary*, 61–9.
67 Benson, *The Working Class in Britain*, 151–5.
68 Dexter, *Rope-Yarns, Marline-Spikes and Tar*, 132.
69 Garahan, *Ship Ahoy!*, 48.

CHAPTER THREE

1 Goffman, *Asylums*.
2 Gorski, 'Employers' Liability and the Victorian Seaman,' 62–75; Gorski, 'Seafarers, Seafaring and Occupational Identity,' 7–8.
3 Dentith, 'Contemporary Working Class Autobiography,' 78.

4 Sager, *Seafaring Labour*, 223–4.
5 For example, Protheroe, *Life in the Mercantile Marine*, 68.
6 Jones, *The Cape Horn Breed*, 279.
7 Farmer, *The Log of a Shellback*, 153, 32.
8 Keane, *On Blue-Water*, 213.
9 Crutchley, *My Life at Sea*, 49.
10 Bestic, *Kicking Canvas*, 26.
11 Lord, *Reminiscences of a Sailor*, 17, 55.
12 Jardine, *Leaves From a Sailor's Diary*, 38–9.
13 Farmer, *The Log of a Shellback*, 236.
14 Adams, *Ships and Women*, 150.
15 Bain, *Life of a Scottish Sailor*, 8–9.
16 Hughes, *Through Mighty Seas*, 156.
17 Lightoller, *Titanic and Other Ships*, 39–42.
18 For these ideas in a literary context, see Shamir, "'The Manliest Relations to Men,'" 75.
19 Berg, *Technology and Toil in Nineteenth Century Britain*, 122–5; Childs, *Labour's Apprentices*, 78–81.
20 Bisset, *Sail Ho!*, 68–9.
21 Stevens, *A Sailor Boy's Experience*, 38.
22 Patterson, *My Vagabondage*, 183.
23 Worsley, *First Voyage in a Square-Rigged Ship*, 73, 85, 114.
24 For example, Farmer, *The Log of a Shellback*, 152; Bullen, *The Log of a Sea-Waif*, 78.
25 Adams, *Ships and Women*, 89–90, 124.
26 Ibid., 200–6.
27 Nelson, *Boys Will Be Girls*, 43–6; Cocks, *Nameless Offences*, 178; Richards, "'Passing the Love of Women,'" 92–122.
28 Clark, *Desire*, 144–58.
29 For example, Aldington, *Death of a Hero*, 23–4.
30 Mason, *Before the Mast in Sailing Ships*, 13, 38, 84–5.
31 Keane, *On Blue-Water*, 189–92, 201–10.
32 Mitchell, *Deep Water*, 33, 42.
33 de Mierre, *Clipper Ships to Ocean Greyhounds*, 91, 55.
34 Dexter, *Rope-Yarns, Marline-Spikes and Tar*, 227–30.
35 Farmer, *The Log of a Shellback*, 51.

36 Mason, *Ocean Echoes*, 64.
37 Sutherland, *At Sea with Joseph Conrad*, 134–5.
38 Lightoller, *Titanic and Other Ships*, 21.
39 Jardine, *Leaves From a Sailor's Diary*, 91–4.
40 Fenton, *The Sea Apprentice*, 76.
41 Wilson, *Autobiography of Ald. John Wilson*, 34–5.
42 Patterson, *My Vagabondage*, 32, 125, 131, 182, 237, 252.
43 Luckin, 'Revisiting the Idea of Degeneration in Urban Britain,' 242–8; Gagnier, *Subjectivities*, 112–13; D'Cruze, *Everyday Violence in Britain*.
44 Bain, *Life of a Scottish Sailor*, 21–3.
45 Jardine, *Leaves From a Sailor's Diary*, 17, 22–3, 34, 55–6, 164–5.
46 Bestic, *Kicking Canvas*, 76–7, 145.
47 Mason, *Before the Mast in Sailing Ships*, 37–8.
48 Anthony Fletcher, *Growing Up in England*, 197–204; Emsley, *Hard Men*, 165.
49 Crutchley, *My Life at Sea*, 17.
50 Mason, *Ocean Echoes*, 10–18, 77.
51 Barker, *The Log of a Limejuicer*, 12–13.
52 Hayes, *Hull Down*, 25.
53 Farmer, *The Log of a Shellback*, 241–3.
54 Ibid., 174–5.
55 Ramsay, *Rough and Tumble on Old Clipper Ships*, 98, 117, 252–4, 260–2, 277.
56 Courtwright, *Violent Land*.
57 Aubert, *The Hidden Society*, 248–58.
58 Bain, *Life of a Scottish Sailor*, 38.

CHAPTER FOUR

1 Hayes, *Hull Down*, 24.
2 Bisset, *Sail Ho!*, 17–19; Bisset's officer certificates, accessed via Ancestry.com.
3 Barker, *The Log of a Limejuicer*, 13, emphasis as in the original.
4 Villiers, *Falmouth for Orders*, 144–6.
5 Jones, *The Cape Horn Breed*, 266.
6 de Mierre, *Clipper Ships to Ocean Greyhounds*, 91.
7 Rostron, *Home From the Sea*, 6–7.
8 Runciman, *Before the Mast – and After*, 37, 70–4.
9 Bisset, *Sail Ho!*, 116.
10 Tosh, *Manliness and Masculinities*, 35.

11 Mason, *Ocean Echoes*, 67.
12 Bain, *Life of a Scottish Sailor*, 21, emphasis as in the original.
13 Runciman, *Before the Mast – and After*, 101.
14 Moffat, *From Ship's Boy to Skipper*, 198–9, 292.
15 Garahan, *Ship Ahoy!*, 228–9.
16 Burton, 'The Making of a Nineteenth-Century Profession,' 110.
17 Randell, *I'm Alone*, 106.
18 Morton, *The Long Wake*, 3.
19 Crutchley, *My Life at Sea*, 5.
20 Keane, *On Blue-Water*, 86.
21 Rostron, *Home From the Sea*, 7.
22 Garahan, *Ship Ahoy!*, 41.
23 Adams, *Ships and Women*, 140.
24 Fenton, *The Sea Apprentice*, 38.
25 Dexter, *Rope-Yarns, Marline-Spikes and Tar*, 4, 87, 110, 131, 264.
26 Mitchell, *Deep Water*, 35, 163, 196, 215, 251.
27 Gagnier, *Subjectivities*, chapter 5.
28 Worsley, *First Voyage in a Square-Rigged Ship*, 76.
29 Ramsay, *Rough and Tumble on Old Clipper Ships*, 22.
30 Lightoller, *Titanic and Other Ships*, 6–7.
31 Ibid., 72–3, 91.
32 For this paragraph and the next see Britten, *A Million Ocean Miles*, 36–44; Britten's officer certificates, accessed via Ancestry.com.
33 Moore, 'Sail, the Last Phase,' 419.
34 Farmer, *The Log of a Shellback*, 7, 15.
35 Morton, *The Long Wake*, 10–12.
36 Jardine, *Leaves From a Sailor's Diary*, 23–5, 39.
37 Runciman, *Before the Mast – and After*, 39.
38 Stevens, *A Sailor Boy's Experience*, 41.
39 Ramsay, *Rough and Tumble on Old Clipper Ships*, 44.
40 Worsley, *First Voyage in a Square-Rigged Ship*, 270–3.
41 Jones, *The Cape Horn Breed*, 25.
42 Adams, *Ships and Women*, 141.
43 Bisset, *Sail Ho!*, 116.
44 Bestic, *Kicking Canvas*, 40.
45 Morton, *The Long Wake*, 12.

46 Lightoller, *Titanic and Other Ships*, 74.
47 Symondson, *Two Years Abaft the Mast*, 69–73.
48 Fenton, *The Sea Apprentice*, 57.
49 Sutherland, *At Sea with Joseph Conrad*, 112.
50 Bain, *Life of a Scottish Sailor*, 125.
51 Ibid., 126–8.
52 McCulloch, *A Million Miles in Sail*, 186–9.
53 Clements, *A Gipsy of the Horn*, 49–51, 85.
54 Adams, *Ships and Women*, 220.
55 Mitchell, *Deep Water*, 196.
56 Bain, *Life of a Scottish Sailor*, 31.
57 Lightoller, *Titanic and Other Ships*, 87–8, 121.
58 Lord, *Reminiscences of a Sailor*, 62.
59 Randell, *I'm Alone*, 110–17.
60 Woolf, 'Joseph Conrad,' 493.
61 Conrad, *A Personal Record*, preface.
62 Bestic, *Kicking Canvas*, 191.

CHAPTER FIVE

1 Witt, '"During the Voyage Every Captain is Monarch of the Ship,"' 165–94; Burton, 'The Making of a Nineteenth-Century Profession,' 97–118.
2 Adams, *Ships and Women*, 124.
3 Mitchell, *Deep Water*, 49, 53.
4 Mason, *Before the Mast in Sailing Ships*, 111-12, 103–4.
5 Worsley, *First Voyage in a Square-Rigged Ship*, 79.
6 Garahan, *Ship Ahoy!*, 17.
7 Runciman, *Before the Mast – and After*, 91.
8 Lightoller, *Titanic and Other Ships*, 25–6, 37–44, 78.
9 Bain, *Life of a Scottish Sailor*, 10, 132–3.
10 Clements, *A Gipsy of the Horn*, 153–4.
11 Hughes, *Through Mighty Seas*, 55, 150.
12 Dexter, *Rope-Yarns, Marline-Spikes and Tar*, 180, 262.
13 Bain, *Life of a Scottish Sailor*, 36.
14 Mason, *Ocean Echoes*, 72.
15 Protheroe, *Life in the Mercantile Marine*, 115, 126.
16 Barker, *The Log of a Limejuicer*, 20–1.

17 Bestic, *Kicking Canvas*, 108–13.
18 Kennerley, 'Nationally-Recognised Qualifications for British Merchant Navy Officers,' 125.
19 Burton, 'The Making of a Nineteenth-Century Profession,' 105.
20 Morton, *The Long Wake*, 17.
21 Crutchley, *My Life at Sea*, 95.
22 Kennerley, 'Aspirant Navigator,' 55.
23 Jones, *The Cape Horn Breed*, 92, 52.
24 Behrman, *Victorian Myths of the Sea*, 63, 96–107.
25 Bisset, *Sail Ho!*, 26.
26 McCulloch, *A Million Miles in Sail*, 78.
27 Jardine, *Leaves From a Sailor's Diary*, 105–7.
28 Barker, *The Log of a Limejuicer*, 217–20.
29 Woodman, *More Days, More Dollars*, 18–20.
30 For example, Hamblen, *The Yarn of a Bucko Mate*.
31 Dexter, *Rope-Yarns, Marline-Spikes and Tar*, 140, 113, 131.
32 Farmer, *The Log of a Shellback*, 58.
33 Ibid., 32–3.
34 Wilson, *Autobiography of Ald. John Wilson*, 37.
35 Rostron, *Home from the Sea*, 24–8.
36 Crutchley, *My Life at Sea*, 9.
37 Lord, *Reminiscences of a Sailor*, 15.
38 Fenton, *The Sea Apprentice*, 41–2.
39 Bisset, *Sail Ho!*, 235.
40 Mason, *Ocean Echoes*, 179–81.
41 Hayes, *Hull Down*, 17.
42 Mitchell, *Deep Water*, 155; Protheroe, *Life in the Mercantile Marine*, 20.
43 Bestic, *Kicking Canvas*, 251.
44 Crutchley, *My Life at Sea*, 67.
45 Dexter, *Rope-Yarns, Marline-Spikes and Tar*, 209, 269.
46 Bisset, *Sail Ho!*, 253.
47 Sutherland, *At Sea with Joseph Conrad*, 149.
48 Lord, *Reminiscences of a Sailor*, 109, 125.
49 Bestic, *Kicking Canvas*, 187.
50 Runciman, *Before the Mast – and After*, 41, 142.
51 McCulloch, *A Million Miles in Sail*, 126.

52 Clements, *A Gipsy of the Horn*, 229.
53 Symondson, *Two Years Abaft the Mast*, 2.
54 Morton, *The Long Wake*, 25.
55 Mitchell, *Deep Water*, 177.
56 Domville-Fife, *Epics of the Square-Rigged Ships*, 175–8.
57 Barker, *The Log of a Limejuicer*, 112, 126, 128, 186.
58 Ibid., 139–40.
59 Symondson, *Two Years Abaft the Mast*, 205.

CHAPTER SIX

1 To paraphrase, among others, Clements, *A Gipsy of the Horn*, 218.
2 Foulke, *The Sea Voyage Narrative*, 7.
3 Blum, *The View from the Masthead*, 118–20.
4 O'Flaherty, *Two Years*, 75–6.
5 Jones, *The Cape Horn Breed*, 22, 69, 97, 100, 112–13, 116.
6 Lightoller, *Titanic and Other Ships*, 1, 69.
7 Mason, *Ocean Echoes*, 4.
8 Clements, *A Gipsy of the Horn*, 212.
9 Bisset, *Sail Ho!*, 49–50.
10 Runciman, *Before the Mast – and After*, 44.
11 Bullen, *The Log of a Sea-Waif*, 28.
12 Farmer, *The Log of a Shellback*, 23.
13 Bisset, *Sail Ho!*, 80.
14 Mason, *Ocean Echoes*, 46–7.
15 Bullen, *The Log of a Sea-Waif*, 19–21.
16 McCulloch, *A Million Miles in Sail*, 127, 149–53, 244.
17 Lightoller, *Titanic and Other Ships*, 9–12.
18 Poggie and Gersuny, 'Risk and Ritual,' 66–72.
19 Bain, *Life of a Scottish Sailor*, 120; Jones, *The Cape Horn Breed*, 234.
20 Ayers, 'The Making of Men,' 66–83.
21 Mitchell, *Deep Water*, 21, 29.
22 Clements, *A Gipsy of the Horn*, 79–81.
23 Farmer, *The Log of a Shellback*, 79–80.
24 Adams, *Ships and Women*, 272.
25 Barker, *The Log of a Limejuicer*, 24–32.

26 Runciman, *Before the Mast – and After*, 44.
27 Ibid., 107–8.
28 Bullen, *The Log of a Sea-Waif*, 130–2.
29 Wilson, *Autobiography of Ald. John Wilson*, 36.
30 Clements, *A Gipsy of the Horn*, 75–6.
31 Dexter, *Rope-Yarns, Marline-Spikes and Tar*, 183–5.
32 Hughes, *Through Mighty Seas*, 90.
33 Morton, *The Long Wake*, 9; Wilson, *Autobiography of Ald. John Wilson*, 36.
34 Symondson, *Two Years Abaft the Mast*, 256–7.
35 Keane, *On Blue-Water.*
36 Bestic, *Kicking Canvas*, 49–50.
37 Barker, *The Log of a Limejuicer*, 75.
38 Mäenpää, 'Sailors and Their Pets,' 480–95.
39 Hughes, *Through Mighty Seas*, 82.
40 Farmer, *The Log of a Shellback*, 162–4.
41 Fenton, *The Sea Apprentice*, 49.
42 Mason, *Ocean Echoes*, 189–90.
43 McCulloch, *A Million Miles in Sail*, 87.
44 Lightoller, *Titanic and Other Ships*, 91–2.
45 Dexter, *Rope-Yarns, Marline-Spikes and Tar*, 239–40.
46 Bestic, *Kicking Canvas*, 22–4, 35.
47 Bain, *Life of a Scottish Sailor*, 37.
48 Rostron, *Home From the Sea*, 36.
49 Farmer, *The Log of a Shellback*, 228.
50 Runciman, *Before the Mast – and After*, 61.
51 Symondson, *Two Years Abaft the Mast*, 337.
52 Adams, *Ships and Women*, 95, 251–3.
53 Farmer, *The Log of a Shellback*, 28, 76.
54 Ibid., 78, 247–9.
55 Clements, *A Gipsy of the Horn*, 46, 161.
56 Ramsay, *Rough and Tumble on Old Clipper Ships*, 40–1.
57 Hughes, *Through Mighty Seas*, 284, 22.
58 Britten, *A Million Ocean Miles*, 31–2.
59 Bestic, *Kicking Canvas*, 255.
60 Adams, *Ships and Women*, 232, emphasis as in the original.

CHAPTER SEVEN

1 Behrman, *Victorian Myths of the Sea*, 59.

2 Atkinson, *Victorian Biography Reconsidered*, 48–52.

3 For example: Dexter, *Rope-Yarns, Marline-Spikes and Tar*, 22; Farmer, *The Log of a Shellback*, v. More generally, see Creighton, '"Women" and Men in American Whaling,' 195–218.

4 Gagnier, *Subjectivities*, 113–14.

5 Foulke, 'Life in the Dying World of Sail,' 105–36; Quinlan, 'Precarious and Hazardous Work,' 281–307; Gorski, 'Employers' Liability and the Victorian Seaman,' 62–75; Carter, *Merchant Seamen's Health*.

6 Johnston and McIvor, 'Dangerous Work, Hard Men and Broken Bodies,' 135–51; Baron, 'Masculinity,' 151–2.

7 Clements, *A Gipsy of the Horn*, 161.

8 Britten, *A Million Ocean Miles*, 33–5.

9 Rostron, *Home From the Sea*, 18.

10 Bisset, *Sail Ho!*, 50.

11 Bullen, *The Log of a Sea-Waif*, 22.

12 Lord, *Reminiscences of a Sailor*, 26.

13 Symondson, *Two Years Abaft the Mast*, 12–21.

14 Evidence for this paragraph and the next comes from Jones, *The Cape Horn Breed*, 53, 95, 101, 135–6; Barker, *The Log of a Limejuicer*, 151–7, 227.

15 Symondson, *Two Years Abaft the Mast*, 18.

16 Villiers, *Falmouth for Orders*, 88.

17 Burnett, *Destiny Obscure*, 56–60.

18 Bisset, *Sail Ho!*, 52.

19 Dexter, *Rope-Yarns, Marline-Spikes and Tar*, 198–200.

20 Mason, *Ocean Echoes*, 77.

21 Bullen, *The Log of a Sea-Waif*, 18.

22 Alsop, 'Jack Tar's Food,' 183–211.

23 Wilson, *Autobiography of Ald. John Wilson*, 35.

24 Jardine, *Leaves From a Sailor's Diary*, 145.

25 Burg, '"Women and Children First,"' 1–9; Delap, '"Thus Does Man Prove His Fitness to Be the Master of Things,"' 45–74.

26 Lord, *Reminiscences of a Sailor*, 36.

27 Farmer, *The Log of a Shellback*, v, 31.

28 Runciman, *Before the Mast – and After*, 63.

29 Rostron, *Home From the Sea*, 11.
30 Barker, *The Log of a Limejuicer*, 81–3.
31 Crutchley, *My Life at Sea*, 43.
32 Worsley, *First Voyage in a Square-Rigged Ship*, 120.
33 Morton, *The Long Wake*, 56.
34 Wilson, *Autobiography of Ald. John Wilson*, 41.
35 Runciman, *Before the Mast – and After*, 167–8.
36 Adams, *Ships and Women*, 143, 147, 191.
37 Fenton, *The Sea Apprentice*, 58.
38 Hayes, *Hull Down*, 16.
39 Protheroe, *Life in the Mercantile Marine*, 7–8.
40 Farmer, *The Log of a Shellback*, 222–4.
41 Clements, *A Gipsy of the Horn*, 126–7.
42 Villiers, *The Set of the Sails*, 232–7.
43 Bestic, *Kicking Canvas*, 115–17.
44 Adams, *Ships and Women*, 91–2, 186–8.
45 Ibid., 29–31, 37–8, 54, 65, 68–71, 75–7, 86, 104, 117–18.
46 Bisset, *Sail Ho!*, 71–5.
47 Lightoller, *Titanic and Other Ships*, 21, 36.
48 Hughes, *Through Mighty Seas*, 203–5.
49 Jardine, *Leaves From a Sailor's Diary*, 149.
50 Moffat, *From Ship's Boy to Skipper*, 289, 306.
51 For example, Jones, *The Cape Horn Breed*, 134–5.
52 Reid, 'Ocean Funerals,' 37–54; Jalland, *Death in the Victorian Family*; Jalland, 'Victorian Death and its Decline,' 230–55.
53 Stewart, 'Burial At Sea,' 276–85.
54 Clements, *A Gipsy of the Horn*, 219.
55 Symondson, *Two Years Abaft the Mast*, 266–70.
56 Stevens, *A Sailor Boy's Experience*, 58.
57 Adams, *Ships and Women*, 91–2.
58 McCulloch, *A Million Miles in Sail*, 137–8.
59 Barker, *The Log of a Limejuicer*, 207–9.
60 Strange, '"She Cried a Very Little,"' 152–3.
61 Fenton, *The Sea Apprentice*, 51.
62 Keane, *On Blue-Water*, 53–5, 211.
63 Dexter, *Rope-Yarns, Marline-Spikes and Tar*, 84.

64 Bullen, *The Log of a Sea-Waif*, 218.
65 Lord, *Reminiscences of a Sailor*, 29–31, 233–4.
66 Barker, *The Log of a Limejuicer*, 214, 232.
67 Crutchley, *My Life at Sea*, 328.
68 Ramsay, *Rough and Tumble on Old Clipper Ships*, 96.
69 McCulloch, *A Million Miles in Sail*, 165.

CHAPTER EIGHT

1 Rouleau, 'Dead Men Do Tell Tales,' 30–62.
2 Gilje, *To Swear Like a Sailor*, 5–6; Parry, 'Sailors' English,' 660–70.
3 Respectively, for example: Lord, *Reminiscences of a Sailor*; Jardine, *Leaves from a Sailor's Diary*.
4 Bisset, *Sail Ho!*, 37.
5 Jones, *The Cape Horn Breed*, 13. For a useful set of diagrams and explanation, see Sager, *Seafaring Labour*, 122–35.
6 Lord, *Reminiscences of a Sailor*, 16.
7 Dexter, *Rope-Yarns, Marline-Spikes and Tar*, 206–8.
8 Protheroe, *Life in the Mercantile Marine*, 138–9.
9 Wilson, *Autobiography of Ald. John Wilson*, 31.
10 Whall, *Ships, Sea Songs and Shanties*, xiii.
11 Garahan, *Ship Ahoy!*, 9, 47–8.
12 Bullen, *The Log of a Sea-Waif*, 335–6.
13 Crutchley, *My Life at Sea*, 16.
14 de Mierre, *Clipper Ships to Ocean Greyhounds*, 32.
15 Fenton, *The Sea Apprentice*, 23.
16 Mitchell, *Deep Water*, 46.
17 Morton, *The Long Wake*, 65.
18 Mason, *Before the Mast in Sailing Ships*, 128, 168.
19 Barker, *The Log of a Limejuicer*; Jones, *The Cape Horn Breed*.
20 Jardine, *Leaves From a Sailor's Diary*.
21 Bercaw Edwards, *Sailor Talk*.
22 Runciman, *Before the Mast – and After*, 40.
23 Farmer, *The Log of a Shellback*, 80.
24 Bender, 'Conrad, the Yarn and the Location of the Marlow Stories,' 168–85.
25 Symondson, *Two Years Abaft the Mast*, 302–4.
26 Lowenthal, *The Past is a Foreign Country*, 235.

27 Dexter, *Rope-Yarns, Marline-Spikes and Tar*, 102.
28 Bain, *Life of a Scottish Sailor*, 23–4.
29 Rostron, *Home from the Sea*, 18.
30 Morton, *The Long Wake*, 25.
31 Lord, *Reminiscences of a Sailor*, 66.
32 Mitchell, *Deep Water*, 139.
33 Fenton, *The Sea Apprentice*, 179.
34 Bestic, *Kicking Canvas*, 117–18.
35 Runciman, *Before the Mast – and After*, 107–8.
36 Milne, 'Collecting the Sea Shanty,' 371–3.
37 Hugill, *Shanties and Sailors' Songs*.
38 Bain, *Life of a Scottish Sailor*, 29–30.
39 Bestic, *Kicking Canvas*, 28–9.
40 Symondson, *Two Years Abaft the Mast*, 13.
41 Clements, *A Gipsy of the Horn*, 232.
42 Mason, *Before the Mast in Sailing Ships*, 157.
43 Symondson, *Two Years Abaft the Mast*, 65.
44 Whall, *Ships, Sea Songs and Shanties*, ix.
45 Bullen, *Songs of Sea Labour*, viii; Mason, *Before the Mast in Sailing Ships*, 66.
46 Milne, 'Collecting the Sea Shanty,' 381–5.
47 Runciman, *Before the Mast – and After*, 58–9.
48 Evidence for the following paragraphs comes from Clements, *A Gipsy of the Horn*, 193–5.
49 Walker, 'In the Inventories of Deceased British Merchant Seafarers,' 330–46.
50 Garahan, *Ship Ahoy!*, 9.
51 Dexter, *Rope-Yarns, Marline-Spikes and Tar*, 170.
52 de Mierre, *Clipper Ships to Ocean Greyhounds*, 94–5.
53 Hilton, *Smoking in British Popular Culture*, 61–76; Kneale, 'The Place of Drink,' 43–59.
54 Adams, *Ships and Women*, 64.
55 Farmer, *The Log of a Shellback*, 140.
56 Jardine, *Leaves From a Sailor's Diary*, 101–2.
57 de Mierre, *Clipper Ships to Ocean Greyhounds*, 12.
58 Crutchley, *My Life at Sea*, 49, 50.
59 Clements, *A Gipsy of the Horn*, 71.
60 Bisset, *Sail Ho!*, 147–8.

61 Wilson, *Autobiography of Ald. John Wilson*, 35.
62 Clements, *A Gipsy of the Horn*, 136–7.
63 Smith, '"The Fancy Work What Sailors Make,"' 104–23.
64 Morton, *The Long Wake*, 52–3.
65 Bestic, *Kicking Canvas*, 226–7; Protheroe, *Life in the Mercantile Marine*, 143.
66 Worsley, *First Voyage in a Square-Rigged Ship*, 136–8.
67 Symondson, *Two Years Abaft the Mast*, 337–8.
68 Ibid., 271.
69 Protheroe, *Life in the Mercantile Marine*, 98.
70 Bullen, *The Log of a Sea-Waif*, 177–8.
71 Hughes, *Through Mighty Seas*, 151.
72 Runciman, *Before the Mast – and After*, 58.

CHAPTER NINE

1 Ingram, 'Saving the Union's Jack,' 49–76; Beaven, Bell, and James, *Port Towns and Urban Cultures*; Milne, *People, Place and Power on the Nineteenth-Century Waterfront*.
2 Barrett, *History from the Bottom Up and the Inside Out*, 38; Hackett, 'A Different Form of "Self,"' 223.
3 Begiato, *Manliness in Britain*, 78.
4 Bullen, *The Log of a Sea-Waif*, 109.
5 Fischer, 'A Dereliction of Duty,' 53–68; Ojala, Pehkonen, and Eloranta, 'Desertions in Nineteenth-Century Shipping,' 122–40.
6 Farmer, *The Log of a Shellback*, 104.
7 Fingard, '"Those Crimps of Hell and Goblins Damned,"' 323–33; Kaukiainen, 'Finnish and International Labour in the Age of Sail,' 101–10.
8 Masefield, *New Chum*, 146–7.
9 McCulloch, *A Million Miles in Sail*, 40.
10 Dexter, *Rope-Yarns, Marline-Spikes and Tar*, 214–15.
11 Lord, *Reminiscences of a Sailor*, 54.
12 Rostron, *Home from the Sea*, 31.
13 Moffat, *From Ship's Boy to Skipper*, 98–9, 209.
14 Crutchley, *My Life at Sea*, 38–40.
15 Mitchell, *Deep Water*, 63, 122–8, 143.
16 Milne, *People, Place and Power on the Nineteenth-Century Waterfront*, chapter 4.
17 Mason, *Before the Mast in Sailing Ships*, 62–3.

18 McCulloch, *A Million Miles in Sail*, 41–6.
19 Down, *On Course Together*; Kverndal, *Seamen's Missions.*
20 Dexter, *Rope-Yarns, Marline-Spikes and Tar*, 215.
21 Bain, *Life of a Scottish Sailor*, 122.
22 Clements, *A Gipsy of the Horn*, 100–1.
23 Mason, *Before the Mast in Sailing Ships*, 49–56.
24 Dennis, 'Seduction on the Waterfront,' 175–201; Kennerley, 'The British Contribution to Seafarers' Welfare,' 65–82.
25 Hinkkanen, 'Expressions of Longing, Sources of Anxiety?,' 63–79.
26 Lightoller, *Titanic and Other Ships*, 30–3, 72–3, 89.
27 Morton, *The Long Wake*, 96.
28 Burton, 'The Myth of Bachelor Jack,' 179–98.
29 Bryder, 'Sex, Race and Colonialism,' 806–22.
30 Walkowitz, *Prostitution and Victorian Society*; Ogborn, 'Law and Discipline,' 28–55; Cook, 'Law,' 64–86.
31 Bestic, *Kicking Canvas*, 131.
32 Bisset, *Sail Ho!*, 94.
33 Szreter and Fisher, *Sex Before the Sexual Revolution*; Burnett, *Destiny Obscure*, 45–6.
34 Machann, 'The Construction of Masculinity in Victorian Autobiography,' 16–17.
35 de Mierre, *Clipper Ships to Ocean Greyhounds*, 82, 88.
36 Jones, *The Cape Horn Breed*, 132, 195.
37 Garahan, *Ship Ahoy!*, 98–9.
38 Barker, *The Log of a Limejuicer*, 25–6.
39 Dexter, *Rope-Yarns, Marline-Spikes and Tar*, 101–2, 233.
40 O'Flaherty, *Two Years*, 114–19.
41 Morton, *The Long Wake*, 19–21.
42 Bisset, *Sail Ho!*, 181–7.
43 Adams, *Ships and Women*, 120–2, 125, 148.
44 Ibid., 168, 238.
45 Bestic, *Kicking Canvas*, 120, 130.
46 Fenton, *The Sea Apprentice*, 145–8.
47 McCulloch, *A Million Miles in Sail*, 186–90.
48 Forman, 'Race and Empire,' 124–5.
49 Mason, *Before the Mast in Sailing Ships*, 131, 162.

50 Mason, *Ocean Echoes*, 40–1, 200.
51 Lord, *Reminiscences of a Sailor*, 107–8, 219–20.
52 Ramsay, *Rough and Tumble on Old Clipper Ships*, 20, 30–5, 106, 134, 290–3.
53 Jardine, *Leaves From a Sailor's Diary*, 81–2, 110–11, 102, 56–7.
54 Clements, *A Gipsy of the Horn*, 212.
55 Hughes, *Through Mighty Seas*, 31–2.
56 Garahan, *Ship Ahoy!*, 285–90; McCulloch, *A Million Miles in Sail*, 81.
57 Bullen, *Confessions of a Tradesman*, viii.
58 de Mierre, *Clipper Ships to Ocean Greyhounds*, 305–9.
59 Patterson, *My Vagabondage*, 324–5.
60 Adams, *Ships and Women*, 304–18.
61 Mason, *Ocean Echoes*, 235.
62 Wilson, *Autobiography of Ald. John Wilson*, 43.
63 Symondson, *Two Years Abaft the Mast*, 369.
64 Ibid., 238.
65 Barker, *The Log of a Limejuicer*, xiv, 241–2.

AFTERLIVES

1 Readman, 'The Place of the Past in English Culture,' 147–200; Daunton and Rieger, *Meanings of Modernity*, 3–6.
2 Malone, *The Last Landfall*; Marlowe, *Coming, Sir!*; and Nixson, *Ring Twice for the Stewardess*, are memoirs of a radio operator, waiter, and stewardess respectively. William McFee based much of his prolific fiction on his years as a ship's engineer.
3 Woodman, *More Days, More Dollars*, chapter 6; Rieger, '"Modern Wonders,"' 152–76.
4 Scott, 'An Assessment of Voyage Memoirs of the Erikson Era,' 322–34.
5 J. Geraint Jenkins, quoted in Day and Lunn, 'British Maritime Heritage,' 302–3; Konvitz, 'Changing Concepts of the Sea,' 1–17.
6 Rosaldo, 'Imperialist Nostalgia,' 107–22; Mangan, '"The Grit of Our Forefathers,"' 113–39.
7 Farmer, *The Log of a Shellback*, 145, 153, 235.
8 Runciman, *Before the Mast – and After*, 221.
9 Ibid., 222–3.
10 Morton, *The Long Wake*, 39, 100.
11 Rostron, *Home From the Sea*, 30, 34, 253.

12 Hayes, *Hull Down*, 18–19.

13 Gräbner, 'Absences and Opacities,' 83–102; Gelb and Gelb, *O'Neill*, 144–68.

14 Hobsbawm, *Industry and Empire*, 207–12.

15 Mason, *Ocean Echoes*, 48, 88.

16 Runciman, *Before the Mast – and After*, 90.

17 Mason, *Before the Mast in Sailing Ships*, 9–10.

18 Sutherland, *At Sea with Joseph Conrad*, 12–18.

19 Dexter, *Rope-Yarns, Marline-Spikes and Tar*, 202.

20 Farmer, *The Log of a Shellback*, 148.

21 Morton, *The Long Wake*, 34.

22 Gamble, 'Theories and Explanations of British Decline,' 1–22.

23 Jamieson, *Ebb Tide in the British Maritime Industries*; Sturmey, *British Shipping and World Competition*.

24 Bisset, *Sail Ho!*, 272, 285, 288.

25 Bullen, introduction to Villiers, *Falmouth for Orders*, xvii–xviii.

Bibliography

MEMOIRS AND PERIOD SOURCES

Adams, Bill. *Fenceless Meadows: Tales of the Sea*. London: Hurst & Blackett, 1924.

– *Ships and Women: An Autobiography.* London: Peter Davies & Lovat Dickson, 1936.

Aldington, Richard. *Death of a Hero.* London: Chatto & Windus, 1929.

Bain, John. *Life of a Scottish Sailor: or, Forty Years' Experience of the Sea.* Nairn: G. Bain, 1897.

Barker, James P. *The Log of a Limejuicer: The Experiences Under Sail of James P. Barker, Master Mariner*. London: Putnam, 1934.

Bestic, A.A. *Kicking Canvas*. New York: E.P. Dutton, 1958.

Bisset, James. *Sail Ho! My Early Years at Sea.* New York: Criterion Books, 1958.

Bone, David W. *Merchantmen at Arms: The British Merchants' Service in the War.* London: Chatto & Windus, 1919.

Britten, Edgar T. *A Million Ocean Miles.* London: Hutchinson, 1936.

Bullen, Frank T. *Confessions of a Tradesman*. London: Hodder & Stoughton, 1908.

– *The Log of a Sea-Waif: Being Recollections of the First Four Years of My Sea Life.* New York: D. Appleton, 1899.

– *The Men of the Merchant Service*. London: John Murray, 1900.

– *Songs of Sea Labour*. London: Orpheus Music Publishing, 1914.

Clements, Rex. *A Gipsy of the Horn: The Narrative of a Voyage Round the World in a Windjammer Twenty Years Ago*. London: Heath Cranton, 1924.

Conrad, Joseph. *A Personal Record*. London: Harper & Brothers, 1912.

Crutchley, William Caius. *My Life at Sea: Being a 'Yarn' Loosely Spun for the Purpose of Holding Together Certain Reminiscences of the Transition Period from Sail to Steam in the British Mercantile Marine (1863–1894)*. London: Chapman & Hall, 1912.

De Mierre, H.C. *Clipper Ships to Ocean Greyhounds*. London: Starke, 1971.

Dean, Harry. *Umbala: The Adventures of a Negro Sea-Captain in Africa and on the Seven Seas in his Attempts to Found an Ethiopian Empire*. London: George G. Harrap, 1934.

Dexter, Walter Ernest. *Rope-Yarns, Marline-Spikes and Tar*. London: William Hodge, 1938.

Dixon, Charles. *See* McCulloch.

Duncan, Norman. 'Youngsters of the Seven Seas.' *Harper's Monthly Magazine*, 1 December 1910, 126–36.

Farmer, H.F. *The Log of a Shellback: A Narrative of Life and Adventure before the Mast in the 'Nineties*. London: H.F. & G. Witherby, 1925.

Fenton, C. *The Sea Apprentice: Being an Account of Two Voyages Round the World under Canvas*. London: P. Allan, 1934.

Garahan, Melbourne. *Ship Ahoy!* London: Chatto & Windus, 1922.

Hamblen, Herbert. *The Yarn of a Bucko Mate*. London: Downey, 1899.

Hayes, Bertram Fox. *Hull Down: Reminiscences of Wind-Jammers, Troops and Travellers*. London: Cassell, 1925.

Hughes, Henry. *Through Mighty Seas: or, The Romance of a Little Wind-Jammer*. London: The Travel Book Club, 1940.

Hurd, Archibald. *History of the Great War Based on Official Documents: The Merchant Navy*. 3 vols. London: J. Murray, 1921–29.

Jardine, John J.M. *Leaves from a Sailor's Diary*. Liverpool: A.W. Duncan, 1924.

Jones, W.H.S. *The Cape Horn Breed: My Experiences as an Apprentice in Sail in the Full-Rigged Ship 'British Isles.'* London: Transworld Publishers, 1957.

Keane, John F. *On Blue-Water: Some Narratives of Sport and Adventure in the Modern Merchant Service*. London: Tinsley Bros, 1883.

Kennedy, Ludovic. 'By Land and Sea.' *Spectator*, 6 April 1956, 460.

Kirkaldy, A.W. *British Shipping: Its History, Organisation and Importance*. London: Kegan Paul, 1919.

Lightoller, C.H. *Titanic and Other Ships.* London: I. Nicholson & Watson, 1935.

Lord, William R. *Reminiscences of a Sailor.* Leith: Mackenzie & Storrie, 1894.

Malone, Desmond. *The Last Landfall.* London: Geoffrey Bles, 1936.

Marlowe, Dave. *Coming, Sir!* London: George G. Harrap, 1937.

Masefield, John. *New Chum.* London: Heinemann, 1944.

Mason, Arthur. *Ocean Echoes: An Autobiography.* New York: H. Holt, 1922.

Mason, John. *Before the Mast in Sailing Ships.* Kirkwall: W.R. Mackintosh, 1928.

McCulloch, John Herries. *A Million Miles in Sail: Being the Story of the Sea Career of Captain C.C. Dixon.* London: Hurst & Blackett, 1933.

Mitchell, Pryce. *Deep Water: The Autobiography of a Sea Captain.* London: Hurst & Blackett, 1934.

Moffat, Henry. *From Ship's Boy to Skipper, with Variations.* Paisley: Alexander Gardner, 1910.

Moore, Alan. 'Sail, the Last Phase.' *Times Literary Supplement*, 9 June 1932, 419.

Morton, Leslie. *The Long Wake.* London: Routledge & Kegan Paul, 1968.

Munro, Neil. 'The Canal Boatman.' In *Echoes of the Sea: Scotland and the Sea*, edited by Brian D. Osborne and Ronald Armstrong, 293–4. Edinburgh: Canongate, 1998.

Nixson, Maida M. *Ring Twice for the Stewardess: The Intriguing Life behind the Scenes on Board Ship.* London: J. Long, 1954.

O'Flaherty, Liam. *Two Years.* London: Jonathan Cape, 1930.

Patterson, J.E. *My Vagabondage: Being the Intimate Autobiography of a Nature's Nomad.* London: Heinemann, 1911.

Protheroe, Charles. *Life in the Mercantile Marine.* London: John Lane, 1903.

Ramsay, Robert. *Rough and Tumble on Old Clipper Ships.* New York: D. Appleton, 1930.

Randell, Jack. *I'm Alone.* Indianapolis: Bobbs-Merrill, 1930.

Rostron, Arthur. *Home from the Sea.* London: Cassell, 1931.

Runciman, Walter. *Before the Mast – and After: The Autobiography of a Sailor and Shipowner.* London: T. Fisher Unwin, 1924.

Stevens, Charles. *A Sailor Boy's Experience.* Napanee, Ontario: C. Stevens & Sons, 1892.

Sutherland, J.G. *At Sea with Joseph Conrad.* Boston: Houghton Mifflin, 1922.

Symondson, F.W.H. *Two Years Abaft the Mast: or, Life as a Sea Apprentice.* Edinburgh: William Blackwood & Sons, 1876.

Villiers, Alan. *Falmouth for Orders: The Story of the Last Clipper Ship Race Round Cape Horn.* London: Geoffrey Bles, 1929.

– *The Set of the Sails: The Adventures of a Cape Horn Seaman*. London: Pan, 1955.

Whall, W.B. *Ships, Sea Songs and Shanties*. Glasgow: J. Brown & Son, 1910.

Williams, Henry Willey. *Some Reminiscences (1838–1918)*. Penzance: J.A.D. Bridger, 1918.

Williams, James H. *Blow the Man Down! A Yankee Seaman's Adventures Under Sail*, edited by Warren F. Kuehl. New York: E.P. Hutton, 1959.

Wilson, John. *Autobiography of Ald. John Wilson, JP, MP: A Record of a Strenuous Life*. Durham: The Durham Chronicle, 1909.

Woolf, Virginia. 'Joseph Conrad.' *Times Literary Supplement*, 14 August 1924, 493–4.

Worsley, Frank. *First Voyage in a Square-Rigged Ship*. London: Geoffrey Bles, 1938.

SECONDARY SOURCES

Allen, Judith A. 'Men Interminably in Crisis? Historians on Masculinity, Sexual Boundaries, and Manhood.' *Radical History Review*, no. 82 (2002): 191–207.

Alsop, James Douglas. 'Jack Tar's Food: Masculine Self-Fashioning in the Age of Sail.' In *The Social History of English Seamen, 1650–1815*, edited by Cheryl A. Fury, 183–211. Woodbridge: Boydell & Brewer, 2017.

Anim-Addo, Anyaa, William Hasty, and Kimberley Peters. 'The Mobilities of Ships and Shipped Mobilities.' *Mobilities* 9, no. 3 (2014): 337–49.

Apollonio, Spencer, ed. *The Last of the Cape Horners: Firsthand Accounts from the Final Days of the Commercial Tall Ships*. Washington, DC: Brassey's, 2000.

Atkinson, Juliette. *Victorian Biography Reconsidered: A Study of Nineteenth-Century 'Hidden' Lives*. Oxford: Oxford University Press, 2010.

Aubert, Vilhelm. *The Hidden Society*. Totowa: Bedminster Press, 1965.

Aurell, Jaume, and Rocio G. Davis. 'History and Autobiography: The Logics of a Convergence.' *Life Writing* 16, no. 4 (2019): 503–11.

Ayers, Pat. 'The Making of Men: Masculinities in Interwar Liverpool.' In *Working Out Gender: Perspectives from Labour History*, edited by Margaret Walsh, 66–83. Aldershot: Ashgate, 1999.

Baird, Donal. *Women at Sea in the Age of Sail*. Halifax: Nimbus, 2001.

Baker, Paul, and Jo Stanley. *Hello Sailor! The Hidden History of Gay Life at Sea*. London: Routledge, 2014.

Balachandran, G. *Globalizing Labour? Indian Seafarers and World Shipping, c.1870–1945*. New Delhi: Oxford University Press, 2012.

Baron, Ava. 'Masculinity, the Embodied Male Worker, and the Historian's Gaze.' *International Labor and Working-Class History* 69, no. 1 (2006): 143–60.

Baron, Ava, and Eileen Boris. '"The Body" as a Useful Category for Working-Class History.' *Labor: Studies in Working Class History of the Americas* 4, no. 2 (2007): 23–43.

Barrett, James R. *History from the Bottom Up and the Inside Out: Ethnicity, Race, and Identity in Working-Class History*. Durham: Duke University Press, 2017.

Bascom, William. 'The Forms of Folklore: Prose Narratives.' *Journal of American Folklore* 78, no. 307 (1965): 3–21.

Beaven, Brad. *Leisure, Citizenship and Working-Class Men in Britain, 1850–1945*. Manchester: Manchester University Press, 2005.

Beaven, Brad, Karl Bell, and Robert James, eds. *Port Towns and Urban Cultures: International Histories of the Waterfront, c.1700–2000*. Basingstoke: Palgrave Macmillan, 2016.

Bederman, Gail. *Manliness and Civilization: A Cultural History of Gender and Race in the United States, 1880–1917*. Chicago: University of Chicago Press, 1995.

Begiato, Joanne. *Manliness in Britain, 1760–1900: Bodies, Emotion, and Material Culture*. Manchester: Manchester University Press, 2020.

Behrman, Cynthia Fansler. *Victorian Myths of the Sea*. Athens: Ohio University Press, 1977.

Bender, Bert. *Sea-Brothers: The Tradition of American Sea Fiction from Moby-Dick to the Present*. Philadelphia: University of Pennsylvania Press, 2015.

Bender, Michael. 'Conrad, the Yarn and the Location of the Marlow Stories.' *Mariner's Mirror* 100, no. 2 (2014): 168–85.

Benson, John. *The Working Class in Britain, 1850–1939*. London: Longman, 1989.

Bercaw Edwards, Mary K. *Sailor Talk: Labor, Utterance, and Meaning in the Works of Melville, Conrad, and London*. Liverpool: Liverpool University Press, 2021.

Berg, Maxine, ed. *Technology and Toil in Nineteenth Century Britain*. London: CSE Books, 1979.

Bérubé, Allan. *My Desire for History: Essays in Gay, Community, and Labor History*. Chapel Hill: University of North Carolina Press, 2011.

Blum, Hester. *The View from the Masthead: Maritime Imagination and Antebellum American Sea Narratives*. Chapel Hill: University of North Carolina Press, 2012.

Bolster, W. Jeffrey. *Black Jacks: African American Seamen in the Age of Sail*. Cambridge, MA: Harvard University Press, 1997.

Bovill, Donald Guy. 'Education of Mercantile Mariners in the North East Ports (1840–1902).' PhD diss., Durham University, 1987.

Boyce, Gordon. *Information, Mediation and Institutional Development: The Rise of Large-Scale Enterprise in British Shipping, 1870–1919*. Manchester: Manchester University Press, 1995.

Boyd, Kelly. *Manliness and the Boys' Story Paper in Britain: A Cultural History, 1855–1940*. Basingstoke: Palgrave Macmillan, 2003.

Bratton, J.S. 'Of England, Home and Duty: The Image of England in Victorian and Edwardian Juvenile Fiction.' In *Imperialism and Popular Culture*, edited by John M. MacKenzie, 73–93. Manchester: Manchester University Press, 1986.

Bristow, Joseph. *Empire Boys: Adventures in a Man's World*. London: Harper Collins, 1991.

Broeze, Frank. 'Militancy and Pragmatism: An International Perspective on Maritime Labour, 1870–1914.' *International Review of Social History* 36, no. 2 (1991): 165–200.

– 'The Muscles of Empire: Indian Seamen and the Raj, 1919–1939.' *Indian Economic and Social History Review* 18, no. 1 (1981): 43–67.

Brown, Michael. 'Cold Steel, Weak Flesh: Mechanism, Masculinity and the Anxieties of Late Victorian Empire.' *Cultural and Social History* 14, no. 2 (2017): 155–81.

Brown, Michael, and Joanne Begiato. 'Visualising the Aged Veteran in Nineteenth-Century Britain: Memory, Masculinity and Nation.' In *Martial Masculinities: Experiencing and Imagining the Military in the Long Nineteenth Century*, edited by Michael Brown, Anna Maria Barry, and Joanne Begiato, 102–36. Manchester: Manchester University Press, 2019.

Bryder, Linda. 'Sex, Race and Colonialism: An Historiographical Review.' *International History Review* 20, no. 4 (1998): 806–22.

Budd, Michael Anton. *The Sculpture Machine: Physical Culture and Body Politics in the Age of Empire*. Basingstoke: Palgrave Macmillan, 1997.

Burg, B.R. '"Women and Children First": Popular Mythology and Disaster at Sea, 1840–1860.' *Journal of American Culture* 20, no. 4 (1997): 1–9.

Burnett, John. *Destiny Obscure: Autobiographies of Childhood, Education, and Family from the 1820s to the 1920s*. London: Allen Lane, 1982.

Burnett, John, David Vincent, and David Mayall. *The Autobiography of the Working Class: An Annotated, Critical Bibliography*. 2 vols. Brighton: Harvester, 1984.

Burton, Valerie. '"As I Wuz A-Rolling Down the Highway One Morn": Fictions of the 19th Century English Sailortown.' In *Fictions of the Sea: Critical Perspectives on the Ocean in British Literature and Culture*, edited by Bernhard Klein, 141–56. Aldershot: Ashgate, 2002.

– 'The Making of a Nineteenth-Century Profession: Shipmasters and the British Shipping Industry.' *Journal of the Canadian Historical Association / Revue de la Société Historique du Canada* 1, no. 1 (1990): 97–118.

– 'The Myth of Bachelor Jack: Masculinity, Patriarchy and Seafaring Labour.' In *Jack Tar in History: Essays in the History of Maritime Life and Labour*, edited by Colin Howell and Richard J. Twomey, 179–98. Fredericton: Acadiensis Press, 1991.

– 'Sourcing Maritime History Over Four Decades: Crew Agreement Scholarship at Memorial University of Newfoundland.' *International Journal of Maritime History*, 31, no. 2 (2019): 308–29.

– '"Whoring, Drinking Sailors": Reflections on Masculinity from the Labour History of Nineteenth Century British Shipping.' In *Working Out Gender: Perspectives From Labour History*, edited by Margaret Walsh, 84–101. Aldershot: Ashgate, 1999.

Carter, Tim. *Merchant Seamen's Health 1860–1960: Medicine, Technology, Shipowners and the State in Britain.* Woodbridge: Boydell, 2014.

Childs, Michael. *Labour's Apprentices: Working-Class Lads in Late Victorian and Edwardian England.* London: Hambledon, 1992.

Clark, Anna. *Desire: A History of European Sexuality*. London: Taylor & Francis, 2012.

Clements, Eric L. *Captain of the Carpathia: The Seafaring Life of Titanic Hero Sir Arthur Henry Rostron*. London: Bloomsbury, 2016.

Cocks, H.G. *Nameless Offences: Homosexual Desire in the Nineteenth Century.* London: I.B. Taurus, 2003.

Cocks, H.G., and Matt Houlbrook, eds. *Palgrave Advances in the Modern History of Sexuality*. Basingstoke: Palgrave Macmillan, 2005.

Cohen, Margaret. *The Novel and the Sea.* Princeton: Princeton University Press, 2010.

Colls, Rob. *Identity of England.* Oxford: Oxford University Press, 2004.

Colville, Quintin, and James Davey, eds. *A New Naval History.* Manchester: Manchester University Press, 2019.

Conley, Mary A. *From Jack Tar to Union Jack: Representing Naval Manhood in the British Empire, 1870–1918.* Manchester: Manchester University Press, 2017.

Connell, R.W. *The Men and the Boys.* Oxford: Wiley, 2013.

Cook, Matt. 'Law.' In *Palgrave Advances in the Modern History of Sexuality*, edited by H.G. Cocks and Matt Houlbrook, 64–86. Basingstoke: Palgrave Macmillan, 2005.

Costello, Ray. *Black Salt: Seafarers of African Descent on British Ships*. Liverpool: Liverpool University Press, 2012.

Courtwright, David T. *Violent Land: Single Men and Social Disorder from the Frontier to the Inner City*. Cambridge, MA: Harvard University Press, 1996.

Craig, Robin. 'Printed Guides for Master Mariners as a Source of Productivity Change in Shipping, 1750–1914.' *Journal of Transport History* 3, no. 2 (1975): 23–35.

Creighton, Margaret S. 'American Mariners and the Rites of Manhood, 1830–1870.' In *Jack Tar in History: Essays in the History of Maritime Life and Labour*, edited by Colin Howell and Richard J. Twomey, 143–64. Fredericton: Acadiensis Press, 1991.

– 'Fraternity in the American Forecastle, 1830–1870.' *New England Quarterly* 63, no. 4 (1990): 531–57.

– '"Women" and Men in American Whaling, 1830–1870.' *International Journal of Maritime History* 4, no. 1 (1992): 195–218.

D'Cruze, Shani, ed. *Everyday Violence in Britain, 1850–1950*. Harlow: Pearson Education, 2000.

Daunton, Martin, and Bernhard Rieger, eds. *Meanings of Modernity: Britain from the Late-Victorian Era to World War II*. Oxford: Berg, 2001.

Davies, Peter N. 'British Shipping and World Trade: Rise and Decline, 1820–1939.' In *Business History of Shipping: Strategy and Structure*, edited by T. Yui and K. Nakagawa, 39–85. Tokyo: University of Tokyo Press, 1985.

Dawson, Graham. *Soldier Heroes: British Adventure, Empire and the Imagining of Masculinities*. London: Routledge, 1994.

Day, Ann, and Ken Lunn. 'British Maritime Heritage: Carried Along by the Currents?' *International Journal of Heritage Studies* 9, no. 4 (2003): 289–305.

Delap, Lucy. '"Thus Does Man Prove His Fitness to be the Master of Things": Shipwrecks, Chivalry and Masculinities in Nineteenth- and Twentieth-Century Britain.' *Cultural and Social History* 3, no. 1 (2006): 45–74.

Dennis, David Brandon. 'Seduction on the Waterfront: German Merchant Sailors, Masculinity and the "Brücke zu Heimat" in New York and Buenos Aires, 1884–1914.' *German History* 29, no. 2 (2011): 175–201.

Dentith, S. 'Contemporary Working Class Autobiography: Politics of Form, Politics of Content.' In *Modern Selves: Essays in Modern British and American Autobiography*, edited by Philip Dodd, 60–80. London: Frank Cass, 1986.

Domville-Fife, Charles W. *Epics of the Square-Rigged Ships: Autobiographies of Sail.* London: Seeley Service, 1958.

Down, Bill. *On Course Together: The Churches' Ministry in the Maritime World Today.* Norwich: Canterbury Press, 1989.

Eakin, Paul. *How Our Lives Become Stories: Making Selves.* Ithaca: Cornell University Press, 2019.

Emsley, Clive. *Hard Men: The English and Violence since 1750.* London: Hambledon & London, 2005.

Evans, Bob. *The Training Ships of Liverpool.* Birkenhead: Countyvise, 2002.

Feys, Torsten. *The Battle for the Migrants: The Introduction of Steam Shipping on the North Atlantic and its Impact on the European Exodus.* St John's, Newfoundland: International Maritime Economic History Association, 2013.

Fingard, Judith. '"Those Crimps of Hell and Goblins Damned": The Image and Reality of Quebec's Sailortown Bosses.' In *Working Men Who Got Wet*, edited by Rosemary Ommer and Gerald Panting, 323–33. St John's: Memorial University, 1980.

Fink, Leon. *Sweatshops At Sea: Merchant Seamen in the World's First Globalized Industry, from 1812 to the Present.* Chapel Hill: University of North Carolina Press, 2011.

Fischer, L.R. 'A Dereliction of Duty: The Problem of Desertion on Nineteenth Century Sailing Vessels.' In *Working Men Who Got Wet*, edited by Rosemary Ommer and Gerald Panting, 53–68. St John's: Memorial University, 1980.

– ed. *The Market for Seamen in the Age of Sail.* St John's: International Maritime Economic History Association, 1994.

Fischer, L.R., and Helge W. Nordvik. 'From Namsos to Halden: Myths and Realities in the History of Norwegian Seamen's Wages, 1850–1914.' *The Scandinavian Economic History Review* 35, no. 1 (1987): 41–66.

Fisher, Michael H. 'Working Across the Seas: Indian Maritime Labourers in India, Britain and in Between, 1600–1857.' *International Research in Social History* 52, Supplement (2006): 21–45.

Fletcher, Anthony. *Growing Up in England: The Experience of Childhood, 1600–1914.* New Haven: Yale University Press, 2008.

Forman, Ross. 'Race and Empire'. In *Palgrave Advances in the Modern History of Sexuality*, edited by H.G. Cocks and Matt Houlbrook, 109–32. Basingstoke: Palgrave Macmillan, 2005.

Foulke, Robert D. 'Life in the Dying World of Sail, 1870–1910.' *Journal of British Studies* 3, no. 1 (1963): 105–36.
– *The Sea Voyage Narrative.* London: Routledge, 2002.
Francis, Martin. 'The Domestication of the Male? Recent Research on Nineteenth and Twentieth-Century British Masculinity.' *Historical Journal* 45, no. 3 (2002): 637–52.
Frost, Diane. *Work and Community among West African Migrant Workers since the Nineteenth Century*. Liverpool: Liverpool University Press, 1999.
Fussell, Paul. *The Great War and Modern Memory.* Oxford: Oxford University Press, 2013.
Gamble, Andrew. 'Theories and Explanations of British Decline.' In *Rethinking British Decline*, edited by Richard English and Michael Kenny, 1–22. Basingstoke: Macmillan Education, 2000.
Gagnier, Regenia. *Subjectivities: A History of Self-Representation in Britain, 1832–1920.* New York: Oxford University Press, 1991.
Gelb, Arthur, and Barbara Gelb. *O'Neill.* London: Cape, 1962.
Gilje, Paul A. *Liberty on the Waterfront: American Maritime Culture in the Age of Revolution*. Philadelphia: University of Pennsylvania Press, 2004.
– *To Swear Like a Sailor: Maritime Culture in America, 1750–1850*. Cambridge: Cambridge University Press, 2016.
Glenn, Myra C. *Jack Tar's Story: The Autobiographies and Memoirs of Sailors in Antebellum America.* Cambridge: Cambridge University Press, 2010.
Goffman, Erving. *Asylums: Essays on the Social Situation of Mental Patients and Other Inmates*. Garden City: Doubleday, 1961.
Gorski, Richard. 'Employers' Liability and the Victorian Seaman.' *Mariner's Mirror* 95, no. 1 (2009): 62–75.
– ed. *Maritime Labour: Contributions to the History of Work at Sea, 1500–2000.* Amsterdam: Aksant, 2007.
– '"Purely a Question of Policy": Undermanning and the Late Victorian Merchant Marine.' *International Journal of Maritime History* 19, no. 1 (2007): 1–34.
– 'Seafarers, Seafaring and Occupational Identity: "Jack Tar" and its Contemporary Uses in Britain c.1815–1914.' University of Hull Research Repository, deposited 31 December 2016.
Gräbner, Cornelia. 'Absences and Opacities: Reading "Hidden" Stories of Seafaring in B. Traven's *Ship of the Dead* and Francisco Goldman's *The Ordinary Seaman.*' *Atlantic Studies: Literary, Cultural, and Historical Perspectives* 15, no. 1 (2018): 83–102.

Graham, Gerald S. 'The Ascendancy of the Sailing Ship, 1850–85.' *Economic History Review* 9, no. 1 (1956): 74–88.

Grass, Sean. *The Commodification of Identity in Victorian Narrative: Autobiography, Sensation, and the Literary Marketplace.* Cambridge: Cambridge University Press, 2019.

Gray, Steven. *Steam Power and Sea Power: Coal, the Royal Navy, and the British Empire, c.1870–1914.* London: Palgrave Macmillan, 2018.

Greenhill, Basil, and Ann Giffard, eds. *Women Under Sail: Letters and Journals Concerning Eight Women Travelling or Working in Sailing Vessels Between 1829 and 1949.* Newton Abbot: David & Charles, 1970.

Griffin, Emma. *Bread Winner: An Intimate History of the Victorian Economy.* New Haven: Yale University Press, 2020.

Hackett, Nan. 'A Different Form of "Self": Narrative Style in British Nineteenth-Century Working-Class Autobiography.' *Biography* 12, no. 3 (1989): 208–26.

Harlaftis, G., S. Tenold, and J. Valdaliso, eds. *The World's Key Industry: History and Economics of International Shipping.* Basingstoke: Palgrave Macmillan, 2012.

Harris, Jose. *Private Lives, Public Spirit: A Social History of Britain, 1870–1914.* Oxford: Oxford University Press, 1993.

Heathorn, Stephen J. *For Home, Country, and Race: Constructing Gender, Class, and Englishness in the Elementary School, 1880–1914.* Toronto: University of Toronto Press, 1999.

Hilton, Matthew. *Smoking in British Popular Culture, 1800–2000.* Manchester: Manchester University Press, 2000.

Hinkkanen, Merja-Liisa. "Expressions of Longing, Sources of Anxiety? The Significance of Contacts with Home for Finnish Sailors in London and Hull in the Late Nineteenth Century." In *People of the Northern Seas*, edited by L.R. Fischer and Walter Minchinton, 63–79. St John's: International Maritime Economic History Association, 1992.

Hobsbawm, E.J. *Industry and Empire: From 1750 to the Present Day.* London: Penguin, 1969.

Hogg, Robert. *Men and Manliness on the Frontier: Queensland and British Columbia in the Mid-Nineteenth Century.* Basingstoke: Palgrave Macmillan, 2012.

Hugill, Stan. *Shanties and Sailors' Songs.* London: Jenkins, 1969.

Hyslop, Jonathan. 'Steamship Empire: Asian, African and British Sailors in the Merchant Marine, c.1880–1945.' *Journal of Asian and African Studies* 44, no. 1 (2009): 49–67.

Ingram, Darcy. 'Saving the Union's Jack: The Montreal Sailor's Institute and the Homeless Sailor, 1862–98.' In *Negotiating Identities in 19th and 20th Century Montreal*, edited by Bettina Bradbury and Tamara Myers, 49–76. Vancouver: University of British Columbia Press, 2005.

Jalland, Patricia. *Death in the Victorian Family.* Oxford: Oxford University Press, 1996.

– 'Victorian Death and its Decline: 1850–1918.' In *Death in England: An Illustrated History*, edited by Peter C. Jupp and Clare Gittings, 230–55. Manchester: Manchester University Press, 1999.

Jamieson, Alan G. *Ebb Tide in the British Maritime Industries: Change and Adaptation, 1918–1990.* Exeter: University of Exeter Press, 2003.

Jasanoff, Maya. *The Dawn Watch: Joseph Conrad in a Global World.* London: William Collins, 2017.

Johnston, Ronnie, and Arthur McIvor. 'Dangerous Work, Hard Men and Broken Bodies: Masculinity in the Clydeside Heavy Industries, c.1930–1970s.' *Labour History Review* 69, no. 2 (2004): 135–51.

Kaukiainen, Yrjö. 'Finnish and International Labour in the Age of Sail.' In *The Market for Seamen in the Age of Sail*, edited by L.R. Fischer, 47–62. St John's: International Maritime Economic History Association, 1994.

Keeling, Drew. *The Business of Transatlantic Migration between Europe and the United States, 1900–1914.* Zurich: Chronos, 2012.

Kelly, Alfred. *The German Worker: Working-Class Autobiographies from the Age of Industrialization.* Berkeley: University of California Press, 1987.

Kennerley, Alston. 'Aspirant Navigator: Training and Education at Sea during Commercial Voyages in British Merchant Ships c.1850 to 1950.' *Great Circle* 30, no. 2 (2008): 41–76.

– 'The British Contribution to Seafarers' Welfare in Mediterranean Ports and Black Sea Ports since the 1820s.' *Mariner's Mirror* 93, no. 1 (2007): 65–82.

– 'Bullen, Frank Thomas (1857–1915), Merchant Seaman and Writer.' *Oxford Dictionary of National Biography*, 23 September 2004.

– *Bullen's Voyages: The Life of Frank T. Bullen, Sailor, Whaler, Author.* Barnsley: Seaforth, 2022.

– 'Global Nautical Livelihoods in the Late Nineteenth Century: The Sea Careers of the Maritime Writers Frank T. Bullen and Joseph Conrad, 1869–1894.' *International Journal of Maritime History* 26, no. 1 (2014): 3–24.

– 'Nationally-Recognised Qualifications for British Merchant Navy Officers, 1865–1966.' *International Journal of Maritime History* 13, no. 1 (2001): 115–35.

– 'Ratings for the Mercantile Marine: The Roles of Charity, the State and Industry in the Pre-Service Education and Training of Ratings for the British Merchant Navy, 1879–1939.' *History of Education* 28, no. 1 (1999): 31–51.

– 'Writing the History of Merchant Seafarer Education, Training and Welfare: Retrospect and Prospect.' *Northern Mariner / Le Marin Du Nord* 12, no. 2 (2002): 1–21.

Kestner, Joseph A. *Masculinities in British Adventure Fiction, 1880–1915*. Farnham: Ashgate, 2010.

Kim, Jongwoo Jeremy. 'Naturalism, Labour and Homoerotic Desire: Henry Scott Tuke.' In *British Queer History: New Approaches and Perspectives*, edited by Brian Lewis, 39–62. Manchester: Manchester University Press, 2013.

Klaus, H. Gustav. 'On the Road: All Manner of Tramps in English and Scottish Writing from the 1880s to the 1920s.' In *A History of British Working Class Literature*, edited by J. Goodridge and B. Keegan, 296–310. Cambridge: Cambridge University Press, 2017.

Klein, Bernhard, ed. *Fictions of the Sea: Critical Perspectives on the Ocean in British Literature and Culture*. Farnham: Ashgate, 2002.

Kneale, James. 'The Place of Drink: Temperance and the Public, 1856–1914.' *Social and Cultural Geography* 2, no. 1 (2001): 43–59.

Konvitz, Josef. 'Changing Concepts of the Sea, 1550–1950.' *Terrae Incognitae* 11, no. 1 (1979): 1–17.

Kubicek, Robert. 'The Proliferation and Diffusion of Steamship Technology and the Beginnings of "New Imperialism."' In *Maritime Empires: British Imperial Maritime Trade in the Nineteenth Century*, edited by David Killingray, Margarette Lincoln, and Nigel Rigby, 100–10. Woodbridge: Boydell, 2004.

Kverndal, Roald. *Seamen's Missions: Their Origin and Early Growth*. Pasadena: William Carey Library, 1986.

Lance, Kate. *Alan Villiers: Voyager of the Winds*. Sydney: University of New South Wales Press, 2009.

Land, Isaac. *War, Nationalism, and the British Sailor, 1750–1850*. Basingstoke: Palgrave Macmillan, 2009.

Lee, Y.S. *Masculinity and the English Working Class: Studies in Victorian Autobiography and Fiction*. Abingdon: Routledge, 2016.

Lewis, Brian. 'Introduction: British Queer History.' In *British Queer History: New Approaches and Perspectives*, edited by Brian Lewis, 1–16. Manchester: Manchester University Press, 2013.

Lowenthal, David. *The Past is a Foreign Country.* Cambridge: Cambridge University Press, 1985.

Luckin, Bill. 'Revisiting the Idea of Degeneration in Urban Britain, 1830–1900.' *Urban History* 33, no. 2 (2006): 234–52.

Lunn, Ken, and Ann Day. 'Britain as Island: National Identity and the Sea.' In *History, Nationhood and the Question of Britain*, edited by Helen Brocklehurst and Robert Phillips, 124–36. Basingstoke: Palgrave Macmillan, 2004.

Machann, Clinton. 'The Construction of Masculinity in Victorian Autobiography.' *Nineteenth-Century Prose* 26, no. 2 (1999): 9–23.

Mäenpää, Sari. 'Galley News: Catering Personnel on British Passenger Liners, 1860–1938.' *International Journal of Maritime History* 12, no. 1 (2000): 243–60.

– 'New Maritime Labour? Catering Personnel on British Passenger Liners, 1860–1938.' PhD diss., University of Liverpool, 2002.

– 'Sailors and Their Pets: Men and Their Companion Animals Aboard Early Twentieth-Century Finnish Sailing Ships.' *International Journal of Maritime History* 28, no. 3 (2016): 480–95.

Mangan, J.A. '"The Grit of Our Forefathers": Invented Traditions, Propaganda and Imperialism.' In *Imperialism and Popular Culture*, edited by John M. MacKenzie, 113–39. Manchester: Manchester University Press, 1986.

Maynard, Steven. 'Queer Musings on Masculinity and History.' *Labour / Le Travail* 42 (1998): 183–97.

Maynes, Mary Jo. *Taking the Hard Road: Life Course in French and German Workers' Autobiographies in the Era of Industrialization.* Chapel Hill: University of North Carolina Press, 1995.

McClelland, Keith. 'Masculinity and the "Representative Artisan" in Britain, 1850–1880.' In *Manful Assertions: Masculinities in Britain Since 1800*, edited by Michael Roper and John Tosh, 74–91. London: Routledge, 1991.

McCord, Norman. *North East England: An Economic and Social History.* London: Batsford, 1979.

McKee, Christopher. *Sober Men and True: Sailor Lives in the Royal Navy, 1900–1945.* Cambridge, MA: Harvard University Press, 2002.

Milne, Graeme J. 'Collecting the Sea Shanty: British Maritime Identity and Atlantic Musical Cultures in the Early Twentieth Century.' *International Journal of Maritime History* 29, no. 2 (2017): 370–86.

– *People, Place and Power on the Nineteenth-Century Waterfront: Sailortown.* Basingstoke: Palgrave Macmillan, 2016.

Nelson, Claudia. *Boys Will Be Girls: The Feminine Ethic and British Children's Fiction, 1857–1917.* New Brunswick: Rutgers University Press, 1991.

O'Hara, Glen. 'The Sea is Swinging into View: Modern British Maritime History in a Globalised World.' *English Historical Review* 124, no. 510 (2009): 1,109–34.

Ogborn, Miles. 'Law and Discipline in Nineteenth Century English State Formation: The Contagious Diseases Acts of 1864, 1866 and 1869.' *Journal of Historical Sociology* 6, no. 1 (1993): 28–55.

Ojala, Jari, Jaakko Pehkonen, and Jari Eloranta. 'Desertions in Nineteenth-Century Shipping: Modelling Quit Behaviour.' *European Review of Economic History* 17, no. 1 (2013): 122–40.

Ojala, Jari, Jari Eloranta, Jaakko Pehkonen, and Anu Ojala. 'Young Lads and Old Tars: Changing Age Structure of the Nordic Sailors, 1750s–1930s.' *Social Science History* 46, no. 4 (2022): 861–86.

Oldenziel, Ruth. *Making Technology Masculine: Men, Women, and Modern Machines in America, 1870–1945.* Amsterdam: Amsterdam University Press, 1999.

Parnaby, Andrew. 'The Many Motivations of Jack Tar.' *Labour / Le Travail* 62 (2008): 199–208.

Parry, J.H. 'Sailors' English.' *Cambridge Journal* 2 (1948–49): 660–70.

Parsons, Joanne, and Ruth Heholt, eds. *The Victorian Male Body.* Edinburgh: Edinburgh University Press, 2018.

Peck, John. *Maritime Fiction: Sailors and the Sea in British and American Novels, 1719–1917.* Basingstoke: Palgrave Macmillan, 2001.

Phillips, Richard. *Mapping Men and Empire: A Geography of Adventure.* London: Routledge, 1997.

Poggie, John J. Jr, and Carl Gersuny. 'Risk and Ritual: An Interpretation of Fishermen's Folklore in a New England Community.' *Journal of American Folklore* 85, no. 335 (1972): 66–72.

Popkin, Jeremy D. *History, Historians, and Autobiography.* Chicago: University of Chicago Press, 2005.

Press, Jon. 'Wages in the Merchant Navy, 1815–54.' *Journal of Transport History* 2, no. 2 (1981): 37–52.

Quinlan, Michael. 'Precarious and Hazardous Work: The Health and Safety of Merchant Seamen 1815–1935.' *Social History* 38, no. 3 (2013): 281–307.

Rakich, Whitney Purvis. 'Savage Fakes: Misdirection, Fraudulence, and Autobiography in the 1920s.' PhD diss., University of New Mexico, 2012.

Readman, Paul. 'The Place of the Past in English Culture, c.1890–1914.' *Past & Present* 186 (2005): 147–200.

Rediker, Marcus. *Between the Devil and the Deep Blue Sea: Merchant Seamen, Pirates and the Anglo-American Maritime World, 1700–1750.* Cambridge: Cambridge University Press, 1987.

Reid, Kirsty. 'Ocean Funerals: The Sea and Victorian Cultures of Death.' *Journal for Maritime Research* 13, no. 1 (2011): 37–54.

Richards, Jeffrey. '"Passing the Love of Women": Manly Love and Victorian Society.' In *Manliness and Morality: Middle-Class Masculinity in Britain and America, 1800–1940*, edited by J.A. Mangan and James Walvin, 92–122. Manchester: Manchester University Press, 1987.

Rico, Monica. *Nature's Noblemen: Transatlantic Masculinities and the Nineteenth-Century American West.* New Haven: Yale University Press, 2013.

Rieger, Bernhard. '"Modern Wonders": Technological Innovation and Public Ambivalence in Britain and Germany, 1890s to 1933.' *History Workshop Journal* 55, no. 1 (2003): 152–76.

Robbins, Keith. *Nineteenth-Century Britain: Integration and Diversity.* Oxford: Clarendon Press: 1988.

Rosaldo, Renato. 'Imperialist Nostalgia.' *Representations* 26 (1989): 107–22.

Rosenwein, Barbara H. 'Worrying About Emotions in History.' *American Historical Review* 107, no. 3 (2002): 821–45.

Rotundo, E. Anthony. *American Manhood: Transformations in Masculinity from the Revolution to the Modern Era.* New York: Basic Books, 1993.

Rouleau, Brian J. 'Dead Men Do Tell Tales: Folklore, Fraternity and the Forecastle.' *Early American Studies* 5, no. 1 (2007): 30–62.

Sager, Eric W. *Seafaring Labour: The Merchant Marine of Atlantic Canada, 1820–1914.* Kingston: McGill-Queen's University Press, 1989.

Saunders, Max. *Self Impression: Life-Writing, Autobiografiction, and the Forms of Modern Literature.* Oxford: Oxford University Press, 2010.

Schell, Jennifer. *A Bold and Hardy Race of Men: The Lives and Literature of American Whalemen.* Boston: University of Massachusetts Press, 2013.

Scholl, Lars U., and Merja-Liisa Hinkkanen, eds. *Sail and Steam: Selected Maritime Writings of Yrjö Kaukiainen.* St John's: International Maritime Economic History Association, 2004.

Scott, Frank. 'An Assessment of Voyage Memoirs of the Erikson Era.' *Mariner's Mirror* 100, no. 3 (2014): 322–34.

Shamir, Milette. '"The Manliest Relations to Men": Thoreau on Privacy, Intimacy, and Writing.' In *Boys Don't Cry? Rethinking Narratives of Masculinity and Emotion in the U.S.*, edited by Milette Shamir and Jennifer Travis, 64–87. New York: Columbia University Press, 2002.

Smith, Crosbie. *Coal, Steam and Ships: Engineering, Enterprise and Empire on the Nineteenth-Century Seas.* Cambridge: Cambridge University Press, 2018.

Smith, Maya Wassell. '"The Fancy Work What Sailors Make": Material and Emotional Creative Practice in Masculine Seafaring Communities.' *Nineteenth-Century Gender Studies* 14, no. 2 (2018): 104–23.

Smith, Sidonie, and Julia Watson. *Reading Autobiography: A Guide for Interpreting Life Narratives.* 2nd ed. Minneapolis: University of Minnesota Press, 2010.

Stenson, Patrick. *Titanic Voyager: The Odyssey of C.H. Lightoller.* Tiverton: Halsgrove, 1998.

Stewart, David J. 'Burial At Sea: Separating and Placing the Dead during the Age of Sail.' *Mortality* 10, no. 4 (2005): 276–85.

– *The Sea Their Graves: An Archaeology of Death and Remembrance in Maritime Culture.* Gainesville: University Press of Florida, 2011.

Strange, Julie-Marie. '"She Cried a Very Little": Death, Grief and Mourning in Working-Class Culture, c.1880–1914.' *Social History* 27, no. 2 (2002): 143–61.

Sturmey, S.G. *British Shipping and World Competition.* St John's: International Maritime Economic History Association, 2010. First published 1962 by Athlone Press (London).

Summerfield, Penny. *Histories of the Self: Personal Narratives and Historical Practice.* London: Routledge, 2019.

Szreter, Simon, and Kate Fisher. *Sex before the Sexual Revolution: Intimate Life in England 1918–1963.* Cambridge: Cambridge University Press, 2010.

Tabili, Laura. *We Ask for British Justice: Workers and Racial Difference in Late Imperial Britain.* Ithaca: Cornell University Press, 1994.

Taillon, Paul Michel. '"What We Want is Good Sober Men": Masculinity, Respectability and Temperance in the Railroad Brotherhoods, c.1870–1910.' *Journal of Social History* 36, no. 2 (2002): 319–38.

Thompson, E.P. *The Making of the English Working Class.* Harmondsworth: Penguin, 1991.

Tosh, John. *Manliness and Masculinities in Nineteenth-Century Britain: Essays on Gender, Family, and Empire.* Harlow: Pearson Longman, 2005.

– *A Man's Place: Masculinity and the Middle-Class Home in Victorian England.* New Haven: Yale University Press, 1999.

Vickers, Daniel, with Vince Walsh. *Young Men and the Sea: Yankee Seafarers in the Age of Sail.* New Haven: Yale University Press, 2005.

Vincent, David. *Bread, Knowledge and Freedom: A Study of Nineteenth-Century Working Class Autobiography.* London: Europa, 1981.

– *Literacy and Popular Culture: England 1750–1914.* Cambridge: Cambridge University Press, 1989.

Walker, Meaghan. 'In the Inventories of Deceased British Merchant Seafarers: Exploring Merchant Shipping and Material Culture, 1860–1880.' *International Journal of Maritime History* 31, no. 2 (2019): 330–46.

Walkowitz, Judith R. *Prostitution and Victorian Society: Women, Class, and the State.* Cambridge: Cambridge University Press, 1980.

Williams, David M. 'The Quality, Skill and Supply of Maritime Labour: Causes of Concern in Britain, 1850–1914.' In *Merchants and Mariners: Selected Maritime Writings of David M. Williams*, edited by Lars U. Scholl, 273–92. St John's: International Maritime Economic History Association, 2000.

Witt, Jann M. '"During the Voyage Every Captain is Monarch of the Ship": The Merchant Captain from the Seventeenth to the Nineteenth Century.' *International Journal of Maritime History* 13, no. 2 (2001): 165–94.

Woodman, Richard. *More Days, More Dollars: The Universal Bucket Chain 1885–1920.* Stroud: History Press, 2010.

Index